Dear Robert

love Happy Cooking

Carla x

East Neuk Festival

2014

carina contini's kitchen garden cookbook

a year of italian scots recipes

F

FRANCES LINCOLN LIMITED
PUBLISHERS

Frances Lincoln Limited
74–77 White Lion Street
London N1 9PF
www.franceslincoln.com

Carina Contini's Kitchen Garden Cookbook
Copyright © Frances Lincoln Limited 2014
Text and photographs copyright © Carina Contini
2014
Artworks on pages 30, 150, 175, 276 © National
Gallery of Scotland

First Frances Lincoln edition 2014

A catalogue record for this book is available
from the British Library.

978-0-7112-3460-4

Printed and bound in China

1 2 3 4 5 6 7 8 9

contents

introduction

I'm blessed to have been surrounded by food all my life. Is it because my Italian roots reveal themselves most obviously through food? Is it my love of wonderful fresh ingredients, simply prepared? Is it because food can bring us closer to people and can enable us to sit with them and share a meal in a busy life? Is it because we cherish the artisan skills of those who are dedicated to growing and gathering the raw materials that make our meals?

Is it our peasant roots that connect us with nature and with the bountiful harvests that Scotland and Italy deliver? Is it because food has always provided our livelihood? Or is it simply our love of eating and of nurturing those who are dearest to us with healthy food that will sustain them even when they aren't by our side?

It's all of the above.

I was born in Edinburgh of parents born in Scotland and Italy. I've lived in Edinburgh for the majority of my life and have only ever holidayed in Italy. I'm embarrassed when I speak Italian, but I cook like an Italian and eat like an Italian of the 1950s – just like my parents. I feel as if I have the best of both worlds and I'm proud to call myself an Italian-Scot.

I love how, in 1954, Elizabeth David described the many virtues of Italian cooking in her book *Italian Food*. She talks of Italians' extravagance with raw ingredients, of their precise awareness of food's quality and freshness, of how a little can be made to go a long way, of culinary skill and care, and of food that is cheap and simple to make.

She describes England's (and Scotland's, of course) homegrown knowledge of preserving, baking and roasting, and of its great wealth of game, but she also talks about the disconnect with food in the Britain of the 1950s and of the lack of ideas and courage in cooking. She yearned to get back to the once-famous sense of quality for which pre-war British food was famous.

With the war over, the limitations of post-war rationing, followed in the 1960s by the technological explosion and in the 1970s by the expansion of supermarkets, all meant that the British slowly lost touch with their food and with an understanding of its origins.

This is slowly changing. Scotland and the UK as a whole have finally regained their desire for good-quality food. Artisan skills are now cherished. We are conscious of waste and its cost at every level. Animal welfare and husbandry are paramount. Home-made wins over shop-bought every time. People have learnt that local, seasonal, sustainable food not only supports the environment but is also cheaper, tastier and healthier. It's a win on every front.

As a Scot, I've been fortunate to have enjoyed the best of Scotland's larder – the finest beef, lamb, shellfish, hardy root vegetables and delicate soft fruits. As an Italian, eating and cooking are in my blood. It was natural for me to be helping Mummy in the kitchen just as it was natural for her to nurture my culinary skills.

My grandparents, having left the mountains in the middle of the Abruzzi, opened an ice cream shop when they arrived in Scotland in 1919. This developed into a thriving café, restaurant and catering business run by my parents for over 70 years. They fed thousands of people with simple, good-quality, seasonal food.

Fast forward almost 100 years, and my husband and I have now taken up the mantle. The journey to our kitchen garden has carried us full circle back to the land. This book touches on some of the stories of our journey and the recipes that form part of it. It also introduces you to the many and varied characters who have helped me develop and refine my Italian-Scots love affair with food.

Mummy taught me well to make the most of what this glorious country has to offer, and to combine it with a little Italian know-how. I hope this book will help me share that passion with you.

Carina

cast of characters

me Number Eight child of Johnny and Gertrude Di Ciacca. Wife to Victor and mother to Orlando, Carla and Arianna. Co-founder of Ristorante Contini and The Scottish Cafe & Restaurant in Edinburgh. Loves a laugh but takes on too much, which makes her grumpy sometimes.

victor Business partner and my darling. Sweetens everyone up and keeps us all in harmony. Has been known to ride horses and dive, and now has his beehives. Always wants to make a friend or customer feel better when they leave than when they arrive. Passionate about Italian wine and adores cleaning the Aga.

orlando Number One son. Orlando Furioso. Orlando the Peacemaker. We waited a long time for our four-and-a-half-kilo, bouncing baby boy and it was love at first sight. Destined to be a Lego designer. As well as keeping the peace, he always makes us laugh. The life and soul of the family.

carla Number One Angel. She's Daddy's darling. Sporty, artistic, energetic, talks for Britain, eats like a little piggy and looks like a thoroughbred race horse. She's Mummy's little chef – always in the kitchen, helping.

arianna Number One Christmas Day Baby. As sweet as honey to look at but you're never quite sure what she's thinking. Has a mind of her own and is always one step ahead of everyone else. Nicknamed Trouble, but she's Mummy's pet.

daddy Johnny Di Ciacca. Daddy was 51 when I was born. He made the best ice cream for over 70 years. Loved a wee nip (actually several big nips), a cigar and a cashmere jumper. Was easily pleased. His laugh was infectious and often got him into trouble. Feared and loved in equal quantities.

mummy Gertrude Di Ciacca. Mother of eight with the constitution of an ox and the elegance of a 1940s American movie star. Loved glam, glitter and parties in her youth. Still loves them in her eighties. Cooked beautiful, homemade, simple food for thousands at the Wemyss Café for over 40 years and never got her apron dirty once!

the magnificent seven The name for the children of Johnny and Gertrude Di Ciacca, until I came along. Four boys, three girls – and then I arrived!

the boys
Number One. Cesidio. The boss. Always right, never wrong.
Number Four Kevin. Mischief. Always in trouble but with a lovely smile.
Number Six. Paul. Everyone's darling.
Number Seven. John Mark. My favourite – if I had to choose!

the girls
Number Two. Anita. Always wanted to be a princess. Still trying.
Number Three. Mary. The worker. Game for a laugh.
Number Five. Joanna. Forever looking for divine inspiration.

margaret Our second mother. Worked for Daddy from the age of 14 until she was 72. Loved every single minute of it. Was there all through our lives and we love her dearly. Always said she never had time to marry as she was too busy loving us.

auntie olive/mum/nonna olivia It's a strange thing when your auntie (twice removed) becomes your mother-in-law. A wonderful cook. Cooked lunch every day for over 50 years for her husband, our darling Nonno Carlo. TripAdvisor five stars for every meal.

auntie gloria Victor's spinster aunt. A baking goddess. Madeira cakes, flourless sponges, jams and puddings – you name it. She is the girl, even aged 85. Still going strong from her head to her hand mixer.

victor & carina contini family All our ventures start here. The journey continues. If you have any questions, please contact www.contini.com

marvellous mr maxwell Edinburgh's best florist. Delivered our first arrangement when we opened Ristorante Contini and continues delivering today.

Top row from left: Victor's legs; Mummy and Daddy; family group with Margaret. Second row from left: Victor, Numbers Seven, Eight and Six; Orlando. Third row from left: Number Four; Arianna. Bottom row from left: Cockenzie Café by John Bellany (1942–2013); Carla.

love happy food (LHF) Our company philosophy. Good food enjoyed with friends and family. That's what life is for.

centotre (now ristorante contini)
Our restaurant at 103 George Street, Edinburgh. Fresh, simple Italian cooking, using produce imported weekly from the markets in Italy. Complemented by the best of Scotland's larder – fish landed by Scottish boats in Scottish ports, best Scottish beef, pork, lamb and game, dairy and vegetables. Seasonal monthly menu.

the scottish cafe & restaurant
In the Scottish National Gallery on The Mound in Edinburgh. Fresh, simple, sustainable Scottish cooking with heritage. Food purchased directly from over 60 Scottish artisan producers. Monthly menu changes with the seasons.

the a team Our 80 plus, sometimes 100, boys and girls, who work so hard to prepare beautiful food, look after our customers and keep the LHF message burning bright. Well done and thank you.

super suzanne Executive chef at Ristorante Contini and The Scottish Cafe & Restaurant. Helps make the A team A Plus. A talented and passionate cook. Tested every recipe in this book – and we had such a laugh along the way. Grazie molto.

lovely lara Manager at Ristorante Contini for many, many years. No favourites. Addicted to Twitter and Facebook. Loves to keep customers up-to-speed and well looked after.

my pals, helen and carol Supported me and Victor hugely during the early days of Ristorante Contini and we love them dearly. Carol – my surrogate sister. Leave us alone and you'll hear us having a carry on before you even see us. Helen – slightly more demure but an amazing cook and an inspiration. Helen and I have lots in common – three children each and restaurants as our business. Her husband Mike, like my darling Victor, is loved by everyone.

mr apple Our amazing Graham Stoddart of Cuddybridge – our 'apple man'. An early supporter of the garden. His inspiration gave us the courage to undertake a project we really didn't have any idea how to start.

robert Robert Wilson of Scotherbs is an absolute gentleman and always there when we need help. Robert, his dear wife Sylvia and their team helped us plant our herb garden in Princes Street Gardens and, more importantly, built Polly the polytunnel at Casa San Lorenzo.

casa san lorenzo Our garden and our home in Midlothian. Named after the patron saint of cooks, comedians and librarians.

Left to right: Suzanne and Carina, shattered after a 14-hour cook-off; Boty and Dani; Gianluigi; Michael and Gianluigi at Ristorante Contini; blueberry muffins; pear tart; Erica digging for victory.

polly the polytunnel It took over eight months to prepare Polly. So when she arrived after the wettest summer we'd had in decades and the wildest, snowiest winter we'd had in years, we had to give her a name. Polly is stronger than Edinburgh Castle rock.

bain-marie (BM) BM and I go back a long way. We either sit together on the stove (pot half-filled with water and a glass or ceramic bowl sitting on top but not touching the water) or cosy up in the oven (deep tray half-filled with water with ramekins or cups sitting inside to help moderate the temperature, keeping the soufflés light and stopping them collapsing).

aperitivo You won't find Aperitivo in the book but he's there. I consume five or six units of alcohol a week. I'd love to be able to drink more but I fall asleep and am no use to anyone. But a little aperitivo – a Martini Rosso, a Campari or a Cosmopolitan on a Sunday – can give me the little pick-me-up that gets me going.

stephen jardine A bit like Aperitivo, you won't find Stephen in the book but he's sitting behind every word and every line. Subtle and reliable. I couldn't have done it without him.

zoe barrie No need to say anything about Zoe. Her beautiful photography speaks quality, attention to detail and a lovely delicate touch.

marvellous manel quiros Filled the gaps with a few extra snaps!

slow food (SF) A big part of our lives. Founded in Italy by Carlo Petrini almost 30 years ago with a focus on cherishing food traditions. We've been believers for years but members since we opened Ristorante Contini. I was asked to join the Slow Food Chef Alliance as its first female chef in 2011. An organization dedicated to good, clean, fair food. Understanding how our global food system works is vital if we're to make the best choices for our environment, our communities and for animal welfare.

contini events Our amazing team headed by Jennie is always available for hand-holding for your special occasions, private parties or corporate events in all our lovely venues. Any number of guests from 14 to 600.

erica Last but no means least. I wanted to end on a high. Erica, our head gardener, has transformed a previously unloved, derelict, domestic garden into a stunning, visual, palate-challenging, recipe-inspiring, fully functioning kitchen garden. Together we've cleared, planted, grown, engaged our team, inspired our children and stimulated our senses. And on top of that, she's provided the gardener's growing notes for this book. Thank you, Erica!

cook's notes

Times and temperatures: I love cooking on a really high heat and in really hot ovens. Consequently, I've been known to have a few crispy outcomes! For this book, therefore, I've given slightly lower temperatures, to be on the safe side. But each oven is different. The more you cook, the more you're able to gauge how long to cook for and at what temperature. So don't be frightened to cook for a little longer if you need it, and for roasts and vegetables, you can turn up the heat and live life in the fast lane if you fancy. My top tip, though, is use a timer. There'll be one on your phone. Use it. You don't want all your hard work to be burnt to a crisp.

Gadgets: I'm not a gadget girl. Mummy has everything – processors, blenders, juicers, you name it. If you have a small kitchen, it can be hard finding space to store these items. My favourite utensils are a wooden spoon and elbow grease, but things are changing. I now have more space and believe it's worth investing in a few time-saving tools. For this book, I bought my first-ever food processor, and it really does make life easier. A tabletop mixer will make you foolproof cakes and meringues, and a mouli is a necessity for some soups. A hand blender or liquidizer is, however, a must. Get a liquidizer if you've got the space, but a hand blender works almost as well and is easier and faster to clean. I also love my pestle and mortar. I almost feel it connects me through the ages all the way back to my Roman ancestors. Using a pestle and mortar is also the most exercise I get some days. If you don't have one, put it on your wish list. It will last forever and if you get into the habit of using it, it can really lift flavours to new heights.

Salt: Where would we be without salt? It balances our palates and our bodies, preserves our food and stimulates our appetite. Too much salt we know isn't good, but too little is equally bad. Maldon Salt has always been a staple in my kitchen but Hebridean Salt from the Isle of Lewis – the first salt to be harvested in Scotland for over 40 years – came into our lives a few years ago and we love it.

Pepper: As well as calling him Orlando Furioso and Orlando the Peacemaker, we also call Orlando our Indian baby. We were lucky enough to visit Colin and Colqin, dear friends who live in Kerala and have the most special pepper plantation in the world. Their main man, Para, and his family, have hand-picked these beautiful little berries to bring us the most fragrant and aromatic white and black pepper you can buy. After eight years of waiting, and nine months after our visit to this heavenly land, Orlando arrived. Amazing!

Olive oil: The Romans introduced olive oil to Britain and it was the main cooking medium until the Norman invasion, when we started using butter. Needless to say, with our Italian heritage, olive oil is a staple. The flavour and uses of each oil are as different from each other as a runny, ripe Gorgonzola is from an aged Blue Stilton. Get to know the different flavours and use them accordingly. We use four main extra virgin oils: Le Ferre, from a co-operative in Puglia, for general cooking, and Fontodi, Capezzana and Selvapiana, each made by famous Chianti Classico wine producers, for salads, sauces and dressings. Each harvest has a different taste and character. We always look forward to November when we get to sample the new bottling for the first time.

Cold pressed rapeseed oil: Unlike olives, rapeseed doesn't have to be pressed until you need it. That makes it very practical as well as sustainable. Though it doesn't have the heritage of olive oils, rapeseed's flavour goes very well with the earthy character of many native British vegetables and grains. If you haven't tried it, give it a go. As a plus, it's also very high in Omega 3, so it's super-healthy.

Freezer: Fresh and simple is how I cook. I have three children and cook for them every day, tending to rely on a plate of pasta and a really quick *sugo* (sauce) made with a tin of tomatoes, a clove of garlic, a generous glug of olive oil and a handful of fresh basil from my windowsill plant. It all goes in the frying pan and is ready faster than cooking the accompanying pasta al dente. Maybe I don't use the freezer much because we hardly ever have leftovers, but a freezer is amazing for excess soup, scones, bread and stews. All freeze really well. My freezer tends to contain nothing more than ice, ice cream and a bottle of vodka – but telling you that is giving away my secrets and my weak spot – that Sunday Cosmopolitan!

Eczema: I wash my hand hundreds of times a week. I've got an obsession. But when you're cooking and handling lots of different ingredients, regardless of how careful or talented you are, you need to wash your hands. And I wash mine so much that if I don't use my Aveeno cream, I end up with eczema. It was suggested for one of the children and now we all use it. It's an oatmeal-based cream that keeps our skins smooth, soft and scratch-free.

Imperial v. metric: Mummy cooks imperial but I cook metric. The children are taught metric at school. I think using metric just makes things easier so I use metric in this book. Buy yourself metric scales if you haven't got them. You'll have a lightbulb moment.

Lemons: Everyone who knows me, knows how much I love lemons. We're spoiled. We get a weekly delivery from Amalfi in Italy for Ristorante Contini. The colour, the smell, the leaves and the flavour are to die for. Their acidity balances the flavours in the food, cuts the fat, helps digestion and boosts the immune system. I hardly ever get a cold and I feel it must be down to all the Vitamin C from the lemons in my cooking. I love them raw, juiced, cooked and pickled. They're essential. Always try to buy unwaxed lemons as they're more versatile and far fresher. But they'll go off faster, so get used to buying lots and using them quickly.

Vinegars: Malt, balsamic, red wine, white wine, cider, raspberry, apple. What a lot of choice! Try and find the styles and producers you like best. They'll add character and a little zing, which is never a bad thing, and added to salads as an alternative to lemon, vinegars can create a whole new experience. They go off though, so don't let them hang around too long.

Pork: Pork isn't a Scottish staple. Bacon and ham are ubiquitous here but, as far as roasts are concerned, lamb, beef and chicken rule the roost (so to speak) in Scotland. But we love pork. It must be our Italian roots. There are many heritage varieties of pig now being reared all over the country. Pork is economical, tasty and very versatile. Slam in the pork for a change!

Herbs and spices: Coriander, cumin, cardamom, turmeric, sumac, ginger. When I was six or seven, these names sounded like the opening sentence of an Aladdin movie. Despite their apparent exoticism, spices were used extensively throughout the Middle Ages and all the way through to Victorian times. The recent fashion for old cookbooks has renewed our interest and released the genie from the bottle.

When it comes to herbs, skip a few hundred years, land in Britain in the 1980s, and there you have herbs. They were suddenly readily available in the supermarkets and we all seemed to go mad for them. For us Italians, these herbs have been fundamental to our cooking since time began. I still get an annual present of dried basil from some nuns in the mountains outside Venice, and we always buy dried oregano and chillies whenever we're in Naples or on the islands near there.

A simple dish can be transformed with a herb or spice. If you have a window ledge or garden, growing fresh herbs is a must. Spices are equally as important in your larder. Use them to get the most from them – stuck at the back of the cupboard gathering dust, they're no use to anyone. If you're lucky enough to travel afar, that's the best way to get local spices. The flavour will be more intense and fresher, and they'll inevitably be much, much cheaper.

Foraged foods: We're slowly rediscovering the wild foraged foods that have been under our feet for years, almost forgotten. All are finding their way back into our kitchens and, most importantly, back into our diets. Foraging is a great way to spend a weekend. If you can find a group trip it's the best way to go. Many leaves have to be blanched before use. Many mushrooms are poisonous. Have fun but don't take any chances!

fourteen months to a kitchen garden

January 2012

House bought. Contractor appointed. Great. Victor and I can start thinking about the garden. Business so easily takes over family in our lives, but we love it!

Enter Mr Apple, aka Graham Stoddart – our apple guru. Graham and his darling wife, Joules, visit the garden. Graham's previous life as a head gardener with the National Trust for Scotland means he's in a good position to advise us two complete novices.

It's January, it's cold, and the ground is brick-hard, but the sunlight is streaming through the clouds and we can see immediately that our garden's a suntrap.

The house is Georgian but there seems to be a large Victorian wall sitting right in the middle of the garden. The one-hectare site has an east-west orientation, two-and-a-half-metre-high walls on two sides, several dead trees, a very large 1.4-metre-deep pond, one dead apple tree and over 500 metres of arm's-depth ivy. Added to that, it's on a sloping site with a three-metre drop at one side. Most noteworthy, there's no evidence that the garden has ever been used to grow food. Mr Apple's eager eye reassures us that all will be good.

Everything needs a name so what should we call the garden? We felt a little divine inspiration was needed. A vision of San Lorenzo appeared (spiritually not literally). I'm a great believer in fate and a bit of faith hasn't done me any harm either. St Lawrence – Italy's San Lorenzo – was a third-century Christian saint who was martyred on an open grill over a raging fire. Halfway through the roasting he was recorded as saying, 'You can turn me now. This side is done.'

We don't want to mimic St Lawrence's experience but as he's the patron saint of cooks and cookery schools, and of librarians and, most importantly, of comedians, we thought that to name our garden after him was very appropriate and was definitely worth a laugh. By coincidence – and I mean coincidence, as I'd never noticed it before – San Lorenzo is also the patron saint of Picinisco, our village in Italy. Every year, on 10 August, there's a procession in the village centred around the statue of San Lorenzo being carried through the cobbled streets and under the ancient archways. So our garden has now been baptized Casa San Lorenzo – the house of Saint Lawrence.

February 2012

It's freezing but it's perfect weather to start clearing the site. Chain saws, axes, hacksaws and other lethal weapons are at the ready to strip back and clear years of overgrown, untended, unloved vegetation. Dead or alive, it must go.

JAN 2012 What a view!   house   house

No ski holiday this year, so the February school holiday has all of us in the garden. Number One son, Orlando, is happy: he's 10 years old and he's got a saw. Mr Apple is in huge trouble as he has taught him how to chop down a tree. I can imagine how grown-up this makes Orlando feel so, Mr Apple, I forgive you.

Victor's in his element. Is it the outdoors, the exercise or standing on the earth where we're going to start growing our own produce for our restaurants?

The garden is isolated so Victor got a real surprise the other day when the local Environmental Health Officer, or EHO for short, appeared. A neighbour living 800 metres along the valley had called to complain about the smoke from our bonfire. Big gardens, particularly our neglected one, produce perennial weeds, dead branches and an abundance of damaged or diseased plants. The amount that needs to be cleared is staggering. We've already filled 10 skips with rubble and builders' waste and hadn't budgeted for getting rid of the garden waste. Having a bonfire party seemed like a practical solution.

Environmentalists may object to the carbon dioxide and the neighbours may object to the smoke, but the ash is invaluable. We'll need tonnes of compost to kick-start the soil. When added to the compost, this ash, packed with potassium, will bring vital benefits. It will help build the plants' immunity to frost, disease and drought, and will help regulate the water in the soil. PS The kids have found some marshmallows and are busy toasting them. Bonfire night in February – what fun!

March 2012

March has been meetings month. Everyone involved has a different opinion on what should be grown where. With so much vegetation, it's been impossible to envisage a clear plan, so last week we commissioned a topographical survey to reveal the true levels and contours of the garden. This will be vital once we've appointed our gardener. Speaking of which, Mr Apple to the rescue. Advert placed for a head gardener in *The Garden* magazine.

The house is being gutted, literally. We now have no more than a roof and some walls. It's a challenge. The rubble, joists and stone are all being stored in the hope that they'll come in handy later on.

Thanks to the survey, we now have a drawing that helps us visualize the positions of the vegetable beds, fruit trees, chicken pen, compost and bonfires. This is exciting stuff. We've made a great start to clearing the site. Maybe we just need a prayer to San Lorenzo to keep the wind blowing in the opposite direction next time Victor's got his matches out. Perhaps that will help to keep the neighbours happy.

April 2012

I've never liked job interviews, whether as interviewer or interviewee. But spring is in the

BRIARY

air and I'm changing my tune. The applicants for our head gardener position have a huge range of previous experience. We've even interviewed a shepherd. But the best man (woman) for the job has got to be Erica Randall, formerly of the Royal Botanic Garden in Edinburgh. Bingo!

Gardener appointed, now we'd better get the Bothy – an old Scots word for a shelter or outhouse – ready. Dave the joiner has converted the derelict stabling. Running water, electricity, a heater, fridge, perfectly positioned potting table, hooks galore for all the tools, and it's ready.

We've sent the soil samples off to the Hutton Institute – one of the Scottish government's main research providers in environmental, crop and food science. The results are back. The soil is slightly acidic – perfect for most crops and excellent for soft fruits. Erica now has the basic information she needs to set a planting scheme in motion.

May Day 2012

Victor has been busy. He's just started his Edinburgh & Midlothian Scottish Beekeepers' Association course. I never thought I'd say that, let alone have a hubby who's a beekeeper. He's got drones, modules, nuclei and queens coming out of his ears. During the Easter holidays we even buzzed over to the house and gardens of Mount Stuart on the Isle of Bute. David, the head gardener there, also keeps bees. Victor's bees will be an important part of our garden. They'll help with early pollination and hopefully we'll end up with a few jars of honey as well.

Thanks to one of our lovely customers, we've bought Welsh black bees. They're native to the British Isles and are known to be particularly happy bees.

From the sweet to the smelly, but equally essential. Lasswade Riding School uses the neighbouring paddock. The cutest ponies have been peeping over the wall, and with ponies also comes the best natural fertilizer! The school has 125 horses so our manure problems are solved.

Operation Volunteer San Lorenzo has now been organized. Erica's band of enthusiastic green-fingered friends are joining us for a day of digging and lifting. We'd hoped that the builder from the house with his boys and a smallish JCB would be able to remove all the nasties from the garden, but the digger has done huge damage to the soil, compacting it really badly. Instead, the volunteers are getting stuck in with some good old-fashioned muscle power.

The transformation after just one day's work is miraculous. The team has cleared all the boundary soil and we're ready for our first planting. The compost area has been created and the majority of the big tree stumps have been removed. The volunteers even planted our first sweet peas, complete with canes.

Suzanne, our Executive Chef, was, as usual, on hand to provide the necessary sustenance – a stunning picnic with all our lovely homemade chutneys and pickles, our own boiled ham, some spring salads and fantastic, hot, homemade bread. It was such fun eating in our garden, together

house   house   soil   APRIL the bothy

with our lovely team. A wonderful reminder of why we've tackled this crazy but joyous adventure. It's teamwork at its best. I'm sure the bees would be proud. This Queen Bee certainly is!

May 2012

The hard work has paid off. Last week we sowed our first crop. After months of planning and preparation, it's a proud moment. Pitchfork in hand, the team has sweated its way through sun, showers and snow to clear the topsoil. There have been days and days of raking and digging. It's been back-breaking work to remove the weeds and their roots without the benefit of machines. But at last the garden is taking shape. Erica has kindly been caressing vegetable plants in her greenhouse, then chauffeuring them to us in the back of her car.

Feeling proud of the garden has coincided with a few discoveries that have made me nostalgic but very happy. For example, I've been looking into the history of the village, Polton Bank. The name Polton Bank comes from two old Scots words for 'pool' and 'farm', so it's thought that the name means simply 'farm by a pool'. The fact that 'farm' is in the name must mean the soil is good!

Loanhead, the village at the top of the valley, one-and-a-half kilometres away, was granted a charter in 1669 to allow a weekly market and annual fair. The region, now classified as a conservation area, has always been largely agricultural, but with the River Esk running through it, the waterpower was soon harnessed and two substantial paper mills were established. The first was Polton Mill, opened in 1750. (To think that the Battle of Prestonpans had taken place only five years before just a few kilometres away on the coast!) By 1790, under new management, Polton Mill became the first ever mill to use chlorine to bleach the paper.

We think our house may have been the home of the mill manager at some stage as the stairs to the garden carry on down to where the mill would have been. The mill closed shortly after the Second World War. The village also had a farm that became the first tuberculosis hospital in the country. Patients were sent there for rehabilitation under the care of Edinburgh's Royal Victoria Hospital. It must be a sign of good clean air in the neighbourhood.

After the Second World War, Italian prisoners of war (POWs) were sent to work on local farms. My own father, who had been born in Picinisco in 1919, had arrived in Cockenzie just before his second birthday. English was his first language as his mother was Nonna Café. That was what we called her because she had a café, and although she was Italian, she'd been born in London in 1888. She moved back to Italy when she was four.

In 1940, when Mussolini joined forces with Hitler, Churchill issued the 'collar the lot' order and my daddy and his daddy were incarcerated. Daddy was interned on the Isle of Man for two years but my grandfather, along with Victor's grandfather, were sent to Canada on the ill-fated Arandora Star. Over 1200 men lost their lives when a German U-boat sunk this beautiful

the bothy   MAY bees   beehive   horse

luxury liner off the coast of Ireland.

In 1942, Daddy was released from the Isle of Man on compassionate grounds, the authorities having realized that those poor Italians and Polish boys who had been locked up had no reason for or intention of collaborating with the enemy. Daddy was allowed home but had to do farm work. He was based in Haddington in East Lothian, but many other men were sent to Polton Farm. Digging a little deeper, I've discovered that all the internees were moved from farm to farm and Daddy was posted to Polton for a short period.

After the war, life carried on much as it had before but tinged with sadness for all the lives lost on both sides.

I was 24 when Daddy died. Losing someone is the same feeling whether you're 20 or 60. You never forget those you love the most and you hold onto anything that brings them back in whatever way. So my journey from town every day, with the chimney stacks of Cockenzie Power Station in the distance and the drive past Polton Farm, is so meaningful for me. I still miss Daddy 20 years on but I do, however, feel very close to him out here.

June 2012

For the first time, Victor and I are beginning to feel we've got a garden. The borders and beds are all neatly marked with twine to ensure they're straight. The pressure-treated wood has been stained to blend with the soil and has been hammered in place. This was noisy work.

The silence in the garden is usually magical but hammering in the planks was louder than a Hibs (our local football team, the Hibernians) fan celebrating a home win, which is a miracle that doesn't happen often enough for my liking.

Erica booked a trailer to head down to the horses and bring back our secret ingredient – the manure – but the driver was ill. The team proved heroic. They jumped in their cars packed with large polythene bags and brought back just enough manure to treat the soil. Erica says we won't have to use manure very often and that certain plants mustn't get any at all due to contamination risks. I'm learning all the time.

The start of the month was energetic but the end has been a dead weight. Despite the calendar telling us it's summer, the elements have taken charge. The ground conditions have dictated the pace of the work and things are slowwwing down ...

Our first deadline is in the diary, so the clock is ticking. We're celebrating Slow Food Week with a five-course tasting menu, but for the first time since we've taken part, we're showcasing our own produce with a Casa San Lorenzo celebration supper. Erica's so anxious to deliver on time that we've even caught her talking to the plants.

Everything's going well but suddenly nature bites back. This time it's not the weather.

Who would have thought that our garden of tranquillity could suddenly turn into an NHS helpline hotspot? With all the Health & Safety requirements and Accident at Work legislation, we've always taken great care to avoid accidents.

MAY seedlings   nonna   view

Garden equipment often comes with safety warnings. Chainsaws, pitchforks, shovels, shears, strimmers and lawn mowers are all lethal weapons in the wrong hands. Steel-tipped boots are a prerequisite for professional gardeners, as a small lapse in concentration can mean the loss of a toe. But we never planned for disease.

Our garden is remote and was very overgrown. Victor's first job had been to cut back all the long grasses and strip out the unwanted shrubs and bushes. About three weeks ago he showed me his right leg. He'd won the Mr Legs competition in Lanzarote in 1980, so I was looking forward to this, but a huge circular spot surrounded by concentric circles had appeared on his calf.

A trip to the pharmacy the next day was followed by some hydrocortisone cream. A few days later the problem appeared to have gone.

Two weeks later, however, and Victor could hardly walk. He had huge pains in his legs and knees. Straight to the GP. Lyme Disease. Ticks from deer live in long grasses and a bite from an infected tick can be fatal if not detected early enough. We're feeling lucky that the doctor diagnosed it right away. Left untreated it can lead to paralysis, rheumatoid arthritis and, in severe cases, brain damage. Thankfully we've caught this early enough and a huge dose of antibiotics is hopefully going to do the trick for this tick. As newcomers to the country, we've loved seeing our wild friends. The roe deer in particular have been a highlight for the children, but the deer fences are going up now, so it's no go for Bambi.

My top tip this month is, keep your trousers tucked into your builders' boots and leave the legs for Lanzarote!

July 2012

Summer! Ari (Arianna, our Number One Christmas Day Baby) asked, why does it rain in Scotland in summer? When you're only six the weather can be confusing. Summer should equal sunshine but up until this little one's six-and-a-half birthday, she hadn't experienced anything like the sizzling 70s. We've had so few hot days never mind hot summers.

Now, though, the rain is really slowing everything down to the point of tears. The soil's so heavy it's making it impossible for us to crack on with the essential digging and planting. The next few beds that need tackling are full of grasses, weeds and, worst of all, slugs that roam from sunrise to sunset. With the mildest spring and the wettest summer, the slugs have come out in their hundreds. On average we're catching 300–400 a day. The children were helping, but at 1p per catch, we needed a more cost-effective solution.

It's old Mother Hen to the rescue. We're going to cage and chicken-wire the bed that needs preparing, then we'll unleash the chickens. We've bought some lovely hens from a local farmer in East Lothian. He said new pullets or young hens are brilliant for eggs but aren't half as good as their old mothers when it comes to the hard work of foraging for grubs and slugs. Hens love doing this and are a vital part of pest

JUNE making timber edges laying path mr legs mixing concrete

19

control in organic gardens. Our old hens will have brutally toughened beaks and feet, which are perfect for all that scrapping and scratching. It's a success. The hens are in heaven and the team can take a break from the really hard, yucky, slug-catching work.

August 2012

Our first real sense of an abundant harvest. We can't believe our luck. Everyone is motivated by outcomes and here at Casa San Lorenzo, we've been motivated by our tummies. Despite the dismal weather, the many green fingers tending the garden have managed to produce the most wonderful treats – red orache, beet leaf, 'Roxy' lettuces, mustard frills, calendula and, best of all, the courgettes, with those stunning yellow flowers that shine out like beacons from amongst their leaves.

More big investments are planned this month. We've started preparations for Polly the polytunnel. We need to build a wall over a metre high and 15 metres long to support Polly and level the ground. It's a pain in the neck!

The pond will also be drained and the lining stripped away. Once drained, it turns out that the pond has left a vast hole in the ground that's rather dangerous, so we've used the rubble from the house to backfill it.

Now we need to start thinking about the wall. I've never been good at spending money where you can't see it. Our new wall is one of those projects where only we'll know how much it cost and how much that hurt. But it's essential as

we need a solid foundation for Polly. If the rain stays away, we hope to have this work finished by the end of the year so we can extend the growing season and really support the garden.

September 2012

A garden is the perfect place to take time and contemplate not only what we eat but also how it gets to our plates. Intensive farming, advances in technology and cold storage have helped keep the cost of food in the supermarkets down, but droughts in America are causing grain prices to increase yet again, together with the price of foods like beef, lamb, dairy and cereals – though basic fruit and vegetable prices haven't increased that much over the last 10 years. By contrast, the cost of producing food by traditional means has increased almost tenfold. Each day I'm amazed at how much time is needed to produce our crops. By the end of the year we'll be growing from just under a hectare of land. This takes two full-time gardeners. The planning is the most time-consuming: you have to consider companion planting, crop rotation, soil type, heritage varieties and season.

Planting is the next killer. It's backbreaking work to prepare the soil both for direct seed sowing and for planting out seedlings. Keeping an eye on things and checking daily that the slugs, the frost or the bugs aren't destroying all your hard work take time but aren't physically hard. Then there's the harvesting. Handpicking is a labour of love. Our humble daily harvest of radishes, leeks, courgettes and salad leaves,

JULY henhouse   hen   cloches

which is enough for about 20 dishes on the menu, takes approximately two hours to pick. The customers can't see the expense that's gone into what they're eating, but they can definitely taste the difference.

October 2012

One year and four months after starting work on the house, we've finally moved into our home. We're exhausted but exhilarated, and the three children are bursting with energy.

Monday saw my first meeting with Erica since we've moved in. What a lovely feeling it was, walking down to the garden from our new home rather than walking through a building site. Apples were on the agenda.

Scotland has a long and wonderful history of apple cultivation. The ability to harvest and store apples made them an ideal crop pre-refrigeration, and the Scottish climate is particularly well suited to heritage varieties. The late nineteenth century saw Scotland at the peak of its power, exporting apples all around the world. Coincidentally, this was when our house was built, too.

Since we haven't inherited any fruit trees in our garden, the challenge is to establish a range of cooking and dessert apples that we'll be able to harvest over an extended period and that will offer a variety of flavours and characteristics.

The team headed down to Harestanes Countryside Visitors' Centre near Jedburgh on 7 October to celebrate the twentieth anniversary of their Apple Day. After much munching and crunching, we chose the top tasters. From

January to March we'll be planting Lord Derby, White Melrose, James Grieve and Chivers Delight, plus six varieties of espalier and cordon apples. All are to be planted along the principal walls and around the front lawn, with each location chosen with the sunlight in mind.

Between the apples we'll be planting redcurrants, two morello cherry trees and one sweet cherry. Lots of thought has gone into the volume of fruit that these will produce as well as how the garden will look once they're established. We'll have to wait about three years to truly reap the benefits of this venture. The apples will be ready just when we finish decorating the house, no doubt. Note to self: remember to have a party!

November 2012

We're very fortunate to call our suppliers our friends. Two of these are Robert Wilson and his darling wife Sylvia, of Scotherbs.

Four years ago we asked for their advice on planting a herb garden in Princes Street Gardens. There was a small abandoned stretch of land adjacent to The Scottish Cafe & Restaurant at the Scottish National Gallery and we just wanted to look after it. Oregano, fennel, rosemary, lavender, lemon thyme, lemon balm, lemon verbena, chives and one sensational cardoon now live happily on this south-east-facing embankment. This little stretch of very sandy soil has fewer than three hours' direct sunlight in winter and six hours in summer. It's wonderful to see the herbs surviving in such an unexpected place.

AUGUST crops

SEPTEMBER fruit trees

It was this project that was the inspiration for our Casa San Lorenzo journey. We've tapped into Robert's skills again this month and asked for advice on a new patch of ground at the back of our kitchen garden cottage. This time we have a sheltered but shaded east-facing border with much heavier soil. Chives, garlic chives, wild thyme, lemon balm and oregano have been planted in the sunnier section, with wild strawberries, wild garlic, wood sorrel, spearmint, Solomon's Seal and shuttlecock ferns in the more shaded area.

It's the perfect time to be planning this part of the garden. The soil is still warm enough for the plants to settle. When spring comes, they'll be established and with a few sunny days and some watering, we'll have our second beautiful herb garden in less than six months. Herbs add such depth of flavour and the finishing touch to any dish. They're my favourite ingredient.

December 2012

My youngest daughter is a Christmas Day baby so, not surprisingly, she loves Christmas carols. Walking around the garden this morning has reminded me of how, when she was very little, we'd often play Jingle Bells in July. The holly and ivy in the garden have brought all those glorious memories back.

The garden has been bursting with holly berries since early November. They make a wonderful food supply for the birds – robins, blackbirds, blue tits, wood pigeons and one stunning pheasant. The glorious green of the holly and ivy leaves has brought a majestic glow to everything. Until now, we've only been thinking of the garden in terms of the food it can produce, but this is an unexpected early Christmas present.

The holly and ivy also provide us with the most beautiful, sustainable and free Christmas decorations we could imagine. We've used them to decorate outside Ristorante Contini. Our dear friend Mr Maxwell has created the most beautiful entrance using evergreens from the garden. It's so exciting to have the garden both for food and to provide this visual feast during our favourite annual celebrations.

January 2013

We've got at least 15 centimetres of snow in the garden and the children are having a ball. The paths between the beds and the natural slope of the garden make the best sledging runs in the world. Snowball fights, snowmen and tracking the furry neighbour – our friendly fox – are the best free fun going, whatever your age.

The garden looks like an Alpine picture postcard, with the snow deep enough to insulate all the kale, garlic and leeks. Their green leaves are just popping out from beneath the fluffy white flakes that are helping to keep them snug. We're all hoping the snow won't last too long and, more importantly, that the temperature won't drop so much that we'll lose our crops. Meanwhile, the Bothy looks like a lovely mountain retreat. Inside, it's perfectly cosy. Outside, in cold frames, our seedlings have

apple tree   NOVEMBER herb garden   raking leaves

been carefully potted so they're ready to be planted directly in the soil in the better weather. We've got crimson-flowered broad beans and sweet peas planned for June, and ten new salad varieties that we hope to be enjoying in May.

The mild weather last week allowed us to get most of the soil cleared and prepared around the edges of the garden for our apple trees. But with the snow, planting them has been put on hold, so this week we've been organizing celeriac, parsnip, carrots and beetroot seed orders. These will be nurtured in the old window frames that were salvaged from the house to make mini cold frames. They've been stripped and are looking magnificent. I love the patience and practicality of gardeners. They don't harm the environment or imperil the food chain. I wish all aspects of our food industry were the same. Our kitchen garden will encourage me to eat more greens – though I doubt I'll ever be a vegetarian – and it will teach me to be patient, practical and sustainable. It will also give us an opportunity to be as happy as the children, whatever our age.

February 2013

Happy Birthday to our lovely kitchen garden. Well, it's a 14-month birthday rather than a one-year birthday, but never mind – I made a carrot cake to celebrate. And the present for the garden (and for Erica) is Polly the polytunnel, bought from Northern Polytunnels. It's huge and took five days to build. Robert of Scotherb fame has very kindly sent down his boys to install it.

They did an incredible job despite the blizzards that we've had over the last few days. It feels good to have finally got Polly in place.

We've had a very exciting and challenging journey, and at times we've really questioned our business decision. The cost of setting up the garden has been far greater than we'd imagined. Sorting out the access and the drainage, and improving the soil condition, not to mention the weather problems and the labour costs, have all impacted more than we budgeted for. So have we done the right thing? Absolutely, yes.

While no one would argue that the invention of central heating, washing machines and fridges hasn't enhanced our lives, we're all aware that too much damage has been done in other areas, in particular in relation to the environment and our eating habits. Buying local, eating in season and maintaining our food heritage must surely be the focus of all our food choices. Growing and cooking our own food, if we can, is the icing on the cake.

Our journey to San Lorenzo has helped us to understand what we love and cherish about our food. Last week, The Scottish Cafe & Restaurant received a three-star rating from the Sustainable Restaurant Association. It's the first gallery restaurant in the UK to receive this honour. Those three stars were nurtured with that love.

Our kitchen garden is now a central part of the sustainable food choices we make and we look forward to sharing all the benefits when our labour of love truly bears fruit.

taking a break   DECEMBER winter garden   HAPPY BIRTHDAY garden (with Polly)

january

January is the month of the year when we can wipe the to-do-list slate clean and start afresh. Weather permitting, the garden looks relatively healthy. There is still a lot of colour and we know we've got a reasonable volume of crops to keep us going.

In season we have cabbage, cauliflower, chicory, chard, pheasant, partridge, red deer, haddock, cod, whiting and pears.

winter chard & bean soup
with chicory toast

Dried beans and pulses give texture to our food and added nutrition in the winter months. I love to use them in stews and chunky soups. Combining dried cannellini beans with chard makes a really hearty winter soup that will warm the whole family. The fennel adds another layer of flavour and the chicory toast makes it into a complete meal.

Victor loves chunky soup while the children prefer it creamier, so I use a food processor or hand-held blender to blend about a quarter of the soup to a smooth consistency once the chard leaves have wilted and after removing the sausage. I then return the blended soup to the rest of the soup in the pan – and everyone is happy.

SERVES 4

500g dried cannellini beans
1 tsp bicarbonate of soda
2 large onions, finely chopped
1 large fennel bulb, finely chopped
500g rainbow chard
2 tbsp extra virgin olive oil
1 litre vegetable stock or ham stock
salt and freshly ground black
 pepper
200g Calabrese sausage or chorizo
 sausage

to finish
2 garlic cloves
salt
large handful of flat-leaf parsley
 leaves
extra virgin olive oil
2 tsp fennel seeds
2 tsp rosemary, leaves only,
 very finely chopped

Soak the beans overnight in a large pot with plenty of cold water, to which you have added the bicarbonate of soda. This helps release the nasty gases that give beans their anti-social side effects. The next day, rinse the beans and return them to the pot with plenty of fresh cold water. Bring to the boil, then drain and rinse under the tap.

Finely chop any coarse chard stalks. In a large soup pan, fry the onion, fennel and the chopped chard stalks in a generous amount of olive oil until soft and golden. The longer and slower this process takes, the better the flavours will be in the finished soup.

Add the stock and the rinsed beans and bring to a simmer. Season to taste with salt and pepper. If you are using ham stock, you may not need to add any salt at this stage. Remove the skin from the sausage and add to the pan in one piece. Simmer for 40–60 minutes until the beans are soft. The time this will take depends on how dry the beans were when you started and how long you soaked them for.

Coarsely chop the chard leaves and finely chop any tender stalks. Add these to the soup and simmer for about 5 minutes, or until the leaves have wilted. Adjust the seasoning. Remove the sausage from the pot. If you want to make the soup a bit creamier, this is the moment to blend a quarter of it, then return the blended soup to the pan. You can either serve the sausage separately or slice it and return it to the soup.

To finish, use a pestle and mortar to cream the garlic with a pinch of salt. Add the parsley leaves and a generous spoonful of the olive oil, and cream together. Finally add the fennel seeds and rosemary and gently work to a runny paste, adding more oil if required. Add a couple of spoonfuls of this finishing touch to the soup.

chicory toast

Salted anchovies have been used in the British Isles since the Roman invasions almost 2000 years ago. Their unique flavour adds depth to any recipe. I always buy them bottled in olive oil, taking the one or two that I need and storing the rest in the fridge for as long as they last, which is often months. I love them and when matched with roast chicory, the flavour is heavenly.

SERVES 4

2 heads of chicory
6–8 tbsp extra virgin olive oil
1 tbsp light honey (such as clover or acacia)
salt and freshly ground black pepper
2 salted anchovies in olive oil
1 garlic clove
small handful of flat-leaf parsley, leaves only,
   coarsely chopped
1 dried red chilli, crumbled
4 thick slices of country or sourdough bread

Preheat the oven to 200°C/400°F/Gas 6. Quarter the chicory lengthways, then quarter it again. Lay the quarters in an ovenproof dish and drizzle with a little olive oil, the honey and a generous sprinkle of salt and freshly ground black pepper. Roast in the preheated oven for 10 minutes, or until the chicory has wilted.

Meanwhile, use a pestle and mortar to cream together the anchovies and garlic. Loosen with some olive oil, then stir in the parsley and chilli. The mixture should make a lumpy sauce rather than a smooth one. Pour about 2 tbsp olive oil on a ridged griddle pan and toast both sides of the bread. When golden, remove the toast and rub with some of the anchovy sauce.

Place the hot chicory on top of the toast and drizzle with more of the anchovy sauce. Finish with a sprinkle of salt and some freshly ground black pepper. Serve hot, though it is also really tasty when eaten cold.

With the addition of the chicory toast, the soup has now been transformed into a balanced main meal that you can enjoy cuddled around a cosy fire. You have the protein of the beans, the vitamins in the greens, the omega oils in the anchovies, and the carbohydrates in the bread.

chicory, orange & pomegranate salad
with mustard dressing

Pomegranates are at their best now. Their colour, flavour and immune-boosting qualities (they are packed with vitamins C and B) make them a must for this time of year. I can find references to lemons, oranges, melons and pineapples having been grown in Scotland in grand Victorian gardens, but of course, I can't find any mention of pomegranates. I love my pomegranates; they last for ages in the fridge, and one of our favourite Puglian holidays was in the middle of a pomegranate orchard, so I can't resist including them in this recipe.

SERVES 4

2 tbsp pumpkin seeds
1 tsp yellow mustard seeds
1 head of chicory, leaves washed
  and dried
1 large orange, skin and pith
  removed and cut into segments
1 pomegranate, seeds only
3 tbsp extra virgin olive oil
1 tbsp lemon juice
salt

Preheat the oven to 180°C/350°F/Gas 4. When the oven is hot, place the pumpkin and mustard seeds on a baking tray and roast for 5 minutes until they are crisp.

Scatter the chicory, orange segments and pomegranate seeds on a large platter and scatter the hot pumpkin and mustard seeds on top.

Mix the olive oil and lemon juice with a generous pinch of salt to make a dressing, then mix well with the salad.

A Hind's Daughter by James Guthrie

The small girl in this picture has just stood up after cutting a cabbage in the family field. James Guthrie (1859-1930) painted this essentially Scottish scene in the Berwickshire village of Cockburnspath, where he opted to stay during the winter, unlike his Glasgow friends, who returned to the city at the end of the summer. The girl's father was a hind – a skilled farm labourer – and cabbage (or kail) was a staple diet of the hinds and their families.

pheasant breasts
with spiced pickled cabbage

Pickled red cabbage has always been a national favourite but eating it hot with some seasonal game beats the cold version hands down. The pheasant breasts are very easy to pan-fry and quick to prepare. Victor has been trying to cut down on carbohydrates for years. This dish doesn't need carbs but a few well-roasted rosemary potatoes never really go amiss.

SERVES 4
1–2 tbsp extra virgin olive oil
4 young pheasant breasts
salt and freshly ground black pepper

Place a heavy frying pan, coated with a little oil, over a medium heat. When it is hot, add the pheasant breasts, skin side down. If the pan is hot enough, you will hear the skin sizzling as soon as it hits the pan. Cook for about 3 minutes until the breasts are seared and can easily be released from the pan. Turn them over and cook for a few minutes more.

Meanwhile, preheat the oven to 180°C/350°F/Gas 4. Transfer the breasts to a roasting tray, season with salt and pepper and place in the preheated oven. Cook for 5–7 minutes until firm to the touch. Remove from the oven, allow to rest for a few minutes, then slice each breast into 3 or 4 pieces and serve with the hot spiced pickled cabbage.

spiced pickled cabbage

SERVES 4
1 large red cabbage
75g fresh ginger, peeled and very finely sliced into matchsticks
200g light brown sugar
250ml malt vinegar
250ml red wine vinegar
2 bayleaves

Prepare the cabbage by removing the outer leaves and the hard heart. Shed as finely as possible with a mandolin or food processor.

Layer the cabbage, ginger and sugar in a large flameproof casserole dish. Pour over the two vinegars, add the bayleaves and bring to the boil. Reduce the heat to a simmer and cover with a lid.

Simmer very slowly for about 2 hours until the cabbage is tender. Stir occasionally. Be patient as it takes time to get the cabbage lovely and soft and totally delicious. Remove the bayleaves and either serve straight away or remove from the heat and reheat when needed. It reheats very well.

cauliflower fritters
with pear, chicory & walnut salad

I loved school dinners but didn't look forward to cauliflower, which was often cooked to death with a minimum of seasoning. However, at home, Mummy prepared fried cauliflower in a rich egg-and-flour batter and it transformed this humble but very beautiful vegetable into a real treat. These fritters make a lovely starter when served with a light salad but they go equally well with roast meat or fish.

I like to cook the fritters at the very last minute as a snack when friends come round for dinner; they go so well with a cold glass of bubbly or a beer. The coriander leaves give an extra little flavour lift, especially if you are having the fritters as a snack, but you can leave it out if you prefer. The parsley on its own gives a clean, crisp flavour that is a bit more elegant. The pear salad makes a refreshing partner to these slightly naughty fritters.

SERVES 4 as a starter
(makes about 12 fritters)

1 small cauliflower, broken
  into florets
4 eggs
25g flat-leaf parsley leaves,
  coarsely chopped
4 tbsp plain flour
1 small garlic clove, crushed
salt and freshly ground black
  pepper
25g coriander leaves,
  coarsely chopped
light olive oil, for frying

Blanch the cauliflower florets by plunging them in boiling salted water for a few minutes until tender but not overcooked. Drain well and set aside.

Put the eggs, parsley, flour and garlic in a large mixing bowl and season with plenty of black pepper and a generous pinch of salt. Add the chopped coriander. Beat with a wooden spoon or balloon whisk until you have a smooth batter. Add the cauliflower and coat it well with the batter. Break the cauliflower up slightly while you are mixing it in as this makes the fritters easier to fry.

Half-fill a shallow frying pan with the olive oil and place over a moderate heat. When the oil is hot, add a drop of the batter. It should bubble immediately; if it spits, the oil is too hot. When the oil is the right temperature, add a few tablespoonsful of batter at a time and fry slowly, turning occasionally until golden all over. Cut a fritter in half to check it is fully cooked, otherwise the centre can be runny and will taste awful.

Remove onto kitchen paper or greaseproof paper to drain and repeat until all the batter is used up. The fritters can be kept in an oven at 150°C/300°F/Gas 2 for up to 30 minutes. Sprinkle with a little salt before serving.

pear, chicory & walnut salad

I love the colour of this salad. The pale elegance of the pear, chicory and yogurt makes it look very delicate but it is really tasty. These January flavours with the little edge of chilli and lime make it feel almost like summer.

SERVES 4

12 walnut halves
2 tbsp extra virgin olive oil, plus extra for frying
4 tbsp natural yogurt
juice of 1 unwaxed lime
50g mint leaves
25g flat-leaf parsley leaves
1 green chilli, deseeded
  and thinly sliced
salt and freshly ground black pepper
2 firm but not hard pears
1 head of chicory, leaves washed and dried

Pan-fry the walnuts in a little olive oil until golden. Remove and set aside.

Place the yogurt, olive oil, lime juice, mint, parsley and chilli in a blender and blend to a smooth sauce. Season to taste with salt and pepper and refrigerate until required.

When ready to serve, peel and deseed the pear and slice it into a bowl. Add the chicory and coat with the sauce. Mix well. Sprinkle with the fried walnuts and serve with the hot cauliflower fritters.

isle of mull macaroni cheese with cauliflower

Macaroni cheese has got to be a favourite for most people. Adding a vegetable such as cauliflower really lightens this dish and makes it extra-tasty and healthier. For some reason, I didn't stay for school lunches on a Wednesday but instead used to walk to the café where Mummy would have macaroni cheese on the menu. The classic Scottish red cheddar that she used gave her macaroni cheese a very different colour to this version – so different that sometimes the annatto colouring would almost dye the plate.

At The Scottish Cafe & Restaurant we champion artisan producers and are so proud of all the wonderful cheese producers that Scotland in particular can now boast. There are too many to name them all, but since day one we've been championing Jeff Rea, Humphrey Errington, Pam Rodway (now retired) and Barry Graham. In honour of them, there is no red cheddar in this dish.

SERVES 4

½ small cauliflower, broken
  into florets
500g macaroni or any short pasta
80g unsalted butter
80g plain flour
salt and freshly ground white
  pepper
½ tsp English mustard powder
600ml full-fat milk
4 tbsp double cream
350g Isle of Mull cheddar,
  finely grated

Blanch the cauliflower florets by plunging them in boiling salted water for a few minutes until tender but not overcooked. Drain well and set aside. Cook the macaroni in boiling salted water until al dente. Drain well and set aside.

Preheat the oven to 200°C/400°F/Gas 6. To make the sauce, melt the butter in a pan over a low heat, then add the flour. Cook for about 3 minutes, stirring continuously until the mixture starts to bubble. Add 1 tsp salt, ½ tsp pepper and the mustard powder. Slowly add the milk and beat with a metal whisk to prevent lumps forming. When the sauce starts to thicken, add the cream and 250g cheddar. Check the seasoning.

Add the cauliflower and macaroni. The mixture will be wet but the macaroni will absorb the sauce as it cooks. Transfer to an ovenproof dish and sprinkle the remaining cheddar on top. Bake in the preheated oven for 20 minutes until bubbling and golden.

At The Scottish Cafe & Restaurant we serve this with a small green salad dressed with a cold-pressed rapeseed oil dressing. This is made with 3 tbsp rapeseed oil to 1 tsp coarse-grain mustard, a small squeeze of lemon and a generous pinch of salt. This adds all the colour you could possibly need.

burns night steak pie

Steak pie was a staple for my parents' caterings. Daddy was always in charge of cutting and serving it. For the big Burns Night suppers we'd sometimes be feeding 400–500 people and all the family would be roped in. Brothers Numbers One and Six were always on mashed potato – that was a man's job. Brother Number Seven was on leeks and I'd be on carrots. It was a military operation that the Scots Guards would be proud of. If you have the time and skill to make your own pastry, I think you're amazing, but ready-made pastry is more than adequate for this dish. The children prefer their pie without beer, so for a sober supper adjust the volume of stock accordingly. And don't forget the mash and buttered carrots!

SERVES 4

1 tbsp extra virgin olive oil
1 large onion, finely chopped
1kg best-quality stewing steak, diced
2 tbsp plain flour, plus extra for dusting
100ml Caledonian Brewery IPA or similar pale ale
300ml home-made beef stock or 2 tsp Bovril dissolved in 300ml boiling water
3 sprigs of thyme
salt and freshly ground white pepper
500g ready-made all-butter puff pastry
full-fat milk, for brushing
egg wash made from 1 egg, beaten (optional)

Preheat the oven to 160°C/325°F/Gas 3. Heat the oil in a flameproof casserole dish over a medium heat. When it is hot, add the onion and fry gently until soft but not brown. Meanwhile, lightly coat the steak with the flour. This will help to thicken the gravy in the pie. Increase the heat under the casserole dish and add the meat. Fry, stirring continuously so the meat doesn't stick. Cook until the meat is browned all over. You may have to do this in batches. Add the ale and cook to reduce, then add just enough stock to cover the meat without drowning it. Season with the thyme, salt and pepper. Cover with a tight-fitting lid and bake in the preheated oven for about 2 hours.

Remove from the oven and check that the steak is tender. If it is not, cook for 30 minutes more. Add a little more water if the stew is looking dry. Meanwhile, remove the pastry from the fridge so it can sit for 1 hour before use. Remove the casserole dish from the oven and leave to cool. Increase the oven temperature to 200°C/400°F/Gas 6.

Choose a 1kg deep pie dish with a rim. Roll the pastry out on a floured surface until it is about 2.5cm bigger all round than the pie dish. Place the pie dish upside-down on top of the pastry and cut around the dish to make a dish-shaped piece of pastry. Fill the pie dish to the rim with stew. Do not over-fill it or the stew will leak out. Dip a pastry brush in a little milk and use to wet the rim of the dish. Use the leftover pastry to make a strip and press it onto the wetted rim. Brush the pastry strip with a little milk.

Gently place the cut-out pastry on top of the stew and press its edge firmly with your thumb and fingers to the pastry strip. Trim off any untidy bits of pastry. Use the flat edge of a knife to press the edges of the pastry strip and the pastry lid together. This will make a nice pattern and help to seal the pie. Then, with the edge of your knife, use a cutting action vertically around the edge of the pastry. This will help to make the pastry light and to rise. Score the top of the pastry and make one slit in the top to let the air escape.

Brush with milk or an egg wash and bake in the preheated oven for 10 minutes until the pastry is golden brown and has risen. Reduce the oven temperature to160°C/325°F/Gas 3 for 15–20 minutes until the filling is piping hot.

For special parties, individual pies are cute. Your tins or dishes will be small so you can get away without edging them with a pastry strip – just like these pies in plaid!

'For the big Burns Night suppers we'd sometimes be feeding 400–500 people and all the family would be roped in.'

the best hot milk mashed potato

SERVES 4
1kg floury potatoes
salt
125ml full-fat milk
½ nutmeg, freshly grated
1 bayleaf
125g unsalted butter
1 tbsp double cream

Peel and cut the potatoes into quarters and put in a pan with a pinch of salt and cold water to cover. Bring to the boil, then reduce the heat and simmer until the potatoes are tender. Drain well and return the potatoes to the pan. Cover the pan with a clean tea towel and place the lid on top.

In a small clean pan heat the milk, nutmeg, bayleaf and butter until the butter has melted and the mixture is warm. Uncover the potatoes, mash them, then strain the warm milk into the pan.

With a wooden spoon or spurtle, beat the potatoes until they are light as a feather. Add the cream for an extra layer of luxury and serve immediately.

buttered carrots

SERVES 4
4 carrots, thickly sliced
1 sprig of mint
50g unsalted butter
salt and freshly ground white pepper

Put the carrots in a pan with cold water to cover and bring to the boil. Add the mint, reduce the heat and simmer for 20 minutes until the carrots are tender. Drain, remove the mint and return the carrots to the pan. Add the butter, salt and pepper, stir well and serve immediately.

chocolate mint delight

Chocolate mint ice cream is a worldwide top seller and my children love it. I've never been able to figure out why. Is it the bright green colour that is the appeal or the flavour? Most children love green goo but resist brushing their teeth as the toothpaste is too minty, so the appeal of this ice cream remains one of life's mysteries. This recipe is a sophisticated version – without the green or the goo.

SERVES 4-6

for the chocolate mousse
250g minimum 40% cocoa
 Valrhona white chocolate
500ml double cream
6 sprigs of mint, leaves only,
 washed
3 eggs, separated

for the sponge
175g 70% cocoa Valrhona dark
 chocolate
6 large eggs, separated
175g golden caster sugar

to decorate
4–6 After Eight mints
few mint leaves
cocoa powder

Make the chocolate mousse. Break up the white chocolate and melt it in a heatproof glass or ceramic bowl over a bain-marie. Do not let the simmering water touch the bottom of the bowl. When the chocolate has melted, set it aside.

Place half the cream and the mint in a small pan and warm them through over a low heat. Remove from the heat and mix the mint through the cream with a wooden spoon to bruise the mint and help release the oils. Strain the warm cream into the melted chocolate and mix well. Add the egg yolks and mix with a wooden spoon.

Beat the egg whites until stiff in a clean, dry bowl, then fold into the chocolate mixture. Transfer to the fridge and chill for about 1 hour until soft-set, then lightly whip the remaining cream and fold into the mousse. Chill for about 1 hour more.

Meanwhile, make the sponge. Line a 25 x 35 x 2cm baking tray with greaseproof paper and preheat the oven to 180°C/350°F/Gas 4. Break up the dark chocolate and melt it in a heatproof glass or ceramic bowl over a bain-marie. Do not let the simmering water touch the bottom of the bowl. Set aside to cool slightly. In a bowl, beat the egg yolks with the sugar until the mixture is light and creamy. Beat the egg whites until stiff in a clean, dry bowl. Add the melted chocolate to the egg-yolk mixture and beat until smooth. Fold in the egg whites, then transfer the mixture to the lined baking tray.

Smooth the mixture level, then place in the preheated oven and bake for about 20 minutes, or until risen and spongy to the touch. Leave to cool in the baking tray. When you are ready to assemble the delight, turn out the sponge and remove the greaseproof paper. Cut out 2 or 3 circles of sponge per person so they fit in 4–6 lovely glasses.

Spoon a generous amount of chocolate mousse into each glass, then a layer of sponge, then a spoonful of mousse, then sponge. Continue layering until the glass is full. Chill for about 1 hour. When you are ready to serve, remove from the fridge. Decorate each glass with a whole After Eight mint, a mint leaf and a dusting of cocoa powder

sticky ginger & date pudding

Aged 85, Auntie Gloria is still a baking goddess. It's a miracle she never married as her baking is so good. There were many men, however, who tried to lure her with their charms but she was having none of it. Instead she dedicated her free hours to perfecting her skills with the oven. This has to be one of her best.

SERVES 6

150g dates, stones removed and coarsely chopped
1 tsp bicarbonate of soda
100g unsalted butter, plus extra for greasing
150g caster sugar
2 eggs
150g self-raising flour
3 tsp ground ginger
2 pieces of stem ginger in syrup, very finely chopped
pouring cream, to serve

for the sticky sauce
300g dark Muscovado sugar
200g unsalted butter
300ml double cream

Place the dates in a pan and add 150ml cold water. Bring to the boil, then remove from the heat and add the bicarbonate of soda. Mash to a smooth paste and set aside for 10 minutes. Meanwhile, make the sticky sauce. Melt the Muscovado sugar, butter and cream in a pan over a low heat. Stir until you have a glossy, smooth, shiny sauce. Set aside.

Preheat the oven to 180°C/350°F/Gas 4 and grease a 20 x 30 x 6cm baking tray or ovenproof dish. In a large mixing bowl, beat the butter and sugar until pale and fluffy, then slowly beat in the eggs, flour and ground ginger. Gently fold in the date mixture and stem ginger until everything has been incorporated. The mixture will be fairly wet.

Pour one-third of the sticky sauce into the bottom of the greased dish, then pour the date/sponge mixture on top. There should be enough room for the sponge to rise. Bake on the middle shelf of the preheated oven for 30–35 minutes. Serve straight from the oven with the remaining sticky sauce, which you can reheat so it's nice and runny. Add a little pouring cream for that extra touch of luxury.

hot orange marmalade creams

This fragrant chilled batter turns into the creamiest, slightly curdled, hot-set custard.
The texture is very unusual but don't worry – the sensation when you eat is a real treat.

SERVES 6

50g unsalted butter, at room
  temperature, plus extra for
  greasing
20g plain flour
75g caster sugar
2 eggs, separated
finely grated zest of 1 unwaxed
  lemon
juice of ½ unwaxed lemon
finely grated zest of 1 orange
juice of ½ orange
150ml full-fat milk
100ml single cream, plus 6 tbsp
  to finish
6 tsp home-made marmalade

Put the butter, flour, sugar, egg yolks, lemon and orange juices and zests, milk and cream in a blender, and blend until smooth. Refrigerate this batter for about 2 hours.

Meanwhile, preheat the oven to 180°C/350°F/Gas 4. Grease 6 individual heat-resistant glasses or ramekins and place in a bain-marie. Put 1 tsp marmalade in each glass.

Beat the egg whites until stiff in a clean, dry bowl. Gently fold the beaten whites into the chilled batter. Divide the mixture between the glasses. Fill the bain-marie with warm water and carefully place in the oven. Bake for 30–40 minutes until golden, topping up the water in the bain-marie if necessary to ensure the marmalade creams cook evenly.

Remove from the oven and spoon 1 tbsp cream into the middle of each pudding to make a well and give an added little hot–cold sensation.

GROWING NOTES

swiss chard
Beta vulgaris subsp. *cicla*

Cultivars grown at Casa San Lorenzo
- 'Rhubarb' – beautiful red stems
- 'Bright Lights' – rainbow mix of vibrant colours including pink, orange, white, red and yellow

Cultivation
- We sow from mid- to late summer to provide a productive winter crop.
- Chard is almost pest-free and will stand through winter with a little fleece protection.

Interesting fact
- Even when the plants have gone to seed the leaves do not become bitter like so many other plants.

winter cabbage
Brassica oleracea Capitata Group

Cultivars grown at Casa San Lorenzo
- 'January King' – beautiful blue-green foliage, often with the edge tinged with red
- 'Ormskirk' – another hardy Savoy cabbage

Cultivation
- We sow at the end of March/early April and prick out the seedlings into individual pots once they have four true leaves. They are transplanted out in June.
- Surround cabbage stems with cardboard collars to prevent cabbage root fly laying their eggs in the soil.
- Earth up stems in autumn to prevent plants moving/falling over due to wind rock.

Interesting fact
- Savoy cabbages are winter-hardy and withstand temperatures as low as -10°C.

cauliflower
Brassica oleracea Botrytis Group

Cultivars grown at Casa San Lorenzo
- 'Romanesco' – vibrant lime-green Italian cultivar for autumn
- 'Triomphant F1' – produces large white curds in winter

Cultivation
- We sow at the end of May and transplant at the beginning of July.
- It is important to keep the soil moist, especially in dry weather, so that growth is not checked.
- Protect from pests (pigeons and butterflies) with a fine mesh.
- Once the curd starts to develop, bend over four or five leaves to protect from rain and frost.

Interesting fact
- With the correct growing conditions, different cultivars can provide cauliflowers nearly all year round.

february

February is cold. It's always a shock how cold it is. The garden is covered in snow and we wish we could be in hibernation. The cloches and Polly the polytunnel keep us in produce and the colours of the garden are all muted and demure.

It's the month for some really hearty dishes to cheer us up. In season we have endive, kale, leeks, purple sprouting broccoli, Brussels sprouts, lobster, haddock, hake and stored apples.

leek & potato soup
with leek & barley bonbons

Leek and potato soup doesn't sound exciting. However, with a little time to really sweat the vegetables at the beginning, and the right amount of liquid so it doesn't become too watery, it is a true classic Scottish soup. If you can find time to make the little bonbons to go with the soup, then the whole experience changes from starter to majestic entrée or a winter night's supper to remember.

SERVES 4
150g unsalted butter
2 tbsp extra virgin olive oil
1 large onion, finely chopped
6 leeks, coarsely chopped,
  white and green parts kept separate
1kg floury potatoes (such as Maris Piper
  or King Edward)
salt and freshly ground white pepper
1 litre home-made chicken stock or boiling water

Heat the butter and oil together in a large pan over a medium heat. When they are hot, add the onion, the white part of the leeks and most of the green part. Reduce the heat and fry until soft, taking time to allow the flavours to develop so you get a really tasty base for the soup.

Meanwhile, peel, wash and cut the potatoes into small cubes. Add to the pan and season with salt and pepper. Add the stock or water and simmer for 35 minutes. Add the remaining green part of the leek and cook for 10 minutes more until the potatoes are soft.

Remove from the heat and transfer one-third of the soup to a clean bowl or pan. Blend until smooth using a hand-held blender, then return the blended soup to the large pan. Season to taste with salt and pepper.

leek & barley bonbons

MAKES approx. 20
50g unsalted butter
1 leek, very finely sliced
100g pearl barley
250ml home-made light chicken or
  vegetable stock, hot
75g Clava Brie or other soft cheese, crumbled
1 tbsp flat-leaf parsley leaves, finely chopped
salt and freshly ground white pepper
1 tbsp plain flour
1 egg white
100g dried breadcrumbs
light olive oil, for frying

Put the butter in a flameproof casserole dish over a medium heat and when it is hot, add the leek and fry until soft. Add the barley and toast for a few minutes. Add the hot stock and cook for 20–30 minutes until the mixture is the consistency of thick porridge. Beat in the cheese and parsley. Season to taste with salt and pepper, remove from the heat and leave to cool.

When cool, fold in the flour. This will help to bind the mixture. Form into small balls the size of large bonbons, then dip in the egg white and then in breadcrumbs. Refrigerate for 30 minutes.

To fry, ideally use a deep fat fryer but if you don't have one, use a large flameproof casserole dish instead. Half-fill with the olive oil and place over a medium heat . Be very careful never to leave the oil unattended. Check the oil is hot by carefully placing one of the bonbons in it. If it bubbles but doesn't spit, the oil is ready.

Fry the bonbons in small batches until crisp and golden. They can be kept in an oven set to 150°C/300°F/Gas 2 for up to 30 minutes. Serve with a sprinkle of salt.

haddock & leek fish cakes
with beetroot tartare sauce

Scotland has a great reputation for fish cakes. There isn't a fishmonger in the country that doesn't sell them. Often, though, they are made with those red rusk breadcrumbs and look fluorescent before they're fried and radioactive afterwards. But home-made fish cakes with fresh breadcrumbs and your favourite fish just can't be beaten. The loveliest thing is that the fish cakes are crispy on the outside and flaky and soft in the middle. With this recipe they have little crunches of leeks and gherkins to give even more flavour and texture. Delicious served with beetroot tartare sauce.

SERVES 4

400g floury potatoes
500g haddock or coley
500ml full-fat milk
salt
few peppercorns
25g unsalted butter
1 leek, thinly sliced
2 small gherkins or cornichons, cut into small cubes
3 stems of dill, finely chopped
freshly ground black pepper
100g plain flour
2 eggs
150g fresh breadcrumbs
100ml light olive oil

Peel and cut the potatoes into quarters and put in a pan with salt and cold water to cover. Bring to the boil, then reduce the heat and simmer until the potatoes are tender.

Meanwhile, put the fish in a pan with the milk, a pinch of salt and the peppercorns. Bring to a simmer over a low heat. Remove from the heat and leave until the milk is tepid. Remove the fish from the milk and flake it, being careful to remove any skin and bones. Leave to cool. Discard the milk and the peppercorns.

Drain the potatoes well and leave to dry in the pan for a few minutes before mashing. Mash with the butter but don't be tempted to add any milk as this will make the mixture too wet. The potato should be fluffy. Leave to cool but don't allow to go completely cold. Blanch the leek by plunging it in boiling salted water for a few minutes until tender but not overcooked. Drain well and set aside.

To form the fish cakes, fold the gherkins and dill into the mashed potato, then adjust the seasoning and add salt and plenty of black pepper. Finally fold in the fish and the leek. Be very gentle, as you don't want the fish to become mushy. Divide into 8 balls and pat to flatten slightly. Refrigerate for 30 minutes.

Remove the fish cakes from the fridge and dip each first in the flour, then in the egg, and finally in the breadcrumbs. Preheat the oven to 180°C/350°F/Gas 4. Heat the olive oil in a 30cm pan over a medium heat. When the oil is hot, add the fish cakes and fry, turning occasionally until golden brown all over. Transfer to a baking tray. Put in the preheated oven to rest for 10 minutes and to ensure they are thoroughly heated through.

beetroot tartare sauce

Traditionally, tartare sauce has a shallot in it but I never like its lingering taste. If you use a pickled beetroot instead, then you get the sharpness without the aftertaste.

SERVES 4
200g home-made mayonnaise (see right)
100g crème fraîche
25g capers in brine, rinsed and drained
10g dill, chopped
1 pickled beetroot, dried on kitchen paper and finely diced

Mix all the ingredients except the beetroot together in a bowl. Finally fold in the beetroot to marble the mixture with its colour.

home-made mayonnaise

SERVES 4
2 egg yolks, chilled
1 tsp Dijon mustard or English
 mustard powder
3 tbsp lemon juice
¼ tsp fine salt
300ml light olive oil or sunflower oil

Put the egg yolks, mustard, lemon juice and salt in a food processor or blender. Set the machine to slow and blend for a minute to combine the ingredients. Then, very, very slowly drizzle in the oil, a tiny amount at a time. When the mixture starts to thicken, gradually add more oil until the texture is that of thick yogurt.

gorgeous goujons

Hake is a fabulous fish. The texture is firm and dense, with many of the characteristics of halibut but the price tag of mackerel. It's ideal for frying and makes gorgeous goujons. These are brilliant served with my endive and yogurt salad.

SERVES 4

500g hake fillet, skin removed
1 egg
salt and freshly ground
 black pepper
200g pinhead oatmeal
light olive oil, for frying

Wash and dry the hake. Cut it into long, thin strips about the size of your thickest finger. Beat the egg with the salt and pepper. Dip the fish in the seasoned egg and then in the oatmeal. Remove onto kitchen paper or greaseproof paper. Preheat the oven to 180°C/350°F/Gas 4.

Half-fill a shallow frying pan with the olive oil and place over a medium heat. When the oil is hot, a drop of the batter should bubble immediately you place it in the oil; if it spits, the oil is too hot. Add the goujons, a few at a time, and fry slowly, turning occasionally until golden all over. Remove with a slotted spoon to a baking tray. Repeat until all the goujons are fried.

Bake in the preheated oven for 10 minutes until crisp. The par-frying and finishing in the oven reduces the amount of oil absorbed by the goujons.

endive & yogurt salad

Endive is such an unusual salad leaf. If it is bitter it can be braised to make it sweeter but if it is young, as here, it adds a crunchy texture and refreshing flavour to a salad served at the end of a meal. The yogurt makes this salad more substantial and marries really well with the endive.

SERVES 4

4 tbsp natural yogurt
2 tbsp extra virgin olive oil
25g flat-leaf parsley, leaves only
50g dill
juice of 1 unwaxed lemon
½ garlic clove
25g small capers in brine, rinsed
 and drained
salt and freshly ground black
 pepper
yellow leaves of 1 small endive,
 washed, broken into small pieces
 and dried

Put the yogurt, olive oil, parsley, dill, lemon juice and garlic in a blender and blend until smooth. Fold in the capers and season to taste with salt and pepper. Refrigerate until required.

To serve, scatter the endive leaves on a large plate or in a bowl and drizzle with the yogurt dressing.

As an alternative to serving the salad alongside the goujons, you can be a bit cheffy. Place the endive on a plate with the gorgeous goujons on top, then drizzle the yogurt dressing over and enjoy while hot. Serve with wedges of lime.

leek & thyme tart

SERVES 4

100g unsalted butter

1kg young leeks, coarse green leaves removed, cut into 1cm slices, washed and well drained

1 sprig of thyme, leaves only

50ml double cream

salt and freshly ground white pepper

500g ready-made all-butter puff pastry

extra virgin olive oil, for greasing

egg wash made from 1 egg, beaten

Put the butter in a large flameproof casserole dish or frying pan over a medium heat until melted. Add the leeks and fry gently until they are soft. If you're using young leeks, this will take 10–15 minutes. Add the thyme and mix through, then add the cream and cook for a few minutes until the mixture thickens. Season to taste with salt and pepper. Remove from the heat and leave to cool for about 15 minutes.

Preheat the oven to 180°C/350°F/Gas 4. Roll out the pastry on a floured surface to the thickness of a 20 pence piece. Cut around a dinner plate to make 2 pastry circles. Lightly oil a large baking tray and place 1 circle of pastry on it.

Gently spoon the leek mixture on top of the pastry, leaving an edge of about 15mm all around. Brush the edge with the egg wash, then place the other pastry circle on top of the leek mixture. Using a fork, press the edges of the pastry together all the way round to seal. Trim off any untidy pieces of pastry. Score the top and make one slit to let the air escape. Brush with more egg wash and bake in the preheated oven for 25 minutes until golden. Easy as pie!

I love tarts with fabulous fillings. Whether they be savoury or sweet, hot or cold, tarts are splendidly versatile. This leek and thyme tart is a delicious, light, warm lunchtime treat. A little leftover slice served cold also makes an irresistible savoury snack when you're peckish.

The French have to be the queens of tarts. I hope that hasn't offended any queens or any tarts! We should thank Mary Queen of Scots for forging the Auld Alliance and for bringing France's rich culinary inheritance to Scotland.

Ready-made puff pastry is my ultimate cheat's ingredient and for this dish it does the job brilliantly.

kale & hake pie

Hake is a great, sustainable local-waters fish and it's hard to beat on quality or price. The rich flakiness of the flesh is perfect for this pie but haddock would make a good alternative. I love meals that don't need much washing-up and with the kale at the bottom of the pie, this is a complete dish that fits the bill perfectly. On a busy school night, it couldn't be better. If you can be bothered, pipe the mashed potatoes on top rather than spooning them on. This makes lovely little potato peaks that will go crispy when baked. They just add that little extra touch of class. Be warned: if you use purple kale, the colour will bleed and you'll end up with a blue pie. Tastes delicious but you may need shades.

MAKES 4 individual pies
150g green curly kale, cut into
  fork-sized pieces
500ml full-fat milk
1 small onion, halved
3 cloves
1 bayleaf, broken in half
500g hake or haddock
50g unsalted butter, plus extra
  for greasing
50g plain flour
salt and freshly ground white
  pepper
200g Isle of Mull cheddar, coarsely
  grated

for the mash topping
500g floury potatoes
50g unsalted butter
1 egg yolk
good splash of full-fat milk
salt and freshly ground white
  pepper

To make the mash topping, peel and cut the potatoes into quarters and put in a pan with salt and cold water to cover. Bring to the boil, then reduce the heat and simmer until the potatoes are tender. Drain really well, then add the butter and egg yolk. Beat well to prevent the egg cooking and add enough milk to make a lovely creamy consistency. Season to taste and set aside.

Blanch the kale by plunging it in boiling salted water for a few minutes until tender but not overcooked. Drain, refresh under cold running water, then drain again really well. Set aside.

Put the milk in a large pan over a low heat. Add the onion, cloves and bayleaf and bring to a simmer.

Add the fish to the milk, increase the heat and bring to the boil. Immediately remove from the heat and leave the fish to poach in the milk for 5 minutes. Leave to cool, then remove the fish from the milk and flake it, being very careful to get rid of the bones. Strain the milk and set aside.

To make the sauce, put the butter in a medium pan over a low heat until it is melted. Add the flour and cook, stirring continuously, for about 3 minutes until the mixture starts to bubble. Season with salt and pepper. Slowly add half the strained milk and beat with a metal whisk or wooden spoon to prevent lumps forming. When the sauce starts to thicken, add half the cheese and adjust the seasoning.

Preheat the oven to 200°C/400°F/Gas 6. Grease 4 individual 400g pie dishes and divide the cooked kale between them. Divide the fish equally between the dishes on top of the kale. Pour the sauce on top of each and spoon or pipe the mashed potatoes on top of the sauce. Bake in the preheated oven for 25 minutes until the potato is golden and crispy.

st valentine's lobster
with lobster claw & potato salad

SERVES 2

1 x 900g lobster per person for
a main dish or half each for
a starter, halved, intestine and
brain sac removed, washed
and claws removed (use the
claws for the salad)
extra virgin olive oil, for drizzling

for the garlic butter

2 sprigs of wild garlic or 1 garlic
clove, crushed
150g unsalted butter
salt
50g flat-leaf parsley leaves,
finely chopped
1 dried red chilli, crumbled

Preheat the grill to its hottest setting or preheat the
oven to 230°C/450°F/Gas 8. Make the garlic butter by
using a mortar and pestle or blender to cream the garlic,
butter, a pinch of salt and the parsley and chilli together.
Place the lobster, flesh side up, on a strong baking tray –
one that won't buckle from the heat. Brush a tablespoon
of garlic butter over the lobster and drizzle with a little
olive oil to prevent the butter from burning too quickly.
Grill or bake for 8–10 minutes until the lobster has
turned pink and the flesh is creamy white. Don't be
tempted to leave the kitchen or get distracted!

lobster claw & potato salad

SERVES 2

2 lobster claws
500g waxy potatoes, boiled in
their skins until tender
1 tbsp baby capers in salt,
rinsed and drained
1 preserved lemon, rinsed and
finely sliced, or 1 unwaxed
lemon, peeled and finely sliced
25g chives, coarsely chopped

25g dill, coarsely chopped
25g flat-leaf parsley leaves,
coarsely chopped
1 garlic clove
1 red chilli, deseeded and finely
chopped
approx. 5 tbsp extra virgin olive oil
juice of 1 unwaxed lemon
salt and freshly ground black
pepper

Place the lobster claws in a pan of cold water. Bring to the
boil over a high heat, then reduce the heat and simmer for
5 minutes. Remove from the heat and leave to cool in the
water. When the claws can be handled, crack them in the
middle with a mallet, remove the shell and flake the meat.
Slice the potatoes into a large bowl. Scatter the lobster meat,
capers, preserved lemon, chives, dill and parsley on top. Peel
and slice the garlic and add to the salad together with the
chilli. Dress with the oil and lemon juice, a good pinch of salt
and plenty of pepper. Mix well and serve with your lovely
St Valentine's lobster.

We were so lucky to have been brought up between two busy harbours. The main catches were lobsters and langoustines. Both, funnily enough, would be my desert-island ingredients. If you are feeling a bit timid, ask your fishmonger to cut the lobster in half. He'll even remove the digestive tract and brain sac if you smile sweetly at him. I've been preparing lobsters for as long as I can remember so it has never bothered me, but I've never plucked a bird – and now that we've got Chicken Licken in the kitchen garden, I've no plans to start.

The lobster claws can be tricky to eat, especially if you're dressed for a romantic supper. (Oh, that takes me back! For 12 years I prepared lobster in one form or another for Victor for his birthday. Since we've had the children, I have cooked lobster on several occasions, but never on Victor's birthday and never for us to eat on our own.) So if you are wooing, entertaining or just have your best frock on, the last thing you want is to be up to your elbows in lobster juices. Instead, I always prepare the claws before they get to the table. This dish uses the claw meat to flesh out a potato salad. The only problem is, it's then too easy to eat. But that's a problem you can manage when it's only once a year.

Some dishes are a labour of love. Lobster Thermidor can be close to heartbreak, but it's worth it. Daddy was born in a very remote village in the Abruzzi mountains in the middle of Italy. He arrived in Scotland in 1921 and lived in a tiny village 16 kilometres outside Edinburgh, with a population of less than 1000. His family made and sold fish and chips and ice cream. It was all very simple and anything but glamorous. But though Daddy worked really hard for his mother, my Nonna, there was no doubt he was spoiled rotten. My aunts always said that Nonna felt guilty that Daddy was the only one of her children who was interned during the war as an enemy alien. A weekly visit to The Pompadour, The Palm Court or Gleneagles was Daddy's special treat. Before and after the Second World War, these famous hotel-restaurants were in the grand old league of the best railway hotels in the country. So with a generous mother and a taste for the good life, Daddy developed a taste for a few good things – Duck à l'orange (my French teacher was very quick to tell me, much to my amazement, that duck wasn't a French word), oysters, and, of course, Lobster Thermidor.

di ciacca lobster thermidor

Because we were a large family, Daddy was only able to indulge his expensive tastes once a year, when we all ate out as a family. That was when he – and Number Eight child, who always managed to sit next to him – would order Lobster Thermidor. If I get to heaven and my Daddy is waiting for me, I bet this is what will be on the table.

SERVES 2

2 x 750g lobsters (refrigerated to chill their nervous system)
salt
2 bayleaves
2 tbsp brandy
60g unsalted butter
60g plain flour
freshly ground black pepper

1 tbsp Worcester sauce
1 tbsp Tabasco sauce
350ml full-fat milk
1 tsp black peppercorns
200g good-quality medium cheddar (such as Isle of Mull), grated
2 tbsp double cream

Place the lobsters in a large pot of ice-cold water (you may need two pots). Add a little salt and a bayleaf. Bring the water to the boil, reduce the heat and simmer for 5 minutes. Remove from the heat and leave the lobsters to cool in the water.

Meanwhile, heat a medium saucepan and when it is hot, add the brandy. Flambé to burn off the alcohol. Add the butter and flour and cook for about 3 minutes, stirring constantly until the mixture starts to bubble. Season to taste with salt, pepper, Worcester sauce and Tabasco sauce. In a separate pan, gently warm the milk with the remaining bayleaf and the peppercorns. Strain the milk, then slowly add it to the butter and flour mixture. Beat well with a metal whisk to prevent lumps forming. When the sauce starts to thicken, add half the grated cheese. Finally add the cream and check the seasoning. Remove from the heat, cover with a lid and set aside.

Start preparing the lobsters by removing the claws. Crack them open, pick out the meat and set it aside. Place the rest of the lobsters on a large chopping board with a damp tea towel underneath so the board doesn't slip. Using a very sharp knife, cut the lobsters in half from head to tail. Remove and discard the brain cavity and the digestive tract from each of the halves. Carefully remove the fleshy tails: these are the jewels in the crown. Cut the tails into about 4 pieces, depending on the size of the lobsters.

Preheat the grill. Choose plates that will go under the grill without cracking and place the empty lobster shells on them. Return the sauce to the heat and let it warm through, taking care not to allow it to boil. Add the lobster flesh to the sauce and stir gently to coat it well. Pour the mixture into the empty lobster shells. Grate the remaining cheese on top and bake under the preheated grill until the cheese is nicely browned. Serve with some steamed rice and pan-fried kale.

raisin & chocolate parfait

Rum and raisins have been partners for years. I like to use Innis & Gunn Rum Beer. It is aged in rum barrels so it has a distinctive hint of that West Indian heritage. The intense chocolatiness of the parfait is an unusual contrast to the beer-soaked raisins. Close your eyes and you could be on holiday in Jamaica!

SERVES 4-6
400g raisins
100ml Innes & Gunn Rum Beer
4 eggs
55g caster sugar
450g 70% cocoa Valrhona dark chocolate
1 tsp vanilla extract
425ml double cream

Soak the raisins in the beer for at least 1 hour. Separate the eggs and beat the yolks with the caster sugar until light. Set aside.

Break up the chocolate and melt it in a heatproof glass or ceramic bowl over a bain-marie. Do not let the simmering water touch the bottom of the bowl. Remove from the heat, then stir in the vanilla extract and soaked raisins. Set aside. Beat the egg whites until stiff in a clean, dry bowl. In a separate bowl, whip the double cream until it forms soft peaks. Gently fold the egg-yolk and sugar and the chocolate and raisin mixtures together, then fold in the egg whites and, finally, the whipped cream.

Carefully divide between 4 or 6 individual ramekin dishes and freeze for 4–5 hours until set. Remove from the freezer 10 minutes before you want to serve the parfaits.

This delicious cheesecake is made all the more gorgeous by the crystallized rose petals. Candied rose petals involve sugar thermometers and tricky temperatures but crystallizing them is so easy and it's especially nice if you can use roses from your own garden. Making them is also a lovely activity for children. My children love them – probably because of the sugar – and the novelty of eating roses is a laugh. Rosewater has a very distinctive aroma and flavour. It's a Marmite moment – you either love it or hate it. My grandmother on Mummy's side, Nonna Flora, was a tremendous baker. When she visited from Glasgow, it was like having a visitor from Australia as her visits were few and very far between. She would arrive looking like the Queen Mother or Barbara Cartland, with flowers, silks, flounces and fluff, and all decked out in fake jewellery from her ears to her fingers. She always wore Floris perfume and the smell was not unlike rosewater. She was cuddly and lovely and this cheesecake reminds me of her for all the pretty, beautiful reasons. The rosewater in this recipe is really very subtle but if you don't like it, you could substitute vanilla extract. Nonna always called me 'pet' or 'petal', so, as my granny would say, 'Petal, it's worth a try.'

rosewater cheesecake

SERVES 8
crystallized rose petals (see below),
  to decorate
a few violets, to decorate

for the base
250g digestive biscuits, crushed into
  the consistency of fine breacrumbs
125g unsalted butter, plus extra for
  greasing

for the first filling
800g full-fat cream cheese

250g caster sugar
100g plain flour
pinch of salt
3 large eggs
400ml soured cream
juice and very finely grated zest
  of 1 small orange

for the second filling
300ml soured cream
1 tbsp icing sugar
4 tsp rosewater
juice of 1 small orange

The day before, preheat the oven to 160°C/325°F/Gas 3. Grease a 24cm springform tin and line the bottom with a circle of baking parchment. To make the base, melt the butter in a pan over a medium heat. Remove from the heat and add the digestive biscuits. Mix well. Spoon the biscuit-crumb mixture evenly over the bottom of the tin and press down gently with the back of the spoon. Bake in the preheated oven for 15 minutes. Remove from the oven and leave to cool in the tin. Increase the oven temperature to 230°C/450°F/Gas 8. Meanwhile, make the first filling. Using an electric mixer, beat the cream cheese until fluffy. Add the sugar, flour and salt and beat until smooth. Using the whisk attachment, beat in the eggs, soured cream, orange juice and zest. The mixture should be smooth and light. Place the cake tin on a baking tray and grease the sides of the tin again. Pour the first filling into the tin, then gently lift the tin and tap it down on a flat surface to release any air bubbles. This ensures the filling cooks evenly. Bake for 15 minutes, then reduce the temperature to 140°C/275°F/Gas 1 and bake for 20 minutes more. The cake should wobble slightly. Open the oven door and leave to cool in the oven for 1 hour. Meanwhile, beat together the ingredients for the second filling until smooth. Add a little more rosewater if you think it needs more impact. Gently pour this over the first filling, then cover with clingfilm and refrigerate overnight. To serve, use a flat knife to release the cake from the sides of the tin and carefully remove the outside ring. Slide the cake, with the baking parchment still in place, onto a large presentation plate. Decorate with a generous scattering of crystallized rose petals (see below) and a few violets.

crystallized rose petals

2 dozen organically grown rose petals
1 egg white, very lightly beaten
125g caster sugar

The day before, lay the rose petals out on greaseproof paper and check that they are clean and dry. Using sharp scissors, cut away any tough edges. Brush the petals with egg white on both sides then dip into the sugar. Gently lay the petals on large sheets of greaseproof paper and leave to dry in a cool room overnight.

hot crème caramel

Crème caramel was one of my favourite childhood desserts. Like so many of the good things in my life, this dish is the absolute opposite of the norm. Mummy made it during the winter months and we always ate it hot from the oven. Chilled crème caramel would have been unthinkable in a house that had no central heating, that backed onto the Firth of Forth and that had an ice-cream shop below the sitting room. Mummy's hot version was essential to warm us up. You get the lovely creamy set custard accompanied by the runny, hot toffee syrup. Serve with a little pouring cream, and you're sorted for a cosy winter treat!

SERVES 4

unsalted butter, for greasing
5 tbsp granulated sugar
1 vanilla pod
600ml full-fat milk
2 tbsp single cream
5 eggs
2 tbsp caster sugar

Grease 4 individual 150ml ramekins and place in a deep ovenproof tray. Preheat the oven to 150°C/300°F/Gas 2.

To make the toffee, put the granulated sugar in a heavy-based pan with a handle that won't conduct the heat.

Place over a low heat and bring to a simmer. The sugar should bubble slowly. Do not stir as this will make the sugar crystallize. After about 5–8 minutes it will start to colour, changing from a clear, almost see-through, colour to a rich golden-brown. It will burn very quickly towards the end so carefully remove from the heat using an oven glove, wait a few moments, and check the colour change. If the toffee isn't dark enough, return to the heat for a few moments. Pour enough toffee into each ramekin to cover the bottom.

To make the custard, cut the vanilla pod lengthways, scrape out the seeds with a sharp knife and put them in a small pan. Add the milk and cream and put the pan over a low heat. Heat gently until hot but not boiling. In a separate bowl, beat the eggs and caster sugar together. Pour the hot milk and cream mixture into the eggs and mix thoroughly. Strain through a sieve into a pouring jug to remove any lumps and the vanilla seeds. Divide the mixture between the ramekins. Put the tray on the top shelf of the preheated oven and half-fill the tray with warm water to create a bain-marie. Bake for 1½ hours until set.

To serve hot, remove each ramekin from the bain-marie using a towel, as the ramekins will be very hot. Run a knife between the edge of the custard and the ramekin, place a plate on top and turn the ramekin over. Still using the towel, lift the ramekin to release the crème caramel. Alternatively, you can make this pudding in the summer, leave it to cool, then refrigerate and serve it straight from the fridge.

GROWING NOTES

leeks
Allium porrum

Cultivars grown at Casa San Lorenzo
- 'Lyon' (also known as 'Prize Taker') – introduced to the UK in 1880 through seed merchants Stuart and Mein of Kelso; ready from September to November
- 'Musselburgh' – Scottish cultivar, named after the East Lothian town where it has grown since the 1830s; winter-hardy; harvest from November to February
- 'Toledo' – very late cropping, December to April

Cultivation
- We sow seed into deep pots in early April and allow them to grow on in the same container until mid-June.
- The leeks are then placed individually into deep holes in the ground. This encourages whiter stems by excluding light from around the plant. Leeks can also be 'earthed up' (soil moved against the stem) to encourage blanching.
- Leeks love moisture, so keep them well watered during dry periods.
- Harvest whilst young for delicious baby leeks.

Interesting fact
- Growing a range of cultivars (early/mid- and late-maturing) gives a continuous supply from September through to April.

endive
Cichorium endivia

Cultivars grown at Casa San Lorenzo
- 'Kimberley' – frisée type with ragged edges
- 'Dafne' – scarole type with broad leaves

Cultivation
- Sow mid- to late summer.
- Plant under cover in autumn.
- Blanch the leaves two weeks prior to harvest by tying them up with string or by placing a plate over the plant to exclude light. This makes the leaves sweeter.

Interesting fact
- Endive is hardier than its close relation, lettuce, and is adapted to the low light levels and cool temperatures of autumn and winter.

march

March in Scotland can be hit or miss. We have seen scorching sunny days and blizzards of snow that would leave a yeti lost.

So though we may still need some comfort food, the lighter, fresher salads are slowly creeping in. We have in season lamb's lettuce, wild garlic, purple sprouting broccoli, spinach, rhubarb, wild salmon, crab, carrots, radishes and whitebait.

spinach & curd cheese drop scones
with scotch bonnet dressing

Drop scones are a Scottish classic. This recipe turns the traditional sweet pancake into a surprisingly satisfying savoury version. I cook these as a first course with everyone standing in the kitchen. Serve with my Scotch Bonnet Dressing.

MAKES 10-12

200g young spinach leaves
25g unsalted butter
salt and freshly ground black
 pepper
225g curd cheese or Crowdie
2 eggs, separated
1 small spring onion,
 very finely sliced
50g plain flour
little freshly grated nutmeg
finely grated zest of
 1 unwaxed lemon

Pan-fry the spinach in a little butter over a low heat just until the leaves have wilted. Season with a little salt and pepper. Transfer to a colander and leave to drain in the sink. When cool, squeeze any excess water from the spinach using your hands, then chop the spinach very finely. Set aside. If the spinach is too chunky, the batter will be very lumpy and difficult to fry.

In a large mixing bowl, use a wooden spoon to cream together the curd cheese, egg yolks, spring onion, flour, nutmeg, lemon zest and black pepper and salt to taste. Fold in the spinach. Beat the egg whites until stiff in a clean, dry bowl, then gently fold them into the spinach mixture. Season to taste with salt and pepper. Preheat the oven to 150°C/300°F/Gas 2.

Heat a non-stick frying pan or flat griddle plate over a medium heat but don't add any butter or oil. It's important that the pan should be at a moderate, even temperature. If it's too hot the batter will burn and if it's too cold, it will stick. Ladle 1 tbsp batter into the hot pan. Leave it until you see the edges changing colour. Using a spatula, flip the drop scone over and cook for 1 minute until the underside has coloured but not burned. Remove from the pan and transfer to an ovenproof dish. Repeat until you have used up all the batter. Keep the scones in a low oven until you are ready to serve.

scotch bonnet dressing

Scotch bonnet chillies are as cute as newborn babies but as hot as little devils. So hot that you will never forget the heat.

SERVES 4 with the scones

200g crème fraîche
50g flat-leaf parsley, leaves only
50g mint leaves
1 Scotch bonnet chilli, top and seeds removed
½ spring onion, chopped
juice of 1 unwaxed lime
2 tbsp extra virgin olive oil
salt and freshly ground black pepper

Blend all the ingredients except the salt and pepper in a blender until smooth. Season to taste with ½ tsp salt and some pepper, then serve. If you are preparing it in advance, the mixture may separate so make sure you give it a good stir before you set it on the table in one of your prettiest bowls.

fried whitebait
with watercress, radish & carrot salad

SERVES 4

600g whitebait

200g plain flour, seasoned with salt,
  freshly ground black pepper and
  2 tsp cayenne pepper

light olive oil or sunflower oil,
  for frying

superfine salt, to serve

Wash and thoroughly dry the whitebait, then dip in the seasoned flour. Shake off any excess flour. Set aside. To deep-fry, half-fill a deep cast-iron pan with the oil and heat over a medium heat. The oil should be hot enough that the fish sizzle when you add them but you don't want the oil to spit. Be very careful and don't leave the pan unattended at any time.

Fry in small batches and as each batch is finished, remove to kitchen paper to drain off any excess oil. Keep the whitebait warm in an oven set to 180°C/350°F/Gas 4. Sprinkle with superfine salt and serve hot, hot, hot.

Deep-frying can be tricky so if you're not confident it's just as easy to shallow-fry these lovely little silvery treats. You'll just have to be prepared to spend a little longer.

The season for fresh whitebait is short so get to know your fishmonger and reserve some when that first catch is landed.

Once a year we'd get a delivery. It was the most special delivery of the whole year and it was better than birthdays or Christmas. (There were eight of us so birthdays and Christmas were about people, never about presents. When I was ten I got a hairbrush. It was a very posh Mason Pearson hairbrush, but come on!) Thankfully, unlike birthdays, food was never a disappointment.

The big delivery that was better than Christmas was 30 kilos of fresh, alive and kicking prawns. We called them prawns but they were enormous, beautiful, sweet, succulent langoustines. Mummy would boil them and we would all sit around the wooden table in the café shelling them. Eat one, shell one, eat one, shell one. There were hundreds left over. So, back to the fryer . . . The remaining langoustines would be taken to the fish and chip shop where they were dipped in a light batter and breadcrumbs, and deep-fried. That's what we called scampi.

I forgive Mummy everything. The hairbrush fades into a distant memory when I remember those scampi. When they were finished, we'd get whitebait. Deep-fried in a proper fryer at the correct temperature with the best fat and a generous sprinkling of superfine salt, whitebait are another taste sensation, from their heads to their tails. It's that combination of the oily flesh, the crispy skin and the salty tang. Well, I no longer have a chip-shop fryer but small batches fried in a shallow pan can be almost as delicious. Whitebait are as cheap as chips, while langoustines are like gold dust, so marvel at the wonderful whitebait.

A family of ten. Only ten?

watercress, radish & carrot salad

SERVES 4

1 tsp black mustard seeds
2 tbsp sunflower seeds
75g watercress
8 radishes, thinly sliced
2 large carrots, cut into ribbons
5 tbsp cold-pressed rapeseed oil
zest and juice of 1 unwaxed lemon
salt

Whitebait are a fairly oily fish, so I think you need a sharpish salad to balance the flavours. The radishes work really well with the nuttiness of the sunflower seeds.

Toast the mustard and sunflower seeds in a dry pan for a few minutes to release the flavours. Set aside to cool. Place the watercress, radishes and carrots in a large salad bowl. Add the cooled seeds and dress with the oil, lemon zest and juice, and a generous pinch of salt.

crab soufflé
with home-made oatcakes

I love going down to the harbour and seeing the crab and lobster boats coming in. The Firth of Forth still provides a substantial proportion of the crabs landed in Scotland but 80 per cent are shipped off to Spain. The hard work involved in boiling and preparing them has never really been a tradition on our native shores; the countries of the Continent appear to value our natural larder more than we do. Crabs, unlike lobsters, are remarkably cheap. The snag is the time you need to prepare them but with a little help from your friendly fishmonger, you will easily get the knack. Alternatively, buy fresh crabmeat. There are many options available from your fishmonger or even the supermarket. Just buy the best you can find and you won't be disappointed if you haven't prepared it yourself.

SERVES 6

60g unsalted butter, plus extra for greasing
60g plain flour
½ tsp mustard powder
300ml full-fat milk, chilled
4 eggs, separated
salt and freshly ground black pepper
200g crabmeat (from 1 large crab)
50g Isle of Mull cheddar
25g dill, very finely chopped

for the sauce
500ml double cream
100g Isle of Mull cheddar, finely grated
salt and freshly ground white pepper

There are loads of useful little videos online that show you how to prepare fresh crab-meat if you're brave enough to try. It's easy – just a little messy!

To make the soufflés, generously grease 6 individual 150ml ramekins. Preheat the oven to 200°C/400°F/Gas 6. Put the butter in a pan over a medium heat. Cook gently until melted, then add the flour. Cook for a few minutes until the mixture starts to bubble. Add the mustard powder and mix through. Slowly add the chilled milk and whisk well to stop the mixture forming lumps. When all the milk has been added, increase the heat and bring to the boil. Remove from the heat and beat in the egg yolks until the mixture is lovely and silky. Season with salt and pepper. Set aside.

Beat the egg whites until stiff in a clean, dry bowl. Fold the crabmeat, cheddar and dill into the sauce until evenly mixed. Gently fold in the beaten egg whites using a metal spoon. Transfer the mixture to the greased ramekins and bake in a bain-marie in the preheated oven for 15 minutes.

While the soufflés are cooking, make the sauce. Heat the cream in a pan over a low heat, then add the cheddar and cook until melted. Season with a little salt and pepper and keep warm over a low heat until the soufflés are golden brown and risen. Using a tea towel to hold the hot ramekins, run a knife between the edge of the soufflé and the ramekin. Upturn onto a soup plate then pour the hot cheese sauce all around. Indulgent, delicious and totally addictive.

home-made oatcakes

I used to make my oatcakes with medium oatmeal and no wheat but my children prefer this recipe, which uses pinhead oatmeal and some flour to help bind the oats. They are crunchier and last longer. Traditionally, oatcakes should also be made with lard or dripping. This was a way to minimize waste: every last, precious bit of fat would be stored and used wherever it was needed, but for me it's a saving too far as the fat can often taste bitter or rancid. This recipe uses cold-pressed rapeseed oil instead as it gives a lovely nutty flavour.

MAKES 24
250g pinhead oatmeal
½ tsp fine salt
1 tsp baking powder
5–6 tbsp plain flour, plus extra for dusting
1 tbsp cold-pressed rapeseed oil, warmed slightly
100ml hand-hot water

Preheat the oven to 200°C/400°F/Gas 6 and line a baking tray with baking parchment. Put the oatmeal, salt, baking powder and about 5 tbsp of the flour in a large bowl. Make a well in the centre of the flour and add the oil. Using a wooden spoon or porridge spurtle, slowly add enough hand-hot water to make a stiff dough. Transfer to a floured surface and roll the dough as thin as you can. Add more flour if necessary to prevent the dough from sticking. Cut into 24 circles with a biscuit cutter or use a side plate to cut a circle, then cut into quarters. Place in the preheated oven and bake for 15 minutes until golden around the edges. Cool on a wire rack.

lemon sole with spinach & loch arthur cheddar

This is a best-seller in both restaurants so I'm slightly reluctant to let you know how easy it is. Our cooking is fresh and simple and we've always been proud of that; I suppose this dish shows it off at its best. At Ristorante Contini we use Parmigiano Reggiano instead of the cheddar but both work equally well.

SERVES 2

2 handfuls of spinach leaves
4 lemon sole fillets, skin removed
12 tbsp double cream
100g Loch Arthur cheddar,
  coarsely grated
salt

Preheat the oven to 180°C/350°F/Gas 4. Place the spinach in four flat piles side by side on a baking tray. You may need 2 baking trays. Place a fillet of sole on top of each pile, then pour the cream over and sprinkle the cheddar on top of that. Season with a little salt. Bake for 12 minutes. The cheese will have melted and the spinach will have wilted under the sole. Heaven! If you have a grill, it's nice to pop the baking tray under it for a few minutes for extra crispness.

spinach, ham & egg pie

This is a winner. I've been making it for as long as I can remember, easily since I was five or six. But I've cracked it now! I've discovered that the buffalo ricotta made by Laverock Hall Farm is absolutely the best. We had always used our dearest friends' Loch Arthur's fresh cow's milk ricotta but the buffalo ricotta is firmer and slightly drier and it really works. Supermarket brands of ricotta don't work as well as they are mostly made with powdered milk and the texture isn't half as good. And here's another opportunity to use ready-made puff pastry. Go for the regular one: the all-butter version is a bit too fatty for this recipe.

SERVES 6-8

100g spinach

unsalted butter or extra virgin olive oil, for frying

4 x 100g buffalo ricotta

8 eggs

100g thick-cut ham (preferably the trimmings from the ham on the bone), cut into small cubes

2 sprigs of rosemary, leaves only, very finely chopped

sea salt flakes and freshly ground black pepper

unsalted butter, softened, for greasing

500g ready-made puff pastry

flour, for dusting

egg wash made from 1 egg, beaten

Pan-fry the spinach in a little butter or olive oil over a medium heat until wilted. Remove from the heat and leave to cool. When cool, squeeze out any moisture. It's vital that you get it all out even if you bruise the spinach. Chop the spinach very finely and set aside. In a large bowl, crumble the ricotta until it is loose. Break in the eggs and mix until they are incorporated. Add the spinach, ham and rosemary. Adjust the seasoning and mix well. Set aside.

Preheat the oven to 200°C/400°F/Gas 6 and grease a 30cm pie tin with the softened butter. Roll the pastry out on a large floured surface so you have enough to cover the bottom and sides of the tin and to make a pastry lid. Ensure there is also enough pastry hanging over the edge of the tin when you line it to help you seal the pie.

Line the tin with the pastry. Dip a pastry brush in the egg wash and use to moisten the edge of the pastry. Place the filling in the pastry-lined tin and carefully place the lid on top. Trim the edges, leaving a border of about 1cm all the way around. Fold the edges together to seal the pie. Score the top of the pie and make one slit in the top to let the air escape. Bake in the preheated oven for 25 minutes. The pie will be risen but not cooked all the way through. Remove from the oven and reduce the heat to 180°C/350°F/Gas 4.

Cut around the edge of the pie to release it from the tin. Now you have to flip the pie over and get it back into the tin the other way up. Tricky! Place a large chopping board over the pie and with a dry tea towel, hold the board to the tin and flip them both over. If the pie is still wet in the middle, liquid may run out so it's best to do this over a sink.

Put the board on the work surface and gently lift the tin off the pie. Carefully slide the pie back into the tin. You'll feel great when it's in. If it breaks slightly around the edges don't worry; just squash it gently back in again. Return to the oven and bake for 15–20 minutes. The pie will be firm to the touch, a lovely golden brown, and will smell heavenly. Turn the pie out of the tin so it is now the right way up on a wire cooling rack. Cool for 15 minutes before cutting. This pie easily lasts for two days if you cover it with tinfoil as soon as it is cool.

broccoli & salmon pancakes

In our house there's always that panic to make sweet pancakes at least once a year, but pancakes aren't just for Shrove Tuesday. They are so easy to make and the savoury ones can easily be prepared in advance. They are also another of those dishes that can become a complete meal without loads of washing-up. Great party and plan-ahead food.

SERVES 4
for the batter
170g plain flour
salt
2 eggs
400ml full-fat milk
50g unsalted butter, melted, plus
  extra for frying

for the filling
400g organic salmon fillet, skin left on
salt
1 bayleaf
250g broccoli, broken into florets
300ml double cream
freshly ground black pepper
300g smoked Dunlop, Gruyère or
  Gouda cheese, coarsely grated

Delicious served with a classic green salad.

Make the batter about 1 hour before you need it. Sieve the flour into a large mixing bowl and add a pinch of salt. Break in the eggs and add the milk and melted butter. Beat with a balloon whisk until smooth, then refrigerate until needed.

Meanwhile, prepare the filling. Put the salmon in a pan of cold water with a small pinch of salt and the bayleaf. Place over a medium heat, bring to the boil, then remove from the heat. Leave the salmon to cool in the water for 10 minutes, then lift it out with a slotted spoon, remove the skin and gently flake. Set aside.

Put the broccoli in a pan of boiling salted water, reduce the heat and simmer gently for about 10 minutes until the broccoli is tender. Drain thoroughly. Add 100ml cream, a generous pinch of salt and plenty of freshly ground black pepper. Blend until smooth using a hand-held blender or food processor. The mixture should be the consistency of béchamel sauce. Gently fold 200g cheese and the salmon flakes into the creamed broccoli.

When you are ready to make the pancakes, heat a non-stick frying pan over a medium heat until it is hot but not roasting. Add a little butter and when it starts to bubble, add a small ladleful of batter – enough to thinly coat the bottom of the pan. Move the pan to help stop the pancake sticking. When tiny bubbles form on the top of the pancake, it is ready to turn. Use a spatula to flip it over. Cook on the other side for a few minutes, then transfer to a plate. Repeat until you have used up all the batter.

Place a generous spoonful of the broccoli and salmon mixture on top of each pancake and roll it up. Lay the rolled pancakes side by side in an ovenproof dish. If you want to, you can refrigerate your pancakes now until you want to use them.

When you are ready to bake them, preheat the oven to 200°C/400°F/Gas 6. Sprinkle the pancakes with the remaining grated cheese and a drizzle of the remaining double cream. Do this at the last minute as the pancakes absorb the cheese and cream really easily and can become stodgy. Bake for about 10 minutes or for 25 minutes if they come from the fridge. Finish by toasting under the grill for a few minutes to give a lovely crispy topping.

Sprouting broccoli warning: I was hooked on sprouting broccoli the first time I tasted it. I was in my early teens and was really getting into cooking. I had to cook for myself one night. Either someone had died or it was snowing, as those were the only reasons I can ever remember cooking just for me. It must have been the snow as I can't remember the funeral.

In my haste, as I was always starving, I quickly washed the broccoli, boiled it, drained it and added some garlic and chilli. The aroma was intoxicating. Mummy would be so proud of me; I was eating vegetables without being forced and I had cooked and would clean up all the dishes.

Yuk! I remember the taste of grit in my mouth and the crunch of the sand between my teeth. It put me off sprouting broccoli for years and now I'm super-paranoid about it. Before I use it, I check that all the sand and grit has really been removed. I love chilli but you can easily leave it out of this recipe if you don't like too much heat.

pork escalopes
with almond & garlic broccoli

One of our very dear customers once said to me that she wanted something devilish! We cook the same food at home and in the restaurant so it never occurred to me that there are times when you may want something a bit more indulgent. These little pork escalopes are pretty devilish but the angel comes with the broccoli, so peace is restored.

SERVES 4

4 x 200g pork escalopes, cut into pieces
  the size and thickness of a pound coin
2 organic free-range eggs
salt and freshly ground black pepper

200g fresh breadcrumbs
grated zest of 2 unwaxed lemons
100g plain flour
50g unsalted butter
2 tbsp extra virgin olive oil

The pork escalopes must be thin enough to cook evenly but not so thin that they collapse when cooked. Your butcher can prepare them but you may need to flatten them a little. If so, place between two sheets of greaseproof paper or clingfilm and gently beat with a rolling pin or hammer. Crack the eggs into a bowl, add the salt and pepper and beat gently with a fork. Mix the breadcrumbs with the grated lemon zest on a large plate and put the flour on another plate. Dip the escalope into the flour, then in the egg, and finally in the breadcrumbs. As each escalope is ready, place it on another plate. Preheat the oven to 180°C/350°F/Gas 4. Put 30g butter and the olive oil in a large frying pan and heat until they start to bubble. Add the escalopes and fry on both sides until the breadcrumbs have started to become golden. Transfer to a baking tray. Add a small knob of the remaining unsalted butter and sprinkle with a little salt. Allow to rest in the preheated oven for about 10 minutes.

almond & garlic broccoli

SERVES 4

100g whole blanched almonds
3 tbsp extra virgin olive oil
100g sprouting broccoli,
  thoroughly washed
salt

1 small dried chilli, crushed
1 small garlic clove, peeled
½ small unwaxed lemon or
  ½ preserved lemon, very thinly
  sliced
freshly ground black pepper

Pan-fry the almonds for a couple of minutes in 1 tbsp olive oil until golden. Remove from the oil, roughly crush them and set them aside. Blanch the well-washed broccoli in boiling salted water for about 5 minutes until tender. Drain and refresh under cold water to help keep the colour and crispness. Drain thoroughly. Heat a large frying pan with 1 tbsp olive oil. Add the chilli and garlic and when they start to bubble, add the broccoli. Keep moving the pan so the broccoli doesn't burn or stick. Add the lemon and remaining olive oil and heat through. Add the crushed almonds and remove from the heat. Season with a generous pinch of salt and some black pepper. This is good served hot or cold.

carrot, clementine & cardamom cake

This is a light cake. The tiny cardamom seeds leave the most romantic, aromatic flavour in your mouth. It's even a very nice, very easy dessert, especially if you're entertaining in the afternoon. You need to assemble this recipe quite quickly, so be organized and weigh everything out before you start.

SERVES 4-6

3 large eggs
150g dark brown sugar
275ml sunflower oil
300g self-raising flour, sieved
1 tsp baking powder
50g dessicated coconut or ground
　hazelnuts
finely grated zest of 2 clementines
300g carrots, finely grated
5 cardamom pods, seeds only,
　or 1 tsp mixed spice
100g sultanas, soaked in the juice
　of 2 clementines for 15 minutes

for the frosting
500g icing sugar, sieved
1 tbsp soured cream
zest of 2 clementines
juice of 1 clementine

Preheat the oven to 180°C/350°F/Gas 4. Line a 23cm cake tin with baking parchment. Put the eggs, sugar and oil in a large bowl and beat together until the mixture is light and fluffy. Using a metal spoon, fold in the flour and baking powder. Add the coconut or hazelnuts, the clementine zest, the carrots and the cardamom seeds or mixed spice.

Drain the sultanas and add them to the mixture. The mixture will be quite solid but don't be tempted to add more liquid as the carrots will soften when cooked and this will help to make the cake moist. Transfer the mixture to the cake tin.

Bake in the preheated oven for 55–60 minutes. The cake is ready when a knife comes out clean from the centre. Transfer to a cooling rack and leave to cool.

Meanwhile, make the frosting. Beat all the ingredients together until creamy and silky. Once the cake is cool, spread the icing on top or serve a slice of plain cake with a dollop of icing on the side to make it look more like a dessert and less like a cake.

cooked cream
with rhubarb compote & toffee brittle

I'll come clean. Our cooked cream recipe is really a very indulgent panna cotta. It's totally luxurious with an unforgettable creamy, silky texture. Traditionally, panna cotta is made using milk or single cream but we use Graham's double cream: it has a 48 per cent fat content. If you're not using this brand of cream, check the fat content as the texture of this pudding will change. Too little fat and the pudding won't set; too much fat and it'll end up like a cooked cream trampoline.

SERVES 5
3 sheets of gold leaf gelatine
750ml double cream
100g caster sugar
1 vanilla pod

Put the gelatine in warm but not hot water to soften for a few minutes. Meanwhile, put the cream and sugar in a heavy-bottomed pan. Split the vanilla pod lengthways, scrape out the seeds with a sharp knife and add the seeds and the pod to the cream. Put the pan over a low heat and, using a wooden spoon, stir to dissolve the sugar. When the cream starts to get hot, a heat haze will rise from it. At this stage remove from the heat and discard the vanilla pod.

Remove the gelatine from the water and squeeze the water out. Add to the cream and stir until dissolved. Pass the cream through a sieve into a pouring jug, then pour into 5 individual 150ml ramekins or moulds. Leave to cool for a few minutes, then cover with clingfilm to stop a skin forming. Refrigerate for 6–8 hours until set, or overnight.

To serve, remove from the fridge. Run a knife between the edge of the cream and the ramekin, then place the ramekin in a small bowl of boiling water for a few seconds to slightly melt the cream. Tip the cream out onto a dessert plate. Serve with a spoonful of rhubarb compote and a sprinkling of toffee brittle.

The beetroot in this recipe helps preserve the lovely pink colour of the rhubarb.

rhubarb compote

SERVES 5
500g rhubarb
250g caster sugar
1 tbsp cold water
1 slice of raw peeled beetroot

Wash and trim the rhubarb and gently scrape with a serrated knife to remove the stringy bits. Cut into 2.5cm cubes and set aside. Dissolve the sugar in the water in a pan over a low heat, then add the beetroot. This will help preserve the lovely pink colour of the rhubarb. Bring to a simmer, then add the rhubarb. Increase the heat, bring to a boil, then reduce the heat and simmer for about 10 minutes until the rhubarb has just started to collapse. Remove from the heat and leave to cool.

toffee brittle

SERVES 5

unsalted butter, softened, for greasing
200g whole blanched almonds, skins removed
200g granulated sugar
100ml cold water
pinch of salt

Preheat the oven to 180°C/350°F/Gas 4. Grease a baking tray. Put the almonds on a second, ungreased baking tray and roast in the preheated oven for 10–15 minutes until golden brown. Set aside. To make the toffee, put the sugar, water and salt in a heavy-based pan with a handle that won't conduct the heat. The handle and the toffee will get extremely hot. Place over a low heat and bring to a simmer. It should bubble slowly. Do not stir as this will make the sugar crystallize. After 5–8 minutes, it will start to colour, changing from a clear, almost translucent colour to a rich golden brown. It will burn very quickly towards the end so carefully remove from the heat using an oven glove, wait a few moments, and check the colour change. Stir in the roasted almonds. Quickly pour the toffee almond onto the greased baking tray and gently move the tray to help the toffee level out. Leave to cool for 5 minutes. When the toffee is cold, break it into small pieces and blend to a coarse, sandy texture in a food processor or blender. Alternatively, if it's been a bad day, put the toffee in a tea towel and beat with a rolling pin. I guarantee you will feel better at the end.

rhubarb meringue pie

Am I rang or am I right, but is meringue one of the best and easiest desserts? If you're not from the East Coast of Scotland you may not have got the joke. They say the old ones are the best ones – a bit like this pie. Lemon meringue pie is wonderful but this rhubarb version feels slightly more like fruit and less like sweeties. That crunchy, crumbly, chewy, soft and fluffy meringue served with some lightly whipped cream combine to make heavenly clouds of decadence. Add these to a pie with a slightly tart rhubarb filling and you're in the land of the gods. I like to add sweet cicely from the garden but it's not essential.

SERVES 6-8

for the pastry
250g plain flour, plus extra for dusting
pinch of salt
120g unsalted butter
70g icing sugar
1 egg yolk

for the filling
1kg rhubarb
500g golden caster sugar
1 tbsp sweet cicely (optional)

for the meringue
6 egg whites
300g golden caster sugar, plus extra for sprinkling

To make the pastry, sieve the flour and salt into a bowl. Grate the butter into the flour and mix with your fingertips until it resembles fine breadcrumbs. Add the icing sugar, mix well, then add the egg yolk. Combine to form a dough. If you need a splash of ice-cold water to help make the dough, don't resist. Refrigerate for about 1 hour.

Roll out the pastry on a floured surface and use to line a 26cm loose-bottomed tin. Leave enough pastry hanging over the edges to help the pastry stay in shape when you bake it. Refrigerate for 30 minutes to stop the pastry shrinking too much.

Meanwhile, preheat the oven to 230°C/450°F/Gas 8 and prepare the filling. Wash and trim the rhubarb and gently scrape with a serrated knife to remove the stringy bits. Cut into 2.5cm cubes. Place in a pan with the sugar over a low heat and simmer for about 5 minutes until the rhubarb has just started to collapse. I don't like rhubarb when it's very, very soft; I prefer to leave some of the texture intact. Remove from the heat. If the rhubarb is very wet, you may need to strain it to give you a more solid filling. While the rhubarb is still warm, add the sweet cicely, if using, and leave to cool.

Remove the pastry-lined tin from the fridge. Place a sheet of baking parchment on top of the pastry and fill with baking beans. Bake in the preheated oven for 10 minutes. When you take the tin from the oven, remove the baking beans and baking parchment, and carefully knock any loose edges of the pastry so the pie has a neat, even edge. Set aside.

To make the meringue, beat the egg whites until stiff in a clean, dry bowl and very gradually add the sugar until you have a translucent, stiff meringue. Fill the tin with the rhubarb filling, then pipe or spoon the meringue on top. Pile it as high as you can. Bake in the preheated oven for 5 minutes until golden, then lower the temperature to 180°C/350°F/Gas 4 and bake for 10 minutes more to cook the meringue. Remove from the oven, sprinkle with a little golden caster sugar and serve piping hot or leave to cool if you prefer.

GROWING NOTES

purple sprouting broccoli
Brassica oleracea Italica Group

Cultivars grown at Casa San Lorenzo
- 'Early Purple Sprouting ' – March harvesting
- 'Late Purple Sprouting' – April harvesting

Cultivation
- Sown in mid-summer for planting out at the end of July once the early broad beans have been cleared.
- They like firm soil that is nutrient-rich and, ideally, neutral.
- Always cover plants with netting to keep both pigeons and butterflies/moths off your plants.
- Cut the spears before the flowers open. Regular harvesting encourages more growth.

Interesting fact
- Broccoli means little sprout or shoot in Italian.

rhubarb
Rheum x *hybridum*

Cultivars grown at Casa San Lorenzo
- 'Victoria'
- 'Timperley Early'

Cultivation
- Give plants a good mulch of compost or well-rotted manure once a year, either in autumn or spring, to boost the plants.
- To tenderize the stems, force the plants every other year by excluding all light in early spring. Cover them with traditional terracotta pots or with an upturned bin.

Interesting facts
- Rhubarb was originally used medicinally to rid the body of impurities.
- It is often treated as a fruit but it is in fact a vegetable.
- The leaves are poisonous to eat (they contain oxalic acid) but can be added to the compost heap where they will rot down.

spinach
Spinacia oleracea

Cultivars grown at Casa San Lorenzo
- 'Medania' – good for both spring and winter baby leaves
- 'Giant Winter' – a large-leafed, hardy winter cultivar

Cultivation
- Winter spinach is sown in August to allow the plants to establish before the cold weather starts.
- We give plants a little protection using low-level cloches covered in horticultural fleece.
- The plants often look stationary until March, when they suddenly produce lots of leaves again as light and temperatures increase.

Interesting fact
- A welcome addition to the hungry gap when the previous year's crops have finished but the spring sowings are not yet ready to harvest.

april

I love April. Spring finally feels like it's coming our way. There is a lot of anticipation for all those new buds that are about to burst into action. Easter is usually being celebrated, lambs appear in the fields and the days are extending. We have plenty of reasons to celebrate.

April is sometimes known as 'the hungry month', but we have rocket, spring onions, pea shoots, wild garlic, mackerel, monkfish and mussels.

The classic Scottish Forfar bridie is world-famous thanks to J. M. Barrie, the author of *Peter Pan*, who came from the tiny village where bridies are known to come from. When I was little, there was a local baker in every village who made very simple cakes, scones, rolls, loaves, pies and bridies. I loved them all. I know there was loads of synthetic cream in some of them as well as additives for every letter in the alphabet, but they tasted great and they were a treat. The bridies and the pies were all made with mince that came straight from the co-op butcher along the road. Yes, flavourings were added to give them a boost, but all the main ingredients were very local.

As an alternative to beef, my recipe uses spring onions, inspired by those delicious Peking spring-onion pancakes that my family love. You can use ready-made flaky pastry but I like the crumbliness of these bridies when you make your own shortcrust pastry. This version uses a mixture of lard and butter. If you don't like lard or can't get hold of it, you can easily use butter on its own. So, for a taste that makes you feel you will never grow up . . .

spring onion bridies

SERVES 4 (2 bridies per person)
full-fat milk or 1 egg, beaten, for brushing

for the pastry
240g plain flour
pinch of salt
60g lard, at room temperature
60g butter, at room temperature

for the filling
100g spring onions, very finely chopped
1 tbsp sesame oil
2 tbsp extra virgin olive oil
good pinch of salt

Start by making the pastry. Work in a cool part of the kitchen. You don't want the mixture to get greasy because you have over-handled it or because the fats have started to melt. The trick is to work as quickly and lightly as possible.

Sieve the flour and salt into a large bowl, then grate the lard and butter into the flour. Using your fingertips, very gently and very quickly crumble everything together until the mixture resembles coarse breadcrumbs. Add a tablespoon of very cold water to bring the breadcrumbs together.

The mixture should leave the bowl clean. If the mixture is still dry, just dip your fingertips in the cold water and work this extra mosisture in. Cover the pastry in clingfilm and refrigerate for at least 30 minutes. Remove from the fridge and allow to come to room temperature before you start to roll it out. Flour the work surface and the rolling pin. Roll out the pastry and cut it into 10cm circles. You should be able to get 8 circles from this quantity of pastry.

Preheat the oven to 200°C/400°F/Gas 6 and line a baking sheet with greaseproof paper. Mix the spring onions in a bowl with the sesame oil, olive oil and salt. Brush the edges of the pastry circles with water. Divide the spring onion mixture between each pastry circle, putting it in the centre. Fold the pastry over to make a semi-circle and, using the back of a fork, press the edges down to seal them. Make sure you have enough mixture in each so you can taste the spring onions, but not so much that you cannot seal the bridie.

Transfer to the prepared baking sheet and brush with a little milk or egg. Bake in the preheated oven for 20 minutes until golden and crispy.

Enjoy your bridies hot in the garden with a glass of Crabbie's Ginger Beer, lots of ice and a big wedge of lime. Flavours of the Orient blended with flavours of Scotland. How exotic!

pea shoot, lanark white & black pudding salad

Haggis and black pudding are two ingredients that visitors to Scotland are always wary to taste. Blood and oats and offal. There are too many excellent artisan producers to mention who have developed traditional recipes and who can claim, with many awards to back them up, that our national haggis and black puddings are world-class. We've used Stornaway black pudding for years; its depth and intensity of flavour is really special. We've also recently started using the black pudding from Ramsay's of Carlukes and boy, does it pack a punch. This salad uses it cut into little squares and fried. That way you get more of the crispy texture and less of the soft, crumbly middle. It works for this recipe but if you prefer to see the black pudding in all its circular glory, you can make it the centrepiece on a plate with all the other ingredients scattered around adoringly.

SERVES 2

2 slices of black pudding, about 1cm thick
extra virgin olive oil, for frying
50g pea shoots, tough stalks removed
100g Lanark White or White Stilton
wedges of lime, to garnish

for the dressing
1 sprig of wild garlic
salt
50g coriander leaves, finely chopped
3–4 tbsp cold-pressed rapeseed oil
3 tbsp apple vinegar
1 small red chilli, deseeded and very finely chopped
1 tsp coriander seeds

Preheat the oven to 180°C/350°F/Gas 4.

Chop the black pudding into small cubes and fry in a little olive oil until crispy. It will crumble but this doesn't matter. Place on a baking tray and dry in the preheated oven until the rest of the dish is ready.

Meanwhile, make the dressing. Cream the garlic and salt to taste together in a pestle and mortar. Fold in the coriander leaves and 3 tbsp oil, then add the vinegar to make the mixture into a loose paste. Fold in the chilli and coriander seeds and add enough extra oil to make the dressing liquid. Set aside.

Scatter the pea shoots in the middle of a large shallow bowl and crumble the Lanark White on top. Add the fried black pudding, then drizzle with the dressing. Serve with wedges of lime.

chicken liver parfaits
with a rocket & raisin salad

SERVES 8
1kg chicken livers
400g unsalted butter
1 sprig of thyme
50ml Springbank single malt whisky
150ml double cream
2 eggs

Grease 8 individual 150ml ramekins and set them aside. Thoroughly clean
the chicken livers by removing the fat and membrane. Melt 150g butter
in a large frying pan, add the thyme and livers and fry for a few minutes
until the livers are pink but not bloody. Add the whisky and flambé to burn
off the alcohol. If you are cooking with gas, allow the liquid in the pan to
catch light. If you are cooking with electricity, you will need to light the
liquid carefully with a match. Remove the thyme, then transfer the livers
to a large bowl or food processor. Add the cream and eggs and blend until
smooth. Strain the mixture through a sieve.

Preheat the oven to 180°C/350°F/Gas 4. Fill the ramekins with the
mixture, then place them in a deep baking tray and half-fill the tray with
warm water. Cover with tinfoil. Cook for 1 hour in the preheated oven
until set. The mixture should have a slight wobble when you remove the
ramekins from the oven. Leave to cool. Meanwhile, melt the remaining
butter in a pan. As the butter melts, the frothy milk solids will come to
the surface leaving the clear fats at the bottom. Spoon off and discard the
frothy solids. Pour the clarified butter over the liver in the ramekins and
leave to set. Transfer to the fridge. These will keep well for up to 4 days.

rocket & raisin salad

Home-made chutney works well with rich chicken liver or game
pâtés. This salad has the same refreshing effect as chutney but is
much faster to prepare.

SERVES 4
100g rocket, washed and dried
100g golden raisins soaked in 2 tbsp sherry
  or red wine vinegar for 20 minutes, then
  drained
1 tbsp extra virgin olive oil
salt

Place the rocket leaves in a large bowl and add the raisins, oil and a pinch
of salt. Mix well and serve immediately.

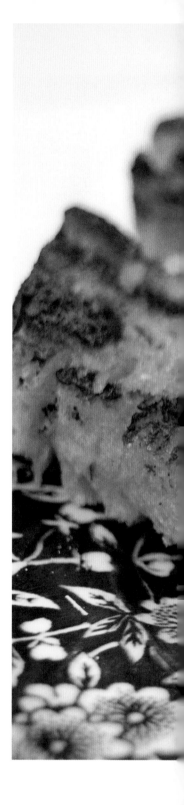

This combination makes a lovely spring starter or a light lunch. The Springbank single malt whisky is aged in Marsala casks and is very milky. Serve with toasted sourdough bread or with the slightly sweet sultana bread on the following pages.

sultana bread

My family think I'm mad. Most of my family are mad so they should know. One thing that gets the 'mad' comment is when I make this bread on big family celebration days. There is never any left over so I can't be that crazy. I've always been spoiled with good food. Sometimes it was cooked by parents, grandmothers or aunties, and sometimes I was given the treat of going to some amazing restaurants. While I can count our family holidays on one or two fingers, I can remember many lunches and nights out. Cosmo's and Denzlers were the big celebration treats but the food that made me feel most grown-up was by Hilary Brown at La Potinière in Gullane. Hilary and Gunn Eriksen of Altnaharrie in Ullapool were Scotland's first female Michelin-starred chefs and both gained fame in the late 70s and early 80s. While I only made it to Ullapool once, just after we got married, Mummy and I would regularly take a run down the coast and have Sunday lunch with David and Hilary. This recipe for sultana bread is inspired by Hilary's Pain aux Noix et Raisins bread from her book, first published in 1990.

I can't over-emphasize the importance of choosing great flour. For this bread there is no better flour than the granary flour made by the Aberfeldy Watermill in Angus - one of a couple of artisan mills in Scotland. It's probably a good idea that this flour may be hard to get hold of because this loaf is so moreish, you don't want to end up making it every day. Doves Farm in Wiltshire also makes great granary flour.

When making bread it's vital to find a really cosy, draught-free spot to leave the bread to rise. In our old house, I used to run the tumble dryer for a cycle, remove the clothes, then put the bread inside. Extreme but necessary.

MAKES 2 x 450g loaves

250ml full-fat milk (such as Graham's Gold)
1 tbsp runny honey
700g Aberfeldy Watermill granary flour
2 tsp dried yeast
2 tsp salt
250g sultanas
225ml hand-hot water
1 egg, beaten, plus extra for brushing
plain flour, for dusting
unsalted butter, softened, or a little extra virgin olive oil, for greasing

Put the milk and honey in a small pan over a low heat until hand-hot. Mix together the flour, yeast, salt and sultanas in a large bowl. Add the warm milk and honey mixture, the water and egg, and mix well. Beat until smooth; you can use an electric mixer with a dough hook. Transfer to a floured surface and knead until smooth and elastic. Add a little more flour if required. Rinse the mixing bowl and grease with a little butter or oil. Place the dough in the bowl, cover with clingfilm and a clean, dry tea towel. Leave in a warm, draught-free place until the dough has doubled in size. This will take about 40 minutes. Meanwhile, grease a baking tray.

Transfer the risen dough to a floured surface. Knead very gently for another few minutes until the dough is elastic again. Divide the dough into 2 equal pieces and place them on the prepared baking tray. It is useful to weigh each half to help ensure the loaves bake evenly. Cover with clingfilm and leave for 30 minutes more until the dough has risen again.

Meanwhile, preheat the oven to 230°C/450°F/Gas 8. Brush the pieces of dough with beaten egg and bake in the middle of the preheated oven for 20–25 minutes. When the loaves are ready, they should sound hollow when the bottom is tapped. Transfer to a wire rack and leave to cool for 10–15 minutes.

smoked mackerel pâté

The mackerel season in Scotland runs from April to October. The natural oils in this national fish give the lovelies flavour and moistness when smoked. This pâté is so soft you can serve it as a dip with crisp vegetables from the garden or in individual pots with some salad leaves and home-made oatcakes (page 75) or potting-shed brown bread (page 189). Here we serve it with a seasonal pea shoot, dried apricot and walnut salad.

SERVES 4
400g smoked mackerel
200g crème fraîche
100ml double cream
finely grated zest of 1 unwaxed
 lemon

6 sprigs of dill, leaves only
juice of 2 unwaxed lemons
½ tsp paprika
salt and freshly ground black
 pepper

Flake the mackerel flesh from the skin. Put the flesh in a food processor with the crème fraîche, cream, lemon zest and dill, and blend. Gradually add enough lemon juice to loosen the mixture. Fold in the paprika and season to taste with salt and pepper. Refrigerate for up to 4 days.

pea shoot, dried apricot & walnut salad

These lovely little pea shoots are an early sign of spring. They give a lift to the dried apricots and walnuts that have provided a great source of vitamins and essential oils over the winter. This salad doesn't have any acid in the dressing but I like to serve the pâté with a wedge of lemon to mellow the fishy, creamy flavour of the mackerel.

SERVES 4
50g walnut pieces
pinch of salt
4 tbsp extra virgin olive oil
1 tbsp walnut oil
small handful of chervil, finely
 chopped

75g pea shoots
100g dried apricots, cut into small
 cubes
50g sunflower seeds, toasted

Toast the walnut pieces in a dry, non-stick frying pan over a medium heat. Using a pestle and mortar, crush the walnuts with the salt, adding a little olive oil to help loosen the mixture. Add the chervil and the walnut oil. Cream to a loose paste. Drizzle over the pea shoots, apricots and sunflower seeds.

spiced rack of lamb
with watercress & orange salad

The Romans brought many things to the British Isles and among them was lamb. The classic marriage of garlic and rosemary with lamb will never go wrong, but this recipe for rack of lamb takes the flavours to a whole new level. It's actually my children's favourite family meal. I love watching them eat it with their hands, then lick their fingers.

SERVES 4

2 racks of 6 ribs of lamb, about
 500g each
2 limes, halved, to serve

for the marinade
300g natural yogurt
1 tbsp light clover or acacia honey
2 tbsp olive oil
100g coriander leaves
100g rocket
3 sprigs of wild garlic
75g fresh ginger, peeled and
 thinly sliced
2 red chillies, deseeded
1 tsp salt

First make the marinade. Blend all the ingredients in a blender or food processor. Pour half over the lamb and refrigerate for up to 24 hours. Keep the rest in the fridge. Remove the lamb from the marinade and leave to rest at room temperature for about 30 minutes.

Preheat the oven to 220°C/425°F/Gas 7. Heat a ridged griddle pan over a medium to hot heat. When it is hot, add the lamb, skin side down, and sear until golden and caramelized. Turn the lamb over and cook on the other side until the meat is coloured all over.

Transfer to a roasting tray and roast in the preheated oven for 20 minutes. The lamb will be medium rare. Cook for longer if you prefer the meat to be less pink. Remove from the oven, leave to rest for 5 minutes, then cut into chops. Serve accompanied by the remaining chilled marinade and some lime halves.

watercress & orange salad

Blood oranges are still in season at this time of year and if you can get your hands on them, the contrast in colour, flavour and texture will really put a spring in your step.

SERVES 4

200g watercress leaves
2 large blood oranges, skin and pith
 removed and cut into 0.5cm slices
4 spring onions, finely sliced
salt
1 tsp sumac

for the dressing
100g mint leaves
100g coriander leaves
200ml Greek yogurt
juice of 1 unwaxed lime
3 tbsp extra virgin olive oil
salt and freshly ground black pepper

First make the dressing. Blend together all the ingredients except the salt and pepper in a blender or food processor. Season to taste.

Arrange the watercress around the edge of a large platter. Place the slices of orange in the middle and sprinkle with the spring onions. Season with a little salt, then spoon the dressing generously over the salad. Finally sprinkle with the sumac.

monkfish &
mussel broth

Despite being Italian, surprisingly, we eat very little garlic. If I make this dish with garlic I feel it oozes from my pores for days. So if I'm speaking to Victor, no garlic. If I'm trying to get my point across, then garlic may be required. If you are feeling brave, you can use a little wild garlic for an extra kick. Monkfish is particularly good for this recipe as it holds its shape when cooked and doesn't disintegrate into the cream.

SERVES 2

1 tbsp extra virgin olive oil
small knob of unsalted butter
2 spring onions, finely sliced
splash of dry white wine
100ml double cream
250g monkfish tail, skin and bones removed and
  cut into large pieces
100g large Shetland or West Coast mussels, barnacles
  and beards removed
small bunch of flat-leaf parsley, finely chopped
2–3 leaves of wild garlic, finely chopped (optional)
salt
toasted sourdough or country bread, to serve

Put the olive oil and butter in a large pan. Heat until they bubble, then add half the spring onions. Cook for a few minutes to release the flavours, then add the white wine. Cook until the alcohol has been cooked off, then add the cream.

Cook over a low heat for a few minutes until the cream comes to a simmer, then add the monkfish and mussels. Cover with a lid and steam for about 5 minutes until all the mussels have opened.

Add the remaining spring onions, the wild garlic, if using, and the parsley. Season to taste with salt. Serve with some toasted sourdough or country bread to soak up all the lovely juices.

chinese marinated sirloin steak
with spinach & chard noodles

It wasn't until the 1960s that Chinese people started to settle in Scotland in any significant numbers. This was a side-effect of the establishment of the People's Republic of China in 1949, followed by mass clearances from Chinese agricultural communities. More Chinese arrived in the aftermath of the Vietnam War. While Chinese tea and the spice trade have long affected our habits and our cooking, Chinese cuisine has only relatively recently influenced us. Thankfully, stir-frying and soy sauce are now common to all our kitchens. Green vegetables take pride of place in most Chinese meals. Chard, spinach, pak choi, bean sprouts and Chinese lettuce can all be easily grown in our climate and are hugely nutritious.

SERVES 4

4 x 250g sirloin steaks
1 tbsp extra virgin olive oil
juice of ¼ unwaxed lime
small handful of coriander leaves,
  coarsely chopped
salt

for the marinade
50ml light soy sauce
1 red chilli, deseeded
100g fresh ginger, peeled and
  sliced
50ml water
4 tbsp clover honey
2 tbsp rice wine vinegar or sake

This dish gives deep flavours to the sirloin and can be cooked at the very last minute if you've got everything ready in advance.

Adding the noodles makes the greens more filling. In our house the children steal the noodles before they reach the table. The adults are always happy to be left with the greens. If you prefer, leave out the noodles and you have a really healthy and super-tasty supper.

First make the marinade. Blend together all the ingredients in a blender or food processor. Put the steaks in a deep dish and pour the marinade over. Turn to ensure they are well coated, then refrigerate for about 2 hours. Remove from the fridge and allow to sit for 10 minutes to bring the steaks to room temperature. Preheat the oven to 180°C/350°F/Gas 4 and heat a ridged griddle pan over a medium to high heat. When the pan is hot, add the olive oil. Remove the steaks from the marinade and place on the griddle pan. Sear until the steaks can easily be removed and are nicely charred, then turn them over and cook on the other side for about 2 minutes. Transfer to a roasting tin and cook in the preheated oven for 3–5 minutes until they are firm to the touch or medium rare. Remove from the oven and allow to rest for a few minutes. Slice the steaks and squeeze over the lime juice. Add the coriander leaves and a pinch of salt, then serve.

spinach & chard noodles

SERVES 4
4 nests of fine egg noodles
2 tbsp extra virgin olive oil
1 garlic clove, finely sliced
1 chilli, deseeded and finely sliced
100g fresh ginger, peeled and sliced
  into fine matchsticks

125g young chard leaves or young
  pak choi
2 tbsp light soy sauce
3 spring onions, cut into quills

Put the noodles in a bowl with boiling water to cover. Leave for 5 minutes, then drain well and set aside. Meanwhile, heat the oil in a large frying pan or wok. When it is hot, add the garlic, chilli and ginger and cook for 10 seconds to release the flavours. Add the chard and soy sauce and increase the heat. Cook until the leaves just start to wilt. You don't want them too soft – a bit of texture is much better. Add the drained noodles and the spring onion, then heat through gently and serve immediately.

chocolate & parma violet mousse

This is the best chocolate mousse recipe in the world when made with your favourite chocolate. Valrhona has always been our chocolate standard-bearer in the kitchen as it tastes perfect and is always reliable for cooking.

SERVES 4-6

400g 70% cocoa Valrhona dark
  chocolate
400g double cream
6 eggs, separated
325g caster sugar
50g crystallized Parma violets,
  slightly crushed, plus extra whole
  violets, to decorate

Break up the chocolate and melt it in a heatproof glass or ceramic bowl over a bain-marie. Do not let the simmering water touch the bottom of the bowl. Meanwhile, warm the cream in a small pan over a low heat but do not allow it to boil. When the chocolate has melted, remove from the heat, stir in the warm cream and mix until smooth. Beat the egg yolks with the sugar until pale and fluffy, then use a wooden spoon to beat this into the chocolate mixture. Leave to cool.

Beat the egg whites until stiff in a clean, dry bowl. Fold the egg whites into the cooled chocolate mixture, then spoon into 4 to 6 individual 150ml glass jars or glasses, layering the crystallized violets between spoonfuls of mousse. Refrigerate for at least 4 hours until the mousse has set. Serve with a Parma violet for decoration.

coffee & coconut cake

Let's face it, there isn't always time to make or eat dessert, but a cake can be made and eaten at any time. Especially if it's grown-up cake. Coffee and walnut cake is one of those things that you only really appreciate when you're older. (I've often thought it a bit strange that coffee cake really only tastes good with a cup of tea, but that might just be me.) Mummy always had a jar of Camp coffee (this has got to be one of the best pieces of branding ever – it makes you feel happy just saying it!) in her cupboard just for making coffee and walnut cake. I'm spoiled with my espresso machine but instant or Camp coffee will work just as well for this recipe. This version with the coconut came about when I burned the walnuts three times in a row. Desiccated coconut came to the rescue. Toasted in a dry non-stick pan for a minute until golden but not brown, the dessicated coconut makes this cake even better than the original. Every cloud does have a silver lining.

SERVES 6

225g unsalted butter, at
  room temperature
225g light brown sugar
2 large eggs
200g self-raising flour, sieved
1 tsp baking powder
50g desiccated coconut, toasted
  (see introduction)
2 shots of espresso, or 2 tsp instant
  coffee dissolved in 50ml hot
  water, or 2 tbsp Camp coffee
  dissolved in 1–2 tbsp full-fat milk
toasted desiccated coconut, to
  decorate

for the frosting
300g icing sugar
50ml double cream
50ml espresso, or 2 tsp instant
  coffee dissolved in 50ml hot
  water, or 2 tbsp Camp coffee
  dissolved in 1–2 tbsp full-fat milk

Preheat the oven to 180°C/350°F/Gas 4. Line the base of two 20cm non-stick cake tins with greaseproof paper.

Cream the butter and sugar in a bowl until light and fluffy. Add one egg at a time with a little of the flour to stop the mixture curdling, then add the remaining flour and the baking powder. Fold in the coconut and espresso. Divide the mixture between the two tins and smooth the mixture level. Bake in the preheated oven for 30 minutes until risen and golden. Remove from the oven, turn the cakes out and cool on a wire rack.

Meanwhile, make the frosting. Beat the icing sugar, cream and espresso together in a bowl until light and fluffy. When the cakes are cool, remove the greaseproof paper and place one sponge on a board or plate. Spread half the frosting on top, then carefully place the other sponge, bottom side up, on top of the frosting. Use a palette knife to smooth the remaining frosting over the cake. Decorate with a generous sprinkle of toasted coconut.

chocolate & lavender truffles

The lavender is very subtle in these delightful and definitely adult truffles. Fresh rosemary, mint leaves or whole cardamom pods can easily be substituted for the lavender but will give an altogether different experience. The truffles will last for four days in the fridge but taste best on the day they are made. If the children help me with these, they always eat them. If they haven't helped, then they tend to think the truffles don't look good enough to eat. They are absolutely good enough to eat, so it's your choice whether you want your wee ones to share them or if you prefer to leave them with the booty from their Easter egg hunt.

MAKES 1 x 350g gift box
140ml double cream
1 sprig of lavender, washed and dried,
 or 1 tsp dried lavender
225g 55% cocoa Valrhona dark chocolate
premium-quality cocoa powder, for dusting

Put the cream and lavender in a pan over a low heat. Remove from the heat when the cream begins to steam but before it boils. Leave to infuse for about 30 minutes. Meanwhile, chop, grate or break up the chocolate into very small pieces and place in a heatproof glass or ceramic bowl over a bain-marie. Do not let the simmering water touch the bottom of the bowl.

Strain the cream into a clean pan and put it back over a low heat but, again, do not let it boil. When the cream is hot, pour it over the chocolate. Stir slowly until the chocolate has melted. Leave to cool, then chill until the mixture is cold enough to handle – about 30 minutes. Using a dessertspoon, shape the mixture into balls, then roll them in cocoa powder. Refrigerate until ready to use.

I prefer to use 55% cocoa chocolate here. I think 70% is too intense for this recipe.

GROWING NOTES

wild garlic
Allium ursinum

There are no cultivars

Cultivation
- We let Mother Nature take care of the wild garlic that grows in the moist shade of the woodland below the productive area of the garden.
- We harvest the young tender leaves in early spring before the flowers open.

Interesting facts
- All parts of the plant are edible – flowers, leaves, seeds and bulb.
- We take care never to over-harvest our patch so there will always be a good supply.

pea shoots
Pisum sativum var. *macrocarpon* or var. *saccharatum*

Cultivars grown at Casa San Lorenzo
- We grow these from the left-over seeds from our normal pea crop, but peas that produce edible pods, such as sugar snap peas, are especially good for pea tips
- 'Oregon Sugar Pod'
- 'Sugar Snap'

Cultivation
- Pea shoots can be grown all year round in a protected environment. We sow them densely (very close, but the seeds never touch each other) into large trays or into lengths of guttering.
- The shoots are cut once the plants produce two or three leaflets, after three to four weeks. A second harvest can be made a few weeks later.

Interesting fact
- Suspend your seeds (lengths of guttering) above ground in a polytunnel or greenhouse to prevent mice helping themselves, especially during the winter months.

rocket
Eruca versicaria

Cultivars grown at Casa San Lorenzo
- 'Discovery' – a long-leafed rocket

Cultivation
- We sow wide bands of rocket early in the season to allow us to harvest large quantities of the leaves. Then in late summer, we sow again for repeat pickings over winter and into spring.
- Rocket benefits from shade, especially during the summer months.

Interesting fact
- Rocket naturally goes to seed quickly, especially in early summer. The flowers, however, are a decorative and peppery addition to any salad, so they are a bit of a bonus.

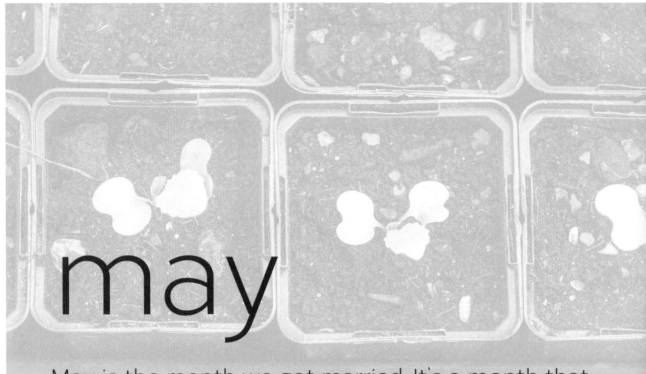

may

May is the month we got married. It's a month that is topped and tailed with Bank Holidays and it feels like summer has arrived. The garden is beginning to blossom and we're starting to get those special flavours that tell us the garden is really working to give us taste as well as substance.

In season we have asparagus, peas, radishes, broad beans, chicory, cod, crab and mackerel.

asparagus & broad bean soup

Classy soups are always a winner, especially asparagus soups. Our habits have changed over the years and we no longer buy asparagus in November even if we see it. Instead, we're relying on the seasons more and more. The challenge when you're growing your own is what to do when you have a glut. Soup is a fantastic way to cope with abundance. You can use cheaper and less delicate ingredients to bulk out a soup but when you have quality and quantity, then the flavour can really shout out loud.

SERVES 4

250g (podded weight) broad beans
1kg asparagus, washed
100g unsalted butter
2 onions, finely chopped
1 leek, very finely chopped
2 celery stalks, very finely chopped
salt
1 litre light chicken stock or vegetable stock
  (optional)
freshly ground black pepper
200ml double cream
50g Maisie's Kebbuck, or similar
  semi-mature cow's milk cheese, grated

Shell the broad beans and put them in a pan of boiling salted water. Simmer for 5–10 minutes, depending on the size of the beans, until tender. Remove from the heat, drain and cool with cold water from the tap. Remove the outer skin of the beans by slitting the top and pushing the beans out onto a plate. This takes time but it's worth the effort. Set the beans aside.

Prepare the asparagus by bending each stalk so the tougher bottom part snaps off. Chop the tender stalks into 2.5cm pieces and chop the top 2.5cm of the tougher bottom of the stalks very finely. Discard the rest of the tough stalks. Melt the butter in a large soup pan and add the onion, leek, celery and tough asparagus stalks. Cook until soft, taking time to let the flavours develop. Season with a good pinch of salt and add the stock or enough boiling water to cover. Simmer for about 20 minutes. Add the tender asparagus stalks and cook for another 10–15 minutes.

Remove the pan from the heat. Save a few aparagus tips for the garnish and pass the rest of the soup through a mouli or sieve to remove any tough stalks. Check the seasoning. The asparagus can be bitter but a generous pinch of salt and pepper will counteract this. Return the soup to the pan, add the broad beans, saving a few for the garnish, and the cream. Heat through gently. Serve hot with some freshly grated cheese sprinkled on top (I love Maisie's Kebbuck because of its texture, delicate flavour and the way it melts). Garnish with the reserved asparagus tips and broad beans.

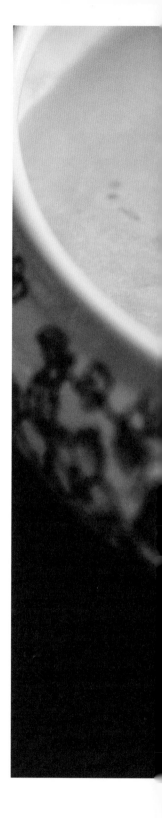

soused mackerel
with chicory, radish & pear salad

Victor knew Carol before I did but thanks to their friendship, Carol is now one of my dearest friends. Victor and Carol get on because they have many things in common; two of them are a pickled fish fanaticism and a raw fish fanaticism. Pickled fish and raw fish don't really do it for me. When we lived in town, Carol would often pop in unexpectedly. Thankfully, Victor always had a stock of pickled herrings or rollmops for those late-night moments when he wanted something tasty and easy to digest. Since moving out of town, we don't get as many visitors, but Victor's pickled fish is safe. I'm not quite sure if this is a win or not, but this recipe for preserving mackerel definitely is a winner.

SERVES 4

4 very fresh mackerel fillets, pin-boned by your friendly local fishmonger
8 sprigs of dill
250ml white wine vinegar and 250ml apple vinegar, or 500ml white wine vinegar
100ml water
4 bayleaves
8 black peppercorns
6 sprigs of curly parsley
1 onion, halved and thinly sliced

A day or two before you want to serve this dish, wash and dry the mackerel and place it skin side down in a shallow ceramic dish. Place the dill on top and set aside.

Put all the other ingredients in a pan and bring to the boil, then reduce the heat and simmer for 10 minutes to intensify the flavours. Pour the hot liquid over the mackerel and quickly cover the whole dish with clingfilm. It is vital that the fish is immersed in the liquid, otherwise it won't cook. Leave to cool, then refrigerate for 1–2 days to allow the flavours to develop. Serve with the chicory, radish and pear salad.

chicory, radish & pear salad

Chicory and pear are a beautiful combination. The bitterness of the leaves and the sweetness of the pears are in perfect harmony. The little crunchy radishes add that extra texture and a bit of a sting, which is always a treat.

SERVES 4

1 pear
2 heads of chicory, leaves washed and dried
4 large radishes, cut into segments

for the dressing
2 Bramley or similar sharp-tasting apples

150ml soured cream
25g sprigs of dill, stalks removed
small handful of flat-leaf parsley leaves
50ml cold-pressed rapeseed oil
2 tbsp apple vinegar
1 tbsp freshly grated horseradish
salt

To make the dressing, peel and core the apples and put in a blender with the remaining dressing ingredients except the salt. Blend until smooth and add salt to taste. Peel, core and slice the pear and arrange it on a serving platter with the chicory and radishes. Pour over a generous spoonful of dressing. Serve immediately to ensure that the salad stays crisp and the pear does not discolour.

pea, criffel & mint barley risotto

Pearl barley is a super alternative to classic Italian risotto rice. The flavour is earthier and the texture more grainy but barley is just as versatile. A generous handful of Parmigiano Reggiano at the end absolutely lifts this dish and gives it all the fame of its glamorous Italian cousin.

SERVES 2 as a main course,
4 as a starter
100g unsalted butter
1 shallot, very finely grated
200g pearl barley
splash of white wine
400–500ml hot vegetable stock or light
  chicken stock
200g fresh peas, podded weight
125g Criffel, Clava Brie or other soft
  cow's milk cheese
125ml double cream
50g Parmigiano Reggiano, finely
  grated, plus extra to serve
small handful of mint leaves

Put half the butter in a heavy-based casserole dish over a low heat. When the butter has melted, add the shallot and sweat until translucent. Add the barley and toast for a few minutes, then add the wine, increase the heat and cook until the wine has evaporated.

Unlike cooking a risotto, where you add the stock gradually, you can now add 400ml stock. Stir gently, reduce the heat and simmer for about 30 minutes.

Add the peas and crumble the Criffel into the barley. Fold through and cook until the Criffel has completely melted. Add a little more stock if necessary. Add the cream and Parmigiano and cook for 1 minute until the mixture has thickened. Coarsely tear the mint leaves and add to the barley, then add the remaining butter. Turn off the heat and leave covered for 5 minutes before serving. Serve sprinkled with some extra freshly grated Parmigiano Reggiano.

Sunday mornings were always a bit of a pain when I was too small to tie my shoelaces and we had to get up at nine to go to Mass. But it was the one day of the week that we always had breakfast together as a family. There being so many children, a lovely lady called Margaret helped out and would have the bacon, eggs and Lorne sausage all ready for us to choose what we wanted for our roll when we came back from church. There were ten of us, remember. Margaret's favourite girl (not me but Sister Number Five) always had her potato pancake, fried with a piece of bacon and a runny egg. The newspapers would be divided out: *The Sunday Times, The Observer* and the *Sunday Mail* for Daddy. By eleven, the girls were off to work at the Wemyss Café and the boys had a carry on.

Now there's no Wemyss Café and we have a little more time on Sundays; a mid-day brunch with this crab and soured cream pâté (easily made the day before) and all the newspapers is a real treat. We've never had weekends off but Victor and I have always tried to have family Sundays. I treasure them as much as I treasure those Sunday mornings all huddled together with our rolls when I was too small to tie my shoelaces.

Margaret with Numbers Seven and Eight (me)

crab & soured cream pâté
with potato pancakes

SERVES 4
100g full-fat cream cheese
300g soured cream
juice of 1 unwaxed lime
very finely grated zest of 2
  unwaxed lemons

1 red chilli, deseeded and very
  finely chopped
25g chives, very finely chopped
25g dill, very finely chopped
500g white crabmeat
salt and freshly ground black pepper

Put the cream cheese in a large bowl and cream it using a rubber spatula. Add all the remaining ingredients except the crabmeat and the salt and pepper and mix together thoroughly. Lightly fold in the crabmeat and season to taste with a good pinch of salt and pepper. Pour into 4 individual ramekins or Kilner jars and refrigerate for about 1 hour before serving.

potato pancakes

These have always been Sister Number Five's favourites. What more can I say? Making these lovely little potato pancakes is a bit like making gnocchi. The potatoes have to be hot and freshly mashed or the pancakes will be like potato bricks.

MAKES 4-6
250g floury potatoes
salt
25g unsalted butter
50g plain flour, sieved

Peel and cut the potatoes into quarters and put in a pan with salt and cold water to cover. Bring to the boil, then reduce the heat and simmer until the potatoes are tender. Drain well and leave to dry in the pan for a few minutes before mashing. Add the butter and a good pinch of salt and mash thoroughly. Beat in the flour with a wooden spoon. If the mixture looks too dry, add more butter. Set aside. Preheat the oven to 140°C/275°F/Gas 1. Heat a dry non-stick frying pan or flat griddle pan over a medium heat. Don't add any fat as this will make the pancakes stick. Form the potato mixture into balls the size of golf balls and flatten them with the palm of your hand. Place on the hot pan and cook until the undersides are coloured. Carefully turn over and cook the other side. You may need to do this in batches. Transfer to an ovenproof dish and put in the preheated oven until you are ready to serve. Alternatively, you can store them on a warm plate covered with a clean tea towel. Keep the pancakes covered so they stay soft.

Serve the chilled pâté and the hot pancakes
with a few salad leaves. Sunny days indeed.

broad bean, pea & ham pasta

I have this constant dilemma. I was born in Edinburgh but Daddy was Italian. Our family has been living in Scotland for almost 100 years. When my children ask, are we Italian or Scottish, the answer is never a clear yes or no. My passport says I'm British. Just as my national identity is shared, so food can also be shared. The ingredients for this recipe were all born in Scotland except the pasta and the Parmigiano Reggiano. So you can decide which nationality is on your plate.

SERVES 2 as a main course,
4 as a starter

160g De Cecco wheel-shaped
  pasta or penne rigate (80g per
  person for a main course, or 40g
  per person for a starter)
salt
50g unsalted butter
½ very small onion, finely chopped
100g smoked streaky bacon, cut
  into small squares
250ml double cream
100g new-season broad beans,
  podded weight, blanched
  and skinned
50g peas, podded weight
50g Parmigiano Reggiano, very
  finely grated, plus extra to garnish
small handful of mixed mint leaves
  and flat-leaf parsley leaves,
  very finely chopped
freshly ground black pepper

Put the pasta in a large pan of boiling salted water and cook until al dente. Meanwhile, make the sauce. Put the butter in a pan over a medium heat and when it has melted, add the onion. Fry until very soft and translucent. Add the bacon and fry until crispy but don't allow it to become too hard. Add the cream and as it starts to thicken, add the broad beans, peas, Parmigiano Reggiano and chopped mint and parsley. Season with a little salt and plenty of pepper. Cook until the cream has thickened and become glossy. If the sauce looks too thick, don't be shy to add a little more cream. Drain the pasta, reserving a little of the pasta water. If you think the sauce needs to be thinned, add some of the pasta water. Serve immediately, sprinkled with more freshly grated Parmigiano Reggiano.

radish, asparagus & broad bean salad
with new potato & white onion omelette

This brightly coloured salad is so jolly and balances the neutral golden tones of the omelette. This is feel-good food before you've eaten it and feel-better food when you've finished it. It's also an easy meal for the children to get stuck into both before and after. My girl's little fingers just love podding all those broad beans.

SERVES 4
250g asparagus, trimmed
50g baby radishes
200g new-season broad beans,
  podded weight, blanched and skinned
15g mint leaves
1 heaped tbsp small capers in salt,
  rinsed and drained
5–6 tbsp extra virgin olive oil
1 tsp Dijon mustard
zest and juice of ½ unwaxed lemon
100g St Andrew's Farmhouse Anster,
  or Cheshire or Lancashire cheese
salt and freshly ground black pepper

Blanch the asparagus by plunging it in boiling salted water for a few minutes until tender but not overcooked. Refresh under cold running water, cut into quills and set aside. Top, tail and slice the radishes thinly so you can see as much of their lovely red skins as possible. Arrange the asparagus, broad beans and radishes on a large platter and sprinkle with the mint leaves and capers. Mix together in a jug the olive oil, mustard and zest and juice of the lemon. Drizzle over the vegetables. Very coarsely shave or crumble the cheese on top and season with a little salt and pepper.

new potato & white onion omelette

Isabel (Isabella to us) was one of my favourite cooks back in the early days of the family business. Almost 20 years later, I'm delighted to say she is happily married and running her own café in Spain. One dish she made that was always perfect was a Spanish omelette. It was totally delicious but full of calories as the potatoes were cooked from raw in oil for what seemed like ages. Here I boil the potatoes in advance and leave them to cool slightly. That way you need less oil. The omelette is still delicious but slightly lighter.

SERVES 4 hungry or 6 not so
hungry people
500g waxy new potatoes
salt
5–6 tbsp extra virgin olive oil
1 large white onion, cut into thin slices
12 eggs
50g flat-leaf parsley leaves, finely chopped
50g mint leaves, finely chopped
freshly ground black pepper

Choose a variety of potato that is quite waxy so the potatoes keep their shape when cooked. If they are new potatoes, I like to leave the skins on but make sure you scrub them well.

Scrub the potatoes and put in a pan with salt and cold water to cover. Bring to the boil, then reduce the heat and simmer until tender. Drain, leave until cool enough to handle, then cut into slices. Set aside. Heat 2–3 tbsp oil in a deep 30cm non-stick frying pan over a medium heat, then add the onion and fry gently until soft and slightly golden. Remove from the pan and set aside. Beat the eggs together in a large bowl, then add the potatoes, parsley, mint and fried onions. Season with a generous pinch of salt and plenty of black pepper. Mix well.

Add the remaining oil to the frying pan to coat the bottom and set over a medium heat. When the oil is hot, add a little of the egg mixture; when it starts to bubble, it means the oil is hot enough. Move the pan to ensure the mixture hasn't stuck to the bottom, then add the rest. Reduce the heat slightly. Using a wooden spoon, occasionally draw the egg mixture from the edges of the pan to the middle, moving the pan gently every so often to prevent any sticking. Continue until the egg mixture has almost all cooked, about 7–10 minutes.

At this point you can either cheat and place the frying pan under a hot grill to finish cooking the egg, or you can be clever and flip it onto a large board or plate, then return it to the pan to cook the other side. This can be messy so it's best to do it over a sink. The omelette is cooked when you can place a knife into the centre and it comes out clean. I usually serve this cold so I don't want the egg to be runny.

baked parsley pesto cod
with broad bean, mint & potato salad

One week we're told we mustn't eat cod as stocks are low, the next we have an excess and the cod is being thrown back into the sea. This week we can eat it, so let's enjoy it while we can as I love cod, especially when it's baked. When given a little kick of garlic and parsley, the flaky white flesh is healthy, tasty and too good to resist.

SERVES 4
extra virgin oil, for greasing
4 x 200g cod fillets
4 tbsp parsley pesto (see below)

Preheat the oven to 200°C/400°F/Gas 6 and lightly oil a baking tray. Wash and dry the cod fillets on kitchen paper, then place them, skin side up, on the oiled baking tray. Spoon a generous tablespoon of pesto onto each fillet. Bake in the preheated oven for 10–12 minutes until the skin is crispy. The fish should be firm to the touch and the flesh translucent.

parsley pesto

Basil pesto – or pesto alla Genovese – is made with basil, pine kernels, garlic and Pecorino Romano. With this parsley pesto I'm using capers and breadcrumbs instead of pine kernels and Pecorino Romano. The preserved lemon adds a fabulous taste and texture that works with fish, meat or chicken.

SERVES 4
1 garlic clove
100g flat-leaf parsley leaves
25g fresh breadcrumbs, very lightly toasted
  in a medium oven for 3–4 minutes
1 preserved or 1 unwaxed lemon, finely chopped
1 tbsp small capers in salt, rinsed
  and drained
75ml extra virgin olive oil
salt and freshly ground black pepper

Finely chop the garlic and parsley and put in a large bowl. Fold in the breadcrumbs, lemon, capers and oil. Season to taste with salt and pepper. Add more oil if the mixture is too dry. You're looking for the consistency of runny raspberry jam – if that's any help! Store in the fridge for up to a week.

broad bean, mint & potato salad

Rather than dress this salad with lemon or vinegar I prefer to serve it with the baked cod. The preserved lemon in the pesto gives all the acidity that you need to balance the meal.

SERVES 4

500g new-season potatoes (such as Royal Kidneys or Jersey Royals)
salt
250g new-season broad beans, podded weight, blanched and skinned
50g mint leaves
25g garlic chives, finely chopped
3–4 tbsp extra virgin olive oil
freshly ground black pepper

Wash the unpeeled potatoes and put in a pan with salt and cold water to cover. Bring to the boil, then reduce the heat and simmer until tender. Drain well and leave to cool. When cool enough to handle, slice thickly onto a large serving platter. Scatter the broad beans, mint and garlic chives on top. Dress with olive oil and season with a little salt and plenty of black pepper.

auntie's apricot meringue

In our house this was always called Auntie Falda's meringue. When you marry within your parents' circle of friends, the home truths always come out. Auntie Falda got the recipe from Auntie Olive (now my mother-in-law – it's a long story), who got the recipe from Auntie Ida in Glasgow. Goodness knows where Auntie Ida got it from! So this is now known as Auntie's Apricot Meringue. The chocolate cream drizzle adds a little extra texture and an extra layer of character to the original.

SERVES 6-8

200g whole hazelnuts, blanched and peeled
extra virgin olive oil, for greasing (optional)
6 egg whites
300g golden caster sugar
1 tsp white wine vinegar
1 tsp vanilla extract

for the apricot cream
250ml double cream, at room temperature
250g dried apricots, cut into small pieces

for the chocolate cream
50g 55% cocoa Valrhona dark chocolate
100ml single cream

Preheat the oven to 180°C/350°F/Gas 4. Put the hazelnuts on a baking tray and toast in the preheated oven until golden but not brown. Remove from the oven and leave to cool. Reset the oven to 190°C/375°F/Gas 5. Put the hazelnuts in a food processor or blender and grind to a fine powder. Set aside. Either generously oil a 30cm ceramic ovenproof dish or line a baking tray with greaseproof paper and draw round a plate to mark a 30cm circle. If you use a dish, the presentation can be better.

Beat the egg whites until stiff in a clean, dry bowl. Very gradually beat in the sugar until the mixture is stiff. Be careful not to overbeat the mixture or the meringue will crystallize when cooking. Gently fold in the ground hazelnuts and finally the vinegar and vanilla extract. Spoon the mixture into the dish or within the circle marked on the greaseproof paper. Bake in the preheated oven for about 30 minutes until the meringue is golden and risen. Remove from the oven and leave to cool.

Meanwhile, make the apricot cream. Put the cream in a bowl and whip it. When it is approaching soft peak stage, add the apricots and fold in until the mixture is light and fluffy. Don't whip the cream once you have added the apricots. If you have baked your meringue on a baking tray, remove the greaseproof paper and put the meringue on a serving plate. Spoon the apricot cream on top of the meringue.

Next make the chocolate cream. Break up the chocolate and melt it in a heatproof glass or ceramic bowl over a bain-marie. Do not let the simmering water touch the bottom of the bowl. When the chocolate has melted, remove from the heat and leave to cool, then drizzle in the cream and gently mix with a knife until smooth. With reckless abandon, drizzle the chocolate cream over the meringue in very thin ribbons.

treacle tart

I could never understand treacle toffees when I was a child, so the thought of treacle tart deterred me for years. Oh what a mistake! I now love treacle tart. There are many recipes that rely on only using golden syrup but obviously the name 'syrup tart' has even less appeal than 'treacle tart'. This recipe uses syrup and treacle. I think the rich deep brown colour of the treacle makes my treacle tart more tempting than the insipid syrup version. If the treacle is too intense for you, then cut it back and add more syrup. Love treacle!

SERVES 6-8

1 x quantity of sweet pastry
  (see recipe, p. 87)
75g treacle
200g golden syrup
225g double cream
2 eggs
75g medium oatmeal
zest of 1 unwaxed lemon
1 tbsp lemon juice
extra-thick fresh cream, to serve

Follow the instructions on page 87 to make the pastry. Preheat the oven to 230°C/450°F/Gas 8. Roll out the pastry and use it to line the bottom of a 26cm loose-bottomed tart tin.

Bake the pastry blind, lined with baking parchment and filled with baking beans, in the preheated oven, for about 10 minutes, as described on page 87, until the pastry is golden. Remove from the oven, leave to cool, then use a palette knife to trim away the edges of the pastry so they are nice and even. Reduce the temperature of the oven to 160°C/325°F/Gas 3.

Mix together the rest of the ingredients except the extra-thick cream in a large bowl with a wooden spoon. The mixture will be runny but don't worry. Pour it into the pastry case and bake for about 40 minutes until the mixture is set. It should wobble slightly when you touch the tin.

Remove from the oven and leave to cool. Serve while still warm with some extra-thick fresh cream.

fly cemetery with nutmeg custard

The name may not be appealing but the taste is a favourite. It's a bit like sugar mice. Who could imagine naming a confectionery after every cook's nightmare? Despite a complete phobia to mice, I've never been deterred by sugar mice so hopefully the name of this dessert won't deter you here. It is, of course, utterly delicious with the nutmeg custard.

SERVES 6-8
225g plain flour, plus extra for dusting
pinch of salt
110g unsalted butter, chilled, plus extra for greasing
1 dessertspoon caster sugar
2 egg yolks
egg wash made from 1 egg, beaten

for the filling
50g light brown sugar
150ml water
500g sultanas
finely grated zest of 1 unwaxed lemon
1 tsp ground cinnamon
10g unsalted butter

First make the pastry. Sieve the flour and salt into a large mixing bowl and coarsely grate the butter on top. Dip the butter into the flour to stop it sticking, then rub the butter into the flour using your fingertips until it resembles coarse breadcrumbs. Add the sugar and mix through, then add the egg yolks and mix thoroughly until the mixture forms a ball. Place on a floured surface and knead gently. Wrap in clingfilm, then transfer to a bowl and refrigerate for about 30 minutes.

To make the filling, put the sugar and water in a pan over a low heat until the sugar has dissolved. Add the remaining ingredients and cook until the water has evaporated and the sultanas look glossy and plump. Remove from the heat and leave to cool. When cool, put one-third of the mixture in a blender and blend until smooth, then return the blended mixture to the remaining filling to help bind the filling together. Set aside. Grease a 20cm square non-stick, loose-bottomed baking tin with butter and preheat the oven to 180°C/350°F/Gas 4. Remove the pastry from the fridge and allow to come to room temperature. Cut the pastry into two pieces, one slightly bigger than the other. Roll out the bigger piece on a floured surface and place it in the tin so it lines the bottom and sides and leaves a little spare hanging over the edges. Fill the tin with the cooled filling. Brush the edges of the tin with a little of the egg wash. Roll out the remaining pastry and lay it on top of the filling. Trim the edges of the pastry and press with your fingers to seal. Score the top of the pastry and make one slit to let the air escape. Brush with the egg wash and bake in the preheated oven for 35–40 minutes until golden. Remove from the oven and sprinkle some caster sugar on top. Leave to cool in the tin.

nutmeg custard

SERVES 6-8 or 4 lovers of custard
400ml single cream
1 nutmeg

3 egg yolks
1 tbsp cornflour
1 tbsp caster sugar

Put the cream in a pan and grate in the nutmeg. Put the pan over a low heat and bring to a simmer. Remove from the heat and leave to infuse for 5 minutes. Meanwhile, beat the egg yolks, cornflour and sugar together in a large glass or ceramic bowl until light and smooth. Strain the warm cream into egg mixture and continue to beat until all the ingredients are incorporated. Strain into a clean pan, place over a low heat and simmer very gently until the custard thickens. Beat with a wooden spoon or balloon whisk to prevent lumps forming. Add more sugar if necessary.

Custard always reminds me of Daddy's ice cream shop. But the little hint of nutmeg makes this more festive and I feel it works really well with the spiced sultanas in the pie.

knickerbocker glory

Knickerbocker Glory is a trademark of the pre-Second World War era. It reminds us very clearly of those self-sufficient days when nothing was ever wasted and treats really were treats. Daddy was two when he arrived from Italy in the back shop of 48 High Street, Cockenzie; he died, aged 72, at 48 High Street, Cockenzie. For 70 years he lived and worked ice cream and only once threw a customer out of his shop. He chucked out loads of kids having a racket, and a good few fishermen who were a bit too friendly after a week at sea and a day in the Thorntree Inn, but he only ever threw out one paying customer. And it was all over a lack of jelly in the Knickerbocker Glories.

   For just six weeks of the year, the café was mobbed and that was when Daddy made his money. All the visitors from the West would descend on the beaches at Port Seton and Seton Sands for their annual holiday before the days of package holidays in Spain and Tenerife. They all wanted ice cream sundaes. For those six glorious summer weeks it was business and nobody would dare interfere. So when Mrs Knickers (who may still be alive, I'm told) sent her and her three children's Knickerbocker Glories back, Daddy was having none of it. Mrs Knickers had a history of complaining. Daddy was always polite, courteous and obliging but this was the final straw. Four Knickerbocker Glories with no jelly went in the bin and I can still see the faces of the three little boys who saw their sundaes flash in front of their eyes as fast as you could say 'Gordon'! What a shame for the sundaes, the boys, my dad who lost the sale, and poor Mrs Knickers, who had a tantrum over jelly.

   The recipe couldn't be simpler. For each Knickerbocker Glory you will need:

the biggest ice cream sundae glass you can get your hands on
50g fruit salad (made with tinned pears, peaches and cherries)
2 generous scoops of vanilla ice cream
1 tbsp home-made raspberry sauce
generous piping of whipped cream
1 wafer biscuit
1 glacé cherry

Fruit first, followed by a scoop of ice cream, more fruit and some raspberry sauce. Then another ball of ice cream topped with whipped cream, more raspberry sauce, a wafer and the crowning glory – a glossy red glacé cherry. Enjoy eating this in your garden as I bet the weather will be better in May than in July.

GROWING NOTES

asparagus
Asparagus officinalis

Cultivars grown at Casa San Lorenzo
- 'Darlise' – early French cultivar
- 'Gijnlim' – bred in the Netherlands; good yield, quality and taste

Cultivation
- Plant asparagus crowns (young plants) in early spring.
- They are a permanent planting so require weed-free, well-prepared soil with plenty of organic matter added well before planting. For best results, choose the warmest, sunniest spot available.
- You cannot harvest in the first year but will obtain a light crop in year two, followed by full harvesting in year three.

Interesting facts
- Allow the ferny foliage to continue growing after the picking season is finished to put energy back into the plant roots.

radishes
Raphanus sativus

Cultivars grown at Casa San Lorenzo
- 'Cherry Belle' – red-skinned and round
- 'Apache F1' – bi-coloured red and white, with a longer root

Cultivation
- We sow in the polytunnel from February onwards for a steady succession.
- We also use them between other crops in spring.
- Watch out for slugs, they love them!

Interesting fact
- Radishes are great used as a fast-maturing crop, either between rows of slower-growing vegetables or to mark a slow-germinating crop, like parsnips or parsley.

broad beans
Vicia fava

Cultivars grown at Casa San Lorenzo
- 'Crimson Flowered' – an old cultivar; decorative with small, tasty beans
- 'Aquadulce Claudia' – great for autumn sowing as it is exceptionally hardy
- 'Witkeim Manita' – fast-growing and delicious

Cultivation
- We tend to sow the beans into root trainers (long cells that encourage root growth downwards) in mid- to late winter in cold frames or in a cold glasshouse. They are transplanted out in February/March, depending on weather conditions. Seeds can be sown direct, but on our heavy soil the seeds tend to rot if the weather is wet.
- Plants are supported with stakes and string as they grow.
- Once the flowers have set, we pinch out the top sappy growth to deter blackfly.
- Sowings in January can ensure a harvest by the end of June/beginning of July.

june

June is the last month of the year before the children's summer holidays. It's the month to get all the jobs done before mayhem kicks in. The garden is beautiful. The edible flowers are popping up all around the raised beds, the courgettes are putting on plenty of growth and the bees are buzzy, buzzy buzzy. I love it.

In season we have beetroot, sorrel, carrots, watercress, courgettes and courgette flowers, and, of course, strawberries, plus lamb, pork, herring, squid and duck.

golden beetroot & butternut squash stew
with caraway soda scones

I've never loved soup. But if you call chunky soup 'stew' on a menu I'll always order it. So I'm going to call this lovely chunky soup 'stew'!

SERVES 4

1 tbsp extra virgin olive oil
2 large onions, cut into small
  pieces
25g fresh ginger, peeled and very
  finely chopped
2 tsp cumin seeds
2 tsp coriander seeds
1 tsp cardamom seeds
400g golden beetroot, peeled and
  cut into small pieces
600g butternut squash, cut into
  small pieces
salt
750ml–1 litre vegetable stock
  or water

to garnish

2 tbsp full-fat natural yogurt
1 spring onion, finely chopped
small handful of coriander leaves
1 red chilli, deseeded and finely
  sliced
juice of ½ unwaxed lime

Heat the oil in a heavy-based casserole dish. When it is hot, add the onion and fry until soft. Add the ginger, cumin, coriander and cardamom seeds and cook for a few minutes to release the flavours. Add the beetroot and squash and cook for a few minutes, stirring, until they are coated in the oil. Season with salt. Add stock or water to just cover the vegetables so you end up with a stew consistency. If you prefer it more soupy, add more stock or water.

Reduce the heat to a simmer, place a piece of greaseproof paper over the pot and cover with a lid. Simmer for 30 minutes until the vegetables are soft. The squash should start to disintegrate while the beetroot will stay firmer, giving a lovely texture. When you are ready to serve, gently marble in the yogurt, then sprinkle over the spring onions, coriander leaves and chilli. Finish with a squeeze of lime juice.

caraway soda scones

The caraway really lifts this very humble but hearty bread. Serve with the stew or, for the start of a summer picnic, with some Crowdie or soft cheese and home-made chutney or relish.

MAKES 12 small scones

10g unsalted butter, melted, plus
  extra, softened, for greasing
180g plain flour
180g wholemeal flour
1 tsp baking powder
½ tsp salt
½ tsp bicarbonate of soda
2 tsp caraway seeds
300ml buttermilk or the same
  volume of full-fat milk mixed with
  1 generous tsp lemon juice and
  left to sit for ½ hour before using
full-fat milk, for brushing

Preheat the oven to 200°C/400°F/Gas 6 and grease a baking tray. Sieve the flours, baking powder, salt, bicarbonate of soda and caraway seeds into a large mixing bowl and form a well in the centre. Pour the melted butter and the buttermilk into the well and mix all the ingredients together. The mixture should be dry enough to handle. Knead for a few minutes until all the ingredients are incorporated, then form into a circle and flatten slightly. Use a scone cutter to cut the scones, then place on the greased baking tray. Brush with a little milk. Bake in the preheated oven for about 15 minutes until the scones are golden and risen. Cool on a wire rack

chargrilled herring
with carrot & courgette salad

SERVES 4
8 herring fillets
extra virgin olive oil, for drizzling
salt, to serve
4 wedges of unwaxed lemon,
 to serve

Herring is a rich fish so I
like to keep it simple. Use
a really hot, ridged griddle
pan or the barbecue if the
weather's good.

Preheat the oven to 180°C/350°F/Gas 4 and heat a ridged griddle pan over a high heat until it is hot. Alternatively, heat up the barbecue. Wash the herring and make sure any loose scales have been removed.

Lay the fish, skin side down, on the griddle or barbecue and cook for about 5 minutes, depending on how thick the fish is. Turn the fish over once it releases easily from the griddle. Cook for another few minutes, then transfer to a baking tray. Put in the preheated oven and bake for 8 minutes until the fish is lovely and opaque, and firm to the touch.

Remove from the oven and drizzle with a little olive oil, a generous sprinkle of salt and a lovely big wedge of lemon. Serve with a generous bowl of crunchy carrot and courgette salad.

Margaret (left) and her cousin, Janet, dressed in their best for church, Eyemouth Harbour c. 1928

Margaret's mother Annie was one of the last of the herring girls. Seeing photographs now, it all looked so beautiful – the girls' heads covered to protect them from the wind, shawls draped over their shoulders, crossed over their bodies and tied behind their waists, and gathered skirts tucked in at the sides with aprons to stop them getting dirty.

But it was a really hard life. The women, mainly young unmarried girls, would follow the native seasonal fish from the east coast of Scotland in the winter and spring down into England for the summer and autumn months. The herrings would be caught and prepared on the harbour jetties. They would be cleaned and packed by the bands of women eager to get as much work done as possible. The fish were packed in large barrels with salt to preserve them, all well before the days of refrigeration.

Margaret spent her childhood along the east coast from Peterhead and Buckie, all the way down to Dunbar and Eyemouth.

carrot & courgette salad

Orange, red and green should never be seen except on an Irish football team. I hope you agree that these colours/flavours can be seen together on a plate as well as on the field.

SERVES 4
1 carrot, cut into ribbons
2 new-season courgettes, cut into thin rounds
50g flat-leaf parsley leaves, coarsely chopped
1 red chilli, deseeded and thinly sliced
1 tbsp parsley pesto (see p.130)
4 tbsp extra virgin olive oil
salt
1 tbsp baby capers in brine, rinsed and drained

Put the carrot, courgettes and parsley leaves in a bowl and scatter with the chilli. Thin the parsley pesto with the olive oil and drizzle on top of the salad. Season to taste with salt and add the capers, then serve.

samphire, chilli & courgette squid

This is a really speedy stir-fry dish. You'll need a little time to make sure everything's prepared before you start cooking, but once you're good to go, you'll be surprised at how quick and easy it is. Be careful not to overcook the squid: it should be on the plate as soon as it's firm to the touch. This is a really great dish for dramatic entertaining if you're in the mood for a bit of a stir.

SERVES 4

100g marsh samphire, thoroughly washed
200g squid, washed and cut into thin rings
2 tbsp extra virgin olive oil
1 garlic clove, thinly sliced
1 red chilli, deseeded and thinly sliced
1 small courgette, topped and tailed, halved
  lengthways and thinly sliced
salt
4 wedges of unwaxed lemon, to serve

Blanch the samphire by plunging it in boiling water for about 15 seconds to help remove some of the salty flavour. Drain and refresh in cold water. Drain well and set aside. Rinse the squid again just before you are due to start cooking. Drain it well and dry it on kitchen paper.

Heat the olive oil in a large frying pan or wok. When it is hot, add the garlic and chilli and cook for 1 minute to release the flavours. Add the courgette and squid, increase the heat and fry over a very hot heat for about 3 minutes. Add the marsh samphire and heat through, then add salt to taste. It may only need a small pinch as the samphire can be very salty. Serve straight away with a wedge of lemon.

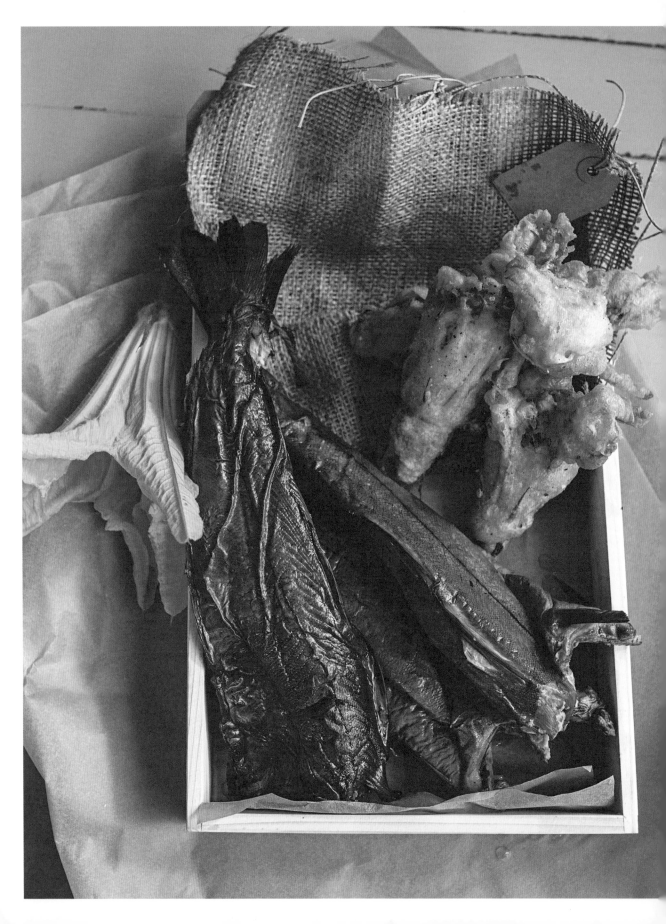

arbroath smokie mousse
with deep-fried courgette flowers

I once watched the famous Spink's Arbroath Smokies family demonstrate how to fillet a smokie. They made it look so easy. Like everything, practice makes perfect. Please be careful to remove all the bones as they can be dangerous.

SERVES 4
4 leaves of gold leaf gelatine
200ml double cream
300g Arbroath Smokies (undyed smoked haddock), bones and skin removed
juice of 1 unwaxed lemon, to taste

Put the gelatine in cold water to soften for a few minutes, then remove from the water and squeeze out any excess. In a small pan over a low heat, warm the cream with the gelatine until the gelatine has dissolved. Put the smoked haddock and cream mixture In a food processor and blend until smooth. Add a little lemon juice to taste. Spoon into 4 individual ramekins or glass jars and refrigerate for 2 hours until set.

deep-fried courgette flowers

Courgettes are a big part of the garden. They take up a lot of space but they are an incredibly bountiful plant. The bees love the flowers, the bright yellow adds sparkle to the garden, and the enormous green leaves hide the beautiful courgettes. The flowers are great in salads, in cream sauces or added at the very last minute to risottos – but they are best deep-fried.

SERVES 4
225g plain flour
pinch of salt
375ml sparkling water, ice-cold
2 egg yolks
8 courgette flowers
vegetable oil or light olive oil, for frying

Sift the flour and salt into a large bowl and use a balloon whisk to beat in the sparkling water and then the egg yolks. Refrigerate this batter for 30 minutes. Meanwhile, prepare the courgette flowers. Gently wipe with a damp cloth and check for insects. You can trim the stem if you like.

Pour at least 2.5cm of oil in a deep frying pan and place over a medium heat. When the oil is hot, a drop of the batter should bubble immediately you place it in the oil; if it spits, the oil is too hot. Dip the courgette flowers in the batter and gently shake off any excess.

Put a batter-coated courgette flower in the hot oil and fry until golden brown, turning occasionally. Remove with a slotted spoon and serve immediately. These are best eaten straight away, so cook them for friends who don't mind standing in the kitchen when you're frying.

If you're feeling adventurous, you can spoon the Arbroath Smokie mousse inside the courgette flowers and then fry them. This produces a really, but really, delicately flavoured starter.

The Shepherd Boy by James Guthrie

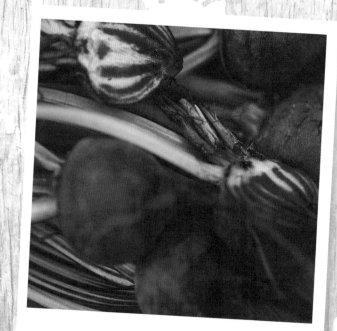

When my daughter Carla was five years old, she asked, 'Why do they kill the baby sheep and not the mummies?' Very good question. It didn't stop her eating her Sunday roast, but it's the thought that counts. Scottish Highland, Shetland or Borders lamb is a Sunday treat in our house. Too early in the season and yes, then it's a luxury, but I prefer it slightly later so the flavour is a little deeper and the legs just slightly bigger. Rosemary is a classic herb for lamb but the Greeks have the winning formula – oregano. Maybe it's because I'm so used to rosemary that the oregano makes me feel more excited, but I genuinely feel it works best.

roast oregano lamb
with beetroot salad & salsa verde

1.5kg leg of lamb on the bone
  (allow about 400g per person)
2–3 tbsp extra virgin olive oil
salt and freshly ground black
  pepper
50g fresh oregano or marjoram
  leaves
4 garlic cloves, unpeeled
375ml dry white wine
sea salt flakes (optional)

Preheat the oven to 230°C/450°F/Gas 8. Put the lamb in a deep roasting tin and rub with the olive oil, salt and plenty of black pepper. Scatter the oregano or marjoram and the garlic on top, then roast in the preheated oven for 15 minutes until the meat starts to sizzle. Add enough wine to generously cover the bottom of the tin. I generally need about half a bottle. Reduce the oven to 180°C/350°F/Gas 4, cover the meat with tinfoil and roast for a further 15 minutes per 500g. Halfway through the cooking time, baste the lamb with the juices. If the juices are drying up, add a little hot water and a good pinch of sea salt flakes. Check the lamb is ready by placing a knife into the thickest part. If the knife goes in easily, it is ready. Remove from the oven, cover with a clean tea towel and leave to rest for 15–30 minutes before carving.

beetroot salad & salsa verde

SERVES 4
50g spinach leaves
2 purple beetroot, cooked and cut
  into small cubes or wedges
2 golden beetroot, cooked and cut
  into small cubes or wedges
50g small olives in brine, pitted
2 tbsp salsa verde (see below)
approx. 50ml extra virgin olive oil
(optional)
salt and freshly ground black
  pepper

for the salsa
50g flat-leaf parsley leaves
50g basil leaves
50g mint leaves
1 garlic clove, finely chopped
2 anchovies, finely chopped
20 small capers in salt, rinsed
  and drained
approx. 75ml extra virgin olive oil
1–2 tbsp red wine vinegar or
  balsamic vinegar
salt

To make the salsa, either use a pestle and mortar to pound together the parsley, basil, mint, garlic, anchovies and capers, or chop these ingredients as finely as you can. Mix with the olive oil and a splash of vinegar (use balsamic vinegar for a more intense flavour). Add salt to taste and set aside. Scatter the spinach leaves over a large serving plate. Scatter the purple and golden beetroot and the olives on top of the spinach. Finally, spoon the salsa over the beetroot and adjust the seasoning. You can add a little extra olive oil to help lubricate the salad if you feel it needs it. Refrigerate for up to 2 hours or serve immediately.

The beetroot salad has been a favourite dish of mine for years. Helen first made it for me. To make it more substantial, you can boil some new potatoes and scatter them next to the beetroot. The contrast in colour is really nice and the flavours work extremely well together.

beetroot & toasted peanut salad

People think of tomatoes as an Italian ingredient but they have a rich Scottish heritage, especially in the Clyde Valley. New-season home-grown tomatoes have a lovely green, slightly acidic flavour and a crisp texture and should be ready at the same time as the first new-season beetroot. Added to the sharpness of the Dunlop and the crunch of the toasted, honeyed peanuts, this is a really tasty, mouthwatering salad, worth waiting for.

SERVES 4

50g unsalted peanuts
salt
1 generous tsp heather honey
50g rocket leaves
2 purple beetroot, cooked and
  cut into quarters
150g new-season slightly
  under-ripe tomatoes
125g Dunlop or similar mature
  cow's milk cheddar
handful of flat-leaf parsley leaves,
  coarsely chopped
12 mint leaves
1 spring onion, finely sliced
50ml extra virgin olive oil
16 pansies or other edible flowers,
  to decorate

Dry-roast the peanuts in a non-stick frying pan over a medium heat. When they start to colour, add a pinch of salt and the honey. Cook for a few seconds. Remove from the heat and leave to cool. When cool, wrap them in a clean, dry tea towel and crush them coarsely with a rolling pin.

Layer the rocket and beetroot on a large plate or platter. Quarter the tomatoes and scatter on top. Crumble the cheese over and sprinkle with the peanuts. Add the parsley, mint and spring onion.

Dress with the olive oil and sprinkle with a little salt. Finally scatter with pansies and you'll have all the flavours and sensations of summer on a plate.

For this photo, Suzanne did her stuff and added a sliced whole cooked beetroot, stalks and all, for decoration. It looks like a beautiful still-life painting.

strawberry & ginger wine syllabub

Light puddings are compulsory on certain occasions. Whether it's sorbets, soufflés or parfaits, they all have their own character. Syllabubs, although very light, are slightly more complicated, given the fact that wine is involved. They are even better when a deliciously intense and luxurious dessert wine is used. Crabbie's Green Ginger Wine has a 13.5% volume, which is as high as most dessert wines, so watch out. No driving after this one. Pudding could put you over the limit.

SERVES 4
300ml double cream
150ml Crabbie's Green Ginger Wine
50g golden caster sugar
300g strawberries, hulled and
  cut into quarters, plus 4 halved
  strawberries, to decorate
8 purple pansies, to decorate

Whip the cream, ginger wine and sugar together in a large bowl until the mixture forms soft peaks. Choose pretty glasses and half-fill them with the cream mixture. Add the quartered strawberries, then top up with more of the cream mixture. Serve each with two strawberry halves and two little purple pansies for that final touch. Your guests will find a strawberry surprise lurking deep inside.

This is so easy yet so delicious. Don't spoil it by using unripe fruit. And only make it if your strawberries are super-sweet and in season, otherwise it will be like eating turnips with ice cream!

very fancy strawberry tarts
with toffee strawberries

Fresh strawberry, raspberry or tayberry tarts made once a year with the first fruits of the new season give a different flavour each month for at least three months. If you have a visitor coming for afternoon tea, these are so easy, as the pastry cases can be made up to a week in advance and stored in an airtight container. The toffee strawberries and cream can be prepared on the day and the tarts assembled just before your guest arrives. The deliciously crisp pastry and soft cream filling with a sharp berry kick make them irresistible.

SERVES 4-6
6 tsp home-made strawberry jam
6 tbsp double cream
4–6 toffee strawberries (see below)

for the pastry
200g unsalted butter, at room
   temperature
100g caster sugar
½ tsp vanilla extract
250g plain flour, sieved,
   plus extra for dusting
90g cornflour

To make the pastry, beat the butter, sugar and vanilla together in a bowl until light and fluffy. Beat in the flour and cornflour. Transfer to a floured surface and knead together to make a firm dough. Refrigerate for 30 minutes. Remove from the fridge and allow to come to room temperature. Roll the pastry out onto a floured surface and use a cutter to cut circles about the thickness of a two-pound coin and large enough to fit your chosen pastry cases. Lay a circle in each pastry case and put the filled cases in a shallow muffin tray. Using a fork, prick a few holes in the pastry, then transfer the tray with the filled pastry cases to the freezer and chill for 30 minutes. This will help stop the pastry from shrinking. Meanwhile, preheat the oven to 180°C/350°F/Gas 4. Bake in the preheated oven for 20 minutes until crisp and golden. Cool for a few minutes, then transfer to a wire cooling rack. To assemble, whip the cream until it forms soft peaks. Place 1 tsp strawberry jam in the bottom of each pastry case, followed by a generous spoonful of whipped cream. Decorate with a toffee strawberry.

toffee strawberries

These are the ultimate extra for my very fancy strawberry tarts. The crunchy toffee, sweet strawberry, soft cream and crumbly pastry will give you every sweet sensation all at once. They use caster sugar for the toffee in the kitchen at The Scottish Cafe & Restaurant but Mummy uses granulated; either is fine.

MAKES 12
150g caster or granulated sugar
12 strawberries, stalks attached

Place the sugar in a heavy-based pan and bring to a simmer. You can move the pan to stop the sugar from sticking, but do not stir it. Simmer until the sugar changes to a light golden toffee shade. This can take 10–15 minutes but don't take your eyes off the pan once you see the colour start to change as it can do so very quickly and you'll have ruined the toffee and your pan. And be super-careful as the pan and the toffee will get extremely hot. Very carefully dip each strawberry into the toffee. If the strawberries have very long stalks, it makes it easier. Alternatively, pierce the top of the strawberry with a fork and use to dip the strawberry in the toffee. Allow any excess toffee to drip off, then transfer to a sheet of greaseproof paper and leave to cool. This will only take a few minutes.

beetroot chocolate cake
with raspberry crème fraîche

This chocolate cake has a fabulous moist texture, similar to a Sacher Torte but without any ground almonds. It's a great choice if you're looking for a slightly more unusual cake. My children love sweets but they don't really like sweet cakes. The beetroot in this recipe helps remove the sweetness, so the children really go for it. It's a great teatime-on-a-Sunday-afternoon kind of cake!

SERVES 6-8
225g 70% cocoa Valrhona dark chocolate
125g unsalted butter, softened
225g golden caster sugar
½ vanilla pod
225g cooked beetroot, peeled and coarsely grated
3 large eggs, lightly beaten
225g self-raising flour, sieved

for the raspberry cream
125g raspberries
250g crème fraîche
squeeze of lemon juice

for the chocolate cream
200g 70% cocoa Valrhona dark chocolate
25g unsalted butter
100g double cream

to decorate
200g mixed berries (such as raspberries, blackberries and small strawberries)
zest of 1 orange

If you like, you can make the cake one or two days before dressing it with the chocolate cream. Keep it in an airtight container and it will stay really moist and fresh.

Preheat the oven to 180°C/350°F/Gas 4 and line a 26cm cake tin with baking parchment. Break up the chocolate and melt it in a heatproof glass or ceramic bowl over a bain-marie. Do not let the simmering water touch the bottom of the bowl. In a separate bowl, beat the butter and sugar together until fluffy. Split the vanilla pod lengthways and scrape out the seeds with a sharp knife. Slowly beat the melted chocolate, vanilla seeds and then the grated beetroot into the butter and sugar mixture. Finally fold in the eggs and flour. Transfer to the cake tin and bake for 40 minutes in the preheated oven until firm to the touch. Remove from the oven, cool for a few minutes, then transfer to a wire cooling rack.

For the raspberry cream, squash the raspberries in a bowl, then fold in the crème fraîche and lemon juice. Set aside.

For the chocolate cream, break up the chocolate and melt it with the butter in a heatproof glass or ceramic bowl over a bain-marie. As soon as the water in the pan comes to the boil, remove the pan and bowl from the heat. Leave the chocolate to melt. Try not to touch it until it has all melted, then gently fold in the cream until the mixture is glossy. When the cake is cool, use a spatula to spread the chocolate cream on top and over the sides.

Decorate with the mixed berries and a sprinkle of orange zest. Serve with the raspberry cream on the side.

GROWING NOTES

beetroot
Beta vulgaris

Cultivars grown at Casa San Lorenzo
- 'Chioggia' – Italian cultivar, great for taste and appearance (white and purple rings)
- 'Boltardy' – ideal for early baby roots
- 'Burpee's Golden' – colourful yellow roots
- 'Egyptian Turnip Rooted' – for flavour!

Cultivation
- Sow outside from late March onwards for harvesting from July to October.
- Earlier and later sowings can be made under cover (in a polytunnel) to extend the harvest into autumn and winter.
- Grow close together for small sweet roots, or allow wider spacing for large beets.

Interesting fact
- Use young leaves for salads, and wilt larger leaves as you would spinach.

strawberries
Fragaria spp.

Cultivars grown at Casa San Lorenzo
- 'Marshmello' – early cultivar suitable for indoor forcing in the polytunnel
- 'Malwina' – late season
- 'Mara des Bois' – perpetual fruits that crop steadily from August through to autumn

Cultivation
- We have planted strawberries beneath the apples that are trained on the garden walls and in vertical planters using recycled pallets.
- We try to protect plants from late frosts with horticultural fleece when the strawberries are in flower.
- Plants are fed with potash using comfrey liquid tea to encourage flowering in spring.
- The plants are watered well once the berries start to develop.

Interesting fact
- We can harvest in June by bringing our 'Marshmello' plants under cover in February. This allows us to have berries almost three weeks earlier than from the plants outdoors.

viola/pansies
Viola spp.

Cultivars grown at Casa San Lorenzo
- All viola flowers are edible; we grow a wide range of cultivars to give different colour combinations

Cultivation
- We sow the seed indoors in February/March into trays and prick them out once they are large enough.
- They are grown on in the polytunnel, then hardened off before planting out in early May.
- The biggest problem is the slugs that munch the young growth.
- We collect seeds from our violas in autumn to propagate more. Plants self-seed easily so we always have young plants to move for harvesting.

july

The sun is up, the sky is blue and it's warm. We may find ourselves searching out some sunshine, but the temperature is always perfect and the garden is looking beautiful. The colours are wonderful at this time of year and the flowers are ablaze with high-summer glory.

In season we have courgettes, fennel, cucumbers, tomatoes, raspberries, blackcurrants and redcurrants.

courgette, green tomato & mint salad

Courgettes are one of the most versatile vegetables. Their beautiful flowers can be fried, stuffed or shredded, while the main show makes the best soups, roasted vegetables or light stews. They enter a whole new world, however, when they are served raw. Courgettes fall into the scientific category of fruits rather than vegetables. Eating them raw increases your vitamin and mineral intake and is of huge benefit for your digestive tract. I prepare many raw courgette salads but always think they taste best with a little chilli – somehow the fiery sting complements the very mellow flavour of the courgettes.

SERVES 4

2 small new-season courgettes
1 small fennel bulb
10 small slightly green,
  crisp tomatoes, cut into quarters
1 small cucumber, peeled,
  deseeded and thinly sliced
1 red chilli, deseeded and
  very finely chopped
large handful of mint leaves
salt
4 wedges of lime, to garnish

for the dressing
100ml soured cream
6 tbsp extra virgin olive oil
50g basil leaves
salt
juice of 1 unwaxed lime

For a more substantial salad, serve with some freshly poached trout or smoked trout flaked on top.

Using a mandolin or the slicer on your grater, slice the courgettes and fennel onto a large serving platter. Scatter the tomato quarters and sliced cucumber on top. Scatter with the chilli and mint and season with a little salt. For the dressing, blend together in a jug the soured cream, olive oil, basil, a little more salt and the lime juice. and drizzle over the salad. Serve with a wedge of lime.

langoustines with cucumber mayonnaise
with courgette & fennel fritters

Freshly boiled langoustines, spicy home-made mayonnaise and the cold crunch of home-grown cucumber are summer flavour sensations. The beetroot tops add a great colour contrast and have a delicious flavour. They work so well with the frisée but if you can't get hold of them, other salad leaves will be just as good.

SERVES 4 as a starter, 2 as
a main course

16 langoustines, shelled, or 8 salted
  anchovies
4 eggs
50ml double cream, chilled
200ml home-made mayonnaise
  (see recipe, p.51)
1 tsp cayenne pepper
juice of ½ unwaxed lemon
  (optional)
1 small cucumber, peeled, halved
  lengthways and deseeded
100g young white and yellow frisée
  salad leaves
25g mini capers in salt, rinsed
  and drained
handful of young beetroot tops

Prepare the langoustines. If they are really fresh, they should still be alive. Hold a langoustine in your left land with the tail pointing to the right. Watch out for the claws as they can scratch. There are five fins at the end of the tail. Gently twist the middle fin and pull it to remove the digestive tract. This requires practice, so take your time. If the tract doesn't come out, don't worry as you can clean the insides after you've cooked the langoustines, but this is more difficult. Once cleaned, rinse the langoustines, then place them in a large pot of slightly salted boiling water. Cover with a lid, bring back to the boil and cook for 2 minutes. Drain immediately and blast with ice-cold water from the tap to stop the langoustines cooking any more and to make them lovely and firm. When cool enough to handle, break the body from the tail. Squeeze the tail between both pairs of thumbs and your first two fingers. Then, turning the tail towards you, gently crack open the shell and remove the beautiful pink flesh. Set aside.

Put the eggs in a pan of tepid water, bring to the boil and simmer for 6 minutes. The whites of the eggs should be set and the yolks soft but not runny. Hold the eggs under cold running water until cool enough to handle. Gently remove the shell. Take care as the yolks are soft. Set aside. Whip the cream until it forms soft peaks. Put the mayonnaise in a small bowl, thin with the cream and add a good pinch of cayenne pepper. Check for seasoning; sometimes you need a squeeze of lemon juice to counteract the sweetness of the cream. Slice the cucumber into semi-circles about 5mm thick and stir into the mayonnaise. Set aside. Put a thin layer of frisée leaves on a large flat plate. Scatter over a few capers and the beetroot tops. Cut the eggs in half and arrange on the frisée leaves. Place the shelled langoustines or anchovies, if using, on top. Drizzle with the flavoured mayonnaise and sprinkle another good pinch of cayenne pepper over the salad.

I most enjoy a meal when there is a balance of hot and cold food. The cucumber mayonnaise can be made in advance and chilled, and just before you're ready to eat, you can fill up with the cheeky and cheap courgette and fennel fritters. Then there is just a little space left for those luxuriously lavish langoustines.

Being brought up between two harbours was better than living next to Disneyland. We spent hours watching the boats and liners in the Firth of Forth, the dramatic changes in the tides and the most glorious sunsets. And almost every Saturday morning in the season, we found a bag of langoustines or a few lobsters in a box on our front doorstep. Daddy was best pals with all the fishermen – the nip and half pint on Saturday nights in the Thorntree Inn may have influenced things!

courgette & fennel fritters

These fritters are made with grated vegetables so they are a cross between a pakora and a fritter. Alternatively, if you want a chunkier nibble, you can cut generous slices of the vegetables and fry them individually in the batter. The Highland Spring Water used for the batter is particularly fizzy. It works well as you need the bubbles to make the batter crispy.

SERVES 4 generously
as a starter
1 fennel bulb, coarsely grated
2 courgettes, coarsely grated
sunflower oil or vegetable oil,
  for frying
salt

for the batter
250g strong white flour
1 tsp cornflour
500ml Highland Spring Water,
  chilled
salt

First make the batter. Sieve the flour and cornflour into a large bowl and use a balloon whisk to beat in the mineral water. Add a pinch of salt and set aside. Line a large baking tray with greaseproof paper and preheat the oven to 160°C/325°F/Gas 3. Add the grated fennel and courgettes to the batter and mix well. The mixture will be quite sloppy but don't worry. Half-fill a deep-fat fryer or deep cast-iron casserole dish with oil. When you are ready to start frying, heat the oil over a medium heat. Once the oil starts to move in the pan, test the temperature. A drop of the batter should bubble immediately you place it in the oil; if it spits, the oil is too hot. The more vegetable mixture you add to the oil, the cooler it will become, so be careful not to fry too much at any one time. When the oil is hot enough, drop in a few spoonfuls of the vegetable mixture. Move the fritters around in the oil with a slotted metal spoon so they get evenly coloured and cooked through. When they are nice and crisp and golden, remove with the slotted spoon and let any excess oil drain off. Transfer to the lined baking tray and keep in the preheated oven while you fry the remaining vegetable mixture. Sprinkle the fritters with a little salt and enjoy with a lovely glass of chilled white wine.

JULY

During my student years, I tried to impress my friends by cooking soufflés. I'd never eaten a really posh soufflé so I thought I did really well. My recipe was more of a kitchen-garden cottage soufflé than a sophisticated château version. Now that I've experienced a few more of life's luxuries and have eaten a few superior soufflés, my kitchen-garden cottage version may only get third-class honours for presentation but is definitely first-class for taste.

The dramatic height of a premier soufflé is hard to master but the impact these little beauties make is based on flavour. Cooking them in a bain-marie means they won't rise as much but neither will they collapse as much, so it's a win-win situation every time. So, don't worry if they don't look like the Eiffel Tower: comparisons with Edinburgh Castle will be more apt!

These savoury walnut scones are a great accompaniment as well as being versatile. They can be eaten at any time – for breakfast, lunch or as a night-time snack instead of toast and butter. When I was in my teens I'd often make scones at 10pm. My brothers and sisters had all married or left home by then, I'd locked up the shop, Mummy and Daddy had their feet up in front of the fire and the ten o'clock news was about to start. So, rather than watch Selina Scott or Moira Stewart, I'd make scones. Much more fun.

courgette & crowdie soufflés
with savoury walnut scones

SERVES 6
50g unsalted butter,
  plus extra for greasing
500g courgettes
salt
50g plain flour

½ nutmeg, freshly grated
150ml full-fat milk
freshly ground white pepper
3 eggs, separated
100g Crowdie or a fresh young
  goat's cheese

Preheat the oven to 180°C/350°F/Gas 4 and grease 6 individual 150ml ramekins. Coarsely grate the courgettes and leave in a colander in the sink with a generous pinch of salt. Melt the butter in a pan over a medium heat, then add the flour and nutmeg. Reduce the heat and cook, stirring frequently, for 4–5 minutes, then add the milk. Season to taste with salt and pepper. Continue cooking until the mixture has thickened, stirring with a balloon whisk to help prevent lumps forming. Add the egg yolks and beat until smooth. With the heat very low, add the Crowdie or goat's cheese and beat again until smooth and thickened. Remove from the heat. Squeeze any excess moisture from the courgettes and add to the mixture. Beat the egg whites until very stiff in a clean, dry bowl, then gently fold into the mixture. Divide between the greased ramekins and set in a bain-marie. Bake for about 25 minutes in the preheated oven, until light, risen and golden. Serve immediately.

savoury walnut scones

MAKES 9-10
50g unsalted butter, chilled, plus
  extra, softened, for greasing
200g self-raising flour, plus extra
  for dusting
1 tsp baking powder
50g ground walnuts
100g your favourite cheddar (leftover
  cheese will do)

1 tsp fine salt
1 tsp cayenne pepper
1 large egg, lightly beaten
4–5 tbsp yogurt
milk or beaten egg, for brushing
9–10 whole walnuts, to decorate

Preheat the oven to 220°C/425°F/Gas 7 and grease a baking tray. Sieve the flour and baking powder into a large bowl and add the ground walnuts. Coarsely grate the butter and cheddar into the flour. Add the salt and cayenne pepper. Rub the mixture together using your fingertips until it resembles fine breadcrumbs. Add the egg and yogurt, and mix until all the ingredients come together. The mixture should be lovely and soft. Add more yogurt if it is too dry. Transfer to a floured surface and knead gently. Roll out to a thickness of 2.5cm and cut out 9–10 circles using a small scone or biscuit cutter. Place on the greased baking tray and brush with a little milk or egg. Decorate each scone with a whole walnut. Bake in the preheated oven for 10–12 minutes until risen and golden.

fennel sea bass

The drama of serving a whole fish, head and tail intact, really depends on your guests. Even some of our best 'foodie' friends in the restaurant don't like the look of those eyes staring at you across the table. Alternatively, you can buy fillets. Small, individual fillets will have come from farmed fish, but if you've got a good fishmonger, ask him to fillet a whole wild sea bass and cut it into pieces. The flesh will be thicker and, given the lower fat content of the wild fish, the flavour will be worth the extra cost. These fillets are perfect with simply sautéed courgettes, spinach and garlic.

SERVES 4
2–3 tbsp extra virgin olive oil,
  plus extra for drizzling
8 sea bass fillets, washed and dried
salt
8 sprigs of fennel, torn

Preheat the oven to 200°C/400°F/Gas 6. Heat the olive oil in a heavy-based frying pan or griddle pan. When the oil is hot, place the fish, skin side down, into the oil. Fry for a few minutes until the skin is coloured. If you are using a griddle pan, the fish will be ready when it releases easily from the pan. Transfer to a baking tray and season with a little salt, the fennel and a drizzle of olive oil. Bake in the preheated oven for 8–12 minutes, depending on the thickness of the fillets, until the flesh is firm to the touch and translucent. Serve immediately.

sautéed courgettes, spinach & garlic

SERVES 4
extra virgin olive oil, for frying
2 courgettes, thinly sliced
400g spinach leaves
4 small garlic cloves, thinly sliced
salt and freshly ground black pepper
juice of ½ unwaxed lemon

Put a little oil in a frying pan that's big enough for all your vegetables. Place over a high heat and when the oil is hot, add the vegetables one at a time, starting with the ones that need cooking the longest. If the courgettes are cut quite small and thin, they will take only a few minutes. Similarly, the spinach only needs a minute or two to wilt slightly. Add the garlic near the end to give a very light aroma that won't overpower either the other vegetables or the lovely salty, iodine flavour of the fresh fish. As you add the vegetables, gently move the pan to stop them sticking or burning. The aim is to keep the vegetables crunchy. Season with the salt, pepper and lemon juice – just enough to give a background taste.

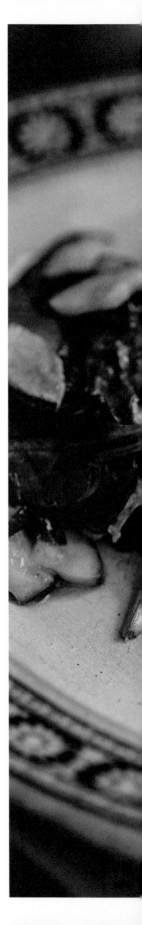

For over ten years now we've been receiving a weekly delivery of fresh vegetables, cheese and fruit from Italy for Ristorante Contini. The ability to buy really fresh produce direct from the busiest market in Europe has inspired our cooking and brought us all the sunshine vitamins, colours and flavours that Scotland can't supply over the hungry winter months. Having the garden, however, is changing all this. We will continue to receive the staple Italian ingredients that we can't grow in any quantity – peppers, violet aubergines, San Marzano tomatoes, Camone tomatoes, puntarelle and so on – but when the sun is shining in Scotland, we'll easily be able to produce courgettes, spinach and garlic in large enough quantities to support our monthly menus.

This is fantastic. Fresher, tastier and home-grown. Courgettes, spinach and garlic are probably our most used produce. The bright green and good feel that you get from eating them, and their ability to work so well on their own or with eggs, fish and white meat like chicken, make them very versatile. This means that we have endless combinations for cooking these ingredients. The sautéed courgettes, spinach and garlic is probably the quickest to prepare and the easiest to cook.

'Our home-grown tomatoes have a unique, lovely green, crisp flavour that's completely different from Italian tomatoes. '

roast fennel & potted salmon
with dill & paprika scones

Fresh fennel and salmon work really well together. These little pots can be prepared in advance and are great if you're entertaining or want to have a light lunch in the garden on a sunny day.

SERVES 6

100g fennel

400g line-caught salmon fillet, skin on

1 bayleaf

6 peppercorns

salt

125g unsalted butter, plus extra for greasing

juice of 1 unwaxed lemon

6 stems of dill

Trim the fennel and shred it very thinly. Place it in a shallow pan with the salmon and cover with cold water. Add the bayleaf, peppercorns and a generous pinch of salt. Bring the water to the boil, remove from the heat and cover with a lid. Leave the salmon to cool; this will take about 1 hour. Grease 6 individual ramekins. Carefully remove the salmon from the pan and place on a plate. Remove the skin and any peppercorns. Gently flake the flesh. Lift the fennel out of the water and pat it dry with kitchen paper. It should be nice and tender. Layer the salmon and fennel in the ramekins and press down gently with the back of a spoon. The mixture must be compact so the butter doesn't run all the way through, so don't be shy about pressing it down. Season with salt if necessary. Squeeze a little lemon juice into each ramekin. Melt the butter in a small pan. As the butter melts, the frothy milk solids will come to the surface leaving the clear fats at the bottom. Spoon off and discard the frothy solids. Carefully pour the clarified butter over each ramekin. While the butter is still warm, lay a sprig of dill on top and gently push it under the butter so the butter sets on top. Transfer to the fridge when cool.

dill & paprika scones

Scones are so easy. They make a great substitute for home-made bread but take no time at all. You can use smoked paprika for a deeper flavour but unsmoked paprika works best for me as it is more delicate and doesn't overpower the dill. These scones are also perfect for afternoon tea. Make them as small as you can and when cold, cut them and serve with some cream cheese, smoked salmon and cayenne pepper.

MAKES 12-14

300g self-raising flour

100g wholemeal flour

1 heaped tsp baking powder

100g unsalted butter, chilled, plus extra for greasing

20g dill

1 tsp salt

½ tsp unsmoked paprika

250ml full-fat milk (reserve a little for brushing)

1 egg

Sieve the flours into a large mixing bowl and add the baking powder. Coarsely grate the butter into the bowl. Gently rub the mixture together using your fingertips until it resembles fine breadcrumbs. Finely chop the dill and add to the mixture with the salt, paprika, milk and egg. Combine the mixture until it forms a ball, then transfer to a floured surface and knead gently. Roll out to a thickness of 2.5cm and cut out 12–14 circles using a small scone or biscuit cutter. They can be refrigerated at this stage until you are ready to bake them, then you can have lovely hot scones with the chilled potted salmon. Before baking, preheat the oven to 230°C/450°F/Gas 8 and grease a baking sheet. Brush the scones with a little milk, then place on the baking sheet in the preheated oven for 10–12 minutes, until golden and risen.

The Eildon Hills and the Tweed by James Ward

In this landscape painting of 1807, James Ward (1769-1859) shows two shepherd boys and their dogs gazing across the Tweed Valley to where an angler fishes peacefully and cattle come down to the river to drink. The Eildon Hills near Montrose in the Borders look like mini volcanoes in the background. Ward visited the Borders in about 1806, at the invitation of Lord Somerville. During his stay he made two studies of the area. This one reflects the atmosphere of Sir Walter Scott's poem, the Lay of the Last Minstrel - 'a kind of Romance of Border Chivalry'.

heavenly tomato & loch arthur omelette

The omelette is my food hero. We've named our chicken run 'Arnold omelette' in honour of the Savoy's famous Arnold Bennett omelette . Omelettes are there when you need comfort and speed, and they are healthy, nutritious, cheap and filling. The other amazing thing is that you can eat omelette for breakfast, lunch, tea or dinner. Whether we thank the Persians, the Romans or the French for omelettes, let's thank the chicken for the eggs. Or do we thank the eggs for the chicken? The secret of success, as always, is the quality of the ingredients. You need the freshest, best eggs and your favourite filling. Orlando's childhood egg allergy stopped me cooking eggs for years, but they're back with a vengeance now. Victor often comes home very late from Ristorante Contini: an omelette and salad fills the gap. It's light, too, so he's not left dozing in front of the TV till the small hours. His choice filling is goat's cheese and spinach. The girls' tea-time favourite is smoked bacon with a little onion and, preferably, boiled new potatoes left from dinner the night before. For me however, my filling of choice has to be cheese and tomato and my favourite, without a doubt, is Loch Arthur cheddar with baby tomatoes. This heavenly omelette becomes totally divine when served with the fennel, raspberry and cucumber salad.

SERVES 1

3 large eggs
salt and freshly ground black
  pepper
1 tbsp extra virgin olive oil
3 or 4 baby tomatoes,
  coarsely sliced
100g Loch Arthur cheddar

Break the eggs into a bowl and add a pinch of salt and pepper to taste. Heat the oil in a 20cm non-stick frying pan over a moderately high heat, then add the tomatoes. Once the tomato skins start to melt but not caramelize, beat the eggs and add to the pan. When the egg starts to solidify around the edges, reduce the heat and very gently draw the edges of the omelette into the middle of the pan. Cook for just 1 minute, until the base of the omelette is defined and cooked. Grate the Loch Arthur cheddar on top and cook for another minute or so until the cheese has melted but the eggs are still quite soft. Remove from the heat and roll the omelette onto a plate. That way the eggs remain soft and the omelette is light and airy.

For breakfast, enjoy the omelette with a cup of Earl Grey tea but for lunch, this fennel, raspberry and cucumber salad adds a lovely crisp texture and crunch to the silky soft, soufflé-like omelette.

fennel, raspberry & cucumber salad

SERVES 4

1 small fennel bulb
1 small cucumber, peeled, halved,
  deseeded and finely sliced
25g flat-leaf parsley leaves,
  coarsely chopped
25g basil or purple basil leaves, torn

100g raspberries
1–3 tbsp extra virgin olive oil
1 tbsp raspberry vinegar or red wine
  vinegar
salt and freshly ground black
  pepper

Trim and finely slice the fennel. Put into a salad bowl with the cucumber, parsley and basil. Sprinkle the raspberries on top. Dress with the oil and vinegar, salt and plenty of black pepper. Taste for balance. If it's too sharp, add a little more oil or salt. Serve immediately.

barley & fennel salad
with toasted coriander seeds & almonds

The nuttiness of the barley and the crunch of the fennel and almonds are a delicious combination. I like to soak my barley in cold water first for about 30 minutes if I'm making a salad. This helps to remove the heavy, starchy taste and leaves a nuttier flavour.

SERVES 4

150g pearl barley
5 tbsp extra virgin olive oil, plus
  extra for frying
2 tsp coriander seeds
100g whole blanched almonds
50g flat-leaf parsley leaves
50g mint leaves
50g coriander leaves
1 large fennel bulb
1 green chilli, deseeded and finely
  chopped
finely grated zest of 1 unwaxed
  lemon
5 tbsp cold-pressed rapeseed oil
juice of 1 unwaxed lemon
salt and freshly ground black
pepper

Put the barley in a large pan and cover with cold water. Leave for about 30 minutes. Rinse and return the barley to the pan. Add 300ml cold water and bring to the boil. Lower the heat and simmer gently for about 20 minutes until the barley is cooked but still has a little bite. Drain any remaining water and leave to cool.

Heat a small spoonful of olive oil in a shallow non stick-frying pan. When the oil is hot, add the coriander seeds and almonds. Cook for a few minutes until the almonds start to colour. Remove the coriander seeds and almonds from the pan with a slotted spoon and leave to cool slightly.

Meanwhile, chop the parsley, mint and coriander very finely. Add to the cooled barley. Trim and thinly slice the fennel and add to the mixture. Add the coriander seeds, almonds, chilli and lemon zest. Dress with the remaining olive oil and the rapeseed oil, the lemon juice and a good pinch of salt. Add pepper to taste.

burnt cream
with blackcurrant compote

They say the origins of this dish are uncertain. Is it French – crème brûlée? Is it Spanish – crema catalana? Or is it British – Trinity Cream? One thing that is known is that an Aberdonian student who was studying in Cambridge persuaded the college cook to try it. Trinity Burnt Cream got the praise but my money is on the Aberdonian as the inventor!

SERVES 4-5

4–5 tbsp blackcurrant compote
 (see below)
1 vanilla pod
500ml double cream
4 large egg yolks
60g golden caster sugar
4–5 tsp granulated or demerara
sugar

The bitter, crisp sugary top, the super-creamy middle and the sweet bursts of blackcurrant make this three treats in one.

Place a spoonful of blackcurrant compote in the bottom of each of 4 or 5 individual 125–150ml ramekins. Refrigerate for about 1 hour. This helps the compote to set so the cream doesn't mix with it when you add it later. Split the vanilla pod lengthways and scrape out the seeds with a sharp knife. Put the seeds and the pod in a pan with the double cream over a medium heat and bring to a simmer. Do not allow to boil. Remove the vanilla pod and discard.

Put the egg yolks and sugar in a glass bowl and strain the hot cream over. Mix well with a wooden spoon or spatula. Preheat the oven to 150°C/300°F/Gas 2. Remove the ramekins from the fridge and place in a deep baking tray. Skim off any foam from the cream mixture, then strain into a jug. Pour the mixture very slowly over the back of a soup spoon onto the compote in each ramekin. This also helps prevent the cream mixture from mixing too much with the compote. Half-fill the baking tray with warm water to make a bain-marie. Carefully place on the middle shelf of the preheated oven.

Bake for about 30 minutes until the creams are set. They will wobble slightly when you move the tray. Be careful not to overcook them or the eggs will curdle and the texture will change from luxuriously smooth to that of curd cheese. Leave to cool in the tray. Preheat the grill to a high setting. Create the 'burnt' part by sprinkling 1 tsp sugar over each ramekin. Blast under the grill until the sugar bubbles. Be careful as it can burn very quickly. Serve immediately, accompanied by the blackcurrant compote.

This is brilliant with vanilla ice cream or thick-set yogurt. A little drizzled over a very young, fresh goat's milk cheese is also a winner.

blackcurrant compote

MAKES 1 x 500g jar
500g blackcurrants, washed
 and stalks removed

150g golden caster sugar
1 tbsp freshly squeezed
 lemon juice

Put 300g blackcurrants in a pan over a medium heat with the sugar and lemon juice. Cook until the sugar has dissolved and the blackcurrants have started to pop. Taste to see if you need to add more sugar. Do this as soon as you can; the sugar must be heated long enough to dissolve, otherwise the compote can be gritty. Remove from the heat and sieve into a bowl. Add the remaining whole blackcurrants. The compote will keep in the fridge for up to 4 days.

cranachan

I'm never, ever surprised by how wonderful the simplest foods are. Cranachan says fresh simple Scottish in a teaspoon. The soft fruit and the whisky are a treat for your tastebuds so choose your whisky wisely. I'd recommend a single malt lowland whisky such as Glenkinchie, made in a lovely little distillery just outside Edinburgh. I've been served this classic dish with chocolate, ginger and various other additions, but simple is by far the best. One bit of heresy I approve of, however, is to make this classic Scottish dessert with an aquavit or raspberry liqueur. It makes it more feminine and really lifts it to a new level. Our favourite is the very special raspberry aquavit from Nonino – Victor's favourite grappa producer from Friuli.

SERVES 4-6
500g raspberries, tayberries
  or brambles
300g medium organic oatmeal
4 tbsp runny clover honey
100ml very light lowland whisky
  or fruit liqueur
500ml double cream

Plump summer raspberries.
What could be tastier?

Preheat the oven to 180°C/350°F/Gas 4. Wash and dry the fruits and set aside. Make the oatmeal topping by mixing together the oatmeal and honey. Place on a flat baking tray and roast in the preheated oven for 8–10 minutes until golden. Be warned, the mixture will be a bit sticky. Remove from the oven and while it is still hot, pour over the whisky or liqueur. The heat of the tray helps evaporate the alcohol and you get lovely crisp topping rather than soggy oats, which are as bad as a kilt caught in the rain. Allow to cool, then crumble the topping with your fingers or with a spoon.

Meanwhile, whip the cream in a bowl until it is lovely and soft but not stiff. Fold half the fruit and the honey together, then add two-thirds of the oatmeal topping and finally fold in the cream. It's nice if the cream turns a little pink. Divide the cream and remaining fruit between chilled glasses and finish with the remaining oatmeal topping.

kitchen garden summer pudding

Everyone loves Victor to bits and thinks he's the best thing since sliced-bread sandwiches filled with butter and home-made jam. This summer pudding is sliced bread with a lovely inside – just like Victor. When you cut into its regal dome and the abundance of summer fruits cascades out, it's like discovering buried treasure. It's Victor in pudding form rather than on a plate for tea-time.

SERVES 5-6

1.5kg mixed soft fruits
  (such as raspberries,
  blackcurrants, redcurrants and
  small strawberries)
1 vanilla pod
2 tbsp water
1 tbsp freshly squeezed
  lemon juice
200g golden caster sugar
6–7 thick slices of day-old
  good-quality white bread
lightly whipped cream, to serve

to decorate
small selection of berries
few mint leaves
few pansies
icing sugar

If you're having a party, then individual summer puddings can be very practical and can look very pretty on the plate. But there's something lovely about a big summer pudding, beautifully decorated and dusted with icing sugar, and sitting on a large platter waiting for everyone to tuck in.

Remove the stalks and hulls from the fruit and wipe with a damp cloth. Set aside. Split the vanilla pod lengthways, scrape out the seeds with a sharp knife and put the seeds in a large pan over a low heat with the water, lemon juice and sugar. When the sugar has dissolved, add the prepared fruit. Cook for 3–4 minutes until the fruits start to release their juices.

Taste to see if you need to add any more sugar. While the fruit is cooking, hold the pan by the handle and move it around. Try not to mix the fruit with a spoon as this can bruise it and make it mushy. Remove from the heat and strain through a sieve into a large bowl. Reserve the juices. Leave the fruit and juice to cool.

Meanwhile, remove the crusts from the bread. Line a 1kg pudding basin with a large sheet of clingfilm. This will help the pudding come out of the basin intact. Now line the basin with bread dipped in the reserved juices. Cut a circle from one slice of bread and place it in the bottom of the basin. Cut another circle that will fit the top of the basin and set it aside. Cut the remaining bread into Mars Bar-shaped pieces that are long enough to reach from the bottom to the top edge of the basin. Arrange these around the inside of the basin. Be as gentle as possible: too much handling or squashing, and the bread will become dense.

When the fruit has cooled, spoon it into the bread-lined basin. Gently press it down so there are no gaps. Place the bread lid on top and gently press it down. Make sure the fruit is completely covered with the bread, then trim off any excess from the edges. Spoon some of the reserved juice over the top to cover, then stand the basin on a large plate and weigh the top down with another plate. The juices may run over so the bottom plate is there to keep your fridge clean. Refrigerate overnight.

To unmould the pudding, stand over the sink and reverse the basin onto the plate. Remove the basin and the clingfilm. Wipe away any excess juices, decorate with a few berries, some mint leaves and some pansies, then dust with icing sugar. Serve with a generous dollop of lightly whipped cream.

GROWING NOTES

tomatoes
Lycopersicon esculentum

Cultivars grown at Casa San Lorenzo
- 'Sungold' – yellow cherry tomato with an excellent flavour
- 'Chocolate cherry' – dark purple cherry tomato

Cultivation
- Tomatoes require a long, warm growing season.
- The seeds are germinated at home on a windowsill in March and transferred to an unheated greenhouse in individual pots in late April/May. Once the plants start to show signs of their first flowers, they are moved into the polytunnel to acclimatize.
- The tomato bed is prepared with a trench filled with compost and comfrey leaves.
- As the tomatoes grow, strings are attached around the stems and secured to an overhead wire.
- Feeding regularly with a high-potash solution helps to promote flowers and then fruits.
- Once the plant has produced five or six trusses (fruiting stems), we pinch out the top of the plant to direct its energies into making fruit not leaf growth.
- As tomatoes develop on the lower trusses of each plant, we remove one or two leaves to allow light and air in to help ripen the fruits.

Interesting fact
- If you end up with lots of green tomatoes at the end of the season, they can be ripened up by placing them in a sunny window.

courgettes and courgette flowers
Cucurbita pepo

Cultivars grown at Casa San Lorenzo
- 'Soleil F1' – narrow, yellow fruits, with dainty flowers
- 'Eight Ball F1' – round green fruits
- 'Defender F1' – traditional long green type, great for both flowers and fruits

Cultivation
- Courgettes are sown indoors in late April/early May into individual pots, in a warm environment.
- As soon as the true plant leaves are up, they are potted into bigger containers to allow these fast-growing plants the space to develop unchecked.
- The plants are hardened off gradually, and planted out in June if the weather permits.
- Courgettes love moisture-retentive, rich soil, so we prepare it well, adding lots of compost.
- From July onwards, the plants tend to romp away, producing a prolific number of flowers and fruits.

Interesting facts
- The courgettes are best picked young for flavour. Often a small courgette can turn into a marrow in just a few days!
- They are good at hiding under the leaves so you have to harvest thoroughly.
- We pick the flowers first thing on a daily basis to ensure they are in the best condition.

august

August is our favourite month. It's Festival time and Edinburgh is in a league of its own. There's the Edinburgh International Festival, the Fringe, the Royal Edinburgh Military Tattoo and so much more. We have a reason to celebrate every day and night of the month.

In season we have celery, runner beans, French beans, garlic, tayberries, gooseberries, potatoes, grouse (from the Glorious Twelfth), watercress, blackberries and blueberries – and the cardoons are going great (Edinburgh Castle) guns in the kitchen garden.

cream of celery & lanark blue soup
with potting-shed brown bread

There are chunky soups, rustic soups and puréed soups, and there are classy soups. Classy soups are made with exquisite ingredients, such as chanterelles, morels, lobster and asparagus. Celery is certainly the most humble of soup ingredients but it shares one thing in common with the classy soup ingredients, and that's sieving! The trick is to blend the soup once it's cooked, sieve it, then finish it. It's the sieving – that extra little bit of elbow grease – that turns this into a soup sensation.

SERVES 4

150g unsalted butter

1 tbsp extra virgin olive oil

2 large onions, finely chopped

2 leeks, white part only, finely chopped

2 heads of celery, leaves reserved

3 large floury potatoes

1 tsp celery salt, plus extra for sprinkling

1 litre chicken stock (see below), hot

125g Lanark Blue, crumbled, plus extra for garnish

125ml double cream

salt and freshly ground white pepper

for the chicken stock (makes approx. 1 litre)

10 chicken thighs or drumsticks

generous pinch of salt

2 litres cold water

1 large bunch of flat-leaf parsley

1 celery stick, halved

Chicken stock can be very fatty so I recommend making it a day in advance. Thoroughly wash the chicken pieces and put them in a 2 litre stockpot. Cover with the cold water, add the salt and bring to the boil. Reduce to a simmer and skim off the scum that comes to the surface. It will take 5–10 minutes of skimming and simmering until the broth clears. Taste. You may need to add a little more salt. Add the celery and parsley and half-cover the pot with a lid. Simmer for 1½ hours. Strain into a jug, leave to cool and refrigerate overnight. When the stock solidifies, the fat will rise to the surface. Remove the fat with a spoon.

Melt the butter and oil in a large pan, add the onions and leeks and sauté until translucent. Add the celery and cook until soft. Take your time. The longer you can cook this without browning, the tastier the soup will be. Meanwhile, peel and dice the potatoes. Season the other vegetables with the celery salt, then add the hot stock and potato. Reduce the heat and simmer for 30 minutes until the vegetables are tender and the liquid has reduced slightly. Add the celery leaves and cook for 5 minutes more until these are soft. Add the Lanark Blue and stir to melt through, then add pepper to taste.

Remove from the heat and leave until cool. Transfer to a blender or food processor and blend until smooth. In small batches, sieve the blended soup into a clean pan using a sieve or a mouli. It's important to put a lot of elbow grease into sieving the final stalks as these will help to thicken the soup. Put the pan over a medium heat and when the soup is hot, add the cream and adjust the seasoning. Serve piping hot sprinkled with a little celery salt and a little extra Lanark Blue crumbled on top.

potting-shed brown bread

MAKES 10 rolls or 1 x 450g
loaf

150g wholemeal flour
350g strong white flour, plus
extra for dusting
1 heaped tsp salt, plus extra for
sprinkling
2 tsp dried yeast
300ml warm water
50g unsalted butter, for greasing
1 shallot, finely sliced, then roasted
with 1 tbsp olive oil at 180°C/350°F
Gas 4 until golden
2 sprigs of rosemary, leaves only,
finely chopped

This is a deceptively easy
recipe. Baked in clay pots
lined with greaseproof paper
makes a lovely statement for
a picnic or outdoor party.

Either line 10 well-washed clay flowerpots with good-quality greaseproof paper or grease a baking tray or a 450g loaf tin. Sieve the flours, salt and yeast into a large bowl. Add the water and mix well, either in a mixer with a dough hook or by hand. Transfer to a floured surface and knead until the dough is smooth. Grease a clean bowl and put the kneaded dough in it. Cover with clingfilm and leave in a warm spot until the dough has doubled in size – 45–60 minutes. Remove the risen dough from the bowl and gently knock it down, then flatten it slightly. Carefully work the shallot and rosemary through the dough by folding the dough over a few times.

Cut the dough into 10 pieces and form into balls. If making a single loaf, omit this stage. Place in the flowerpots or on the greased baking tray. If making a single loaf, place the dough in the greased loaf tin. Cover with clingfilm and a clean towel and leave to prove for another 15 minutes, until doubled in size again. Preheat the oven to 230°C/450°F/Gas 8. At the bottom of the oven place a deep baking tray with a cup of hot water splashed into it. This will help the bread to form a nice crust. Uncover the dough and sprinkle a little salt on top. Bake in the preheated oven for 15 minutes for the rolls or 25 minutes for the loaf, until golden brown. If you are using clay pots, turn the rolls out after 20 minutes and continue cooking on a baking tray to ensure they are cooked all the way through. The rolls can be transferred back to the flowerpots for serving. Cool on a wire rack.

summer broth of clams, french beans & pesto genovese

Warm summer evenings may be few and far between but this dish will give you that summery feeling regardless of the weather. Surf clams can be gritty so it's a good idea to leave them in a large pot or bowl of cold water in the fridge for a few hours and change the water several times to help remove any sand. Unlike mussels, there are usually only a few bad clams, but remember to discard any that float and any that remain open when they are drained of the water.

SERVES 4

2 tbsp extra virgin olive oil
1 small onion, very finely chopped
1kg surf clams
200g French beans, cut into 2cm quills
generous splash of dry white wine
100ml double cream
1 heaped tbsp pesto Genovese (see below)
pinch of salt

The broth comes from the wine and the juices from the clams. There will be just enough for great dunking.

Heat the olive oil in a large, deep pan. When it is hot, add the onion. Fry until translucent, then add the clams, beans and wine. Cook for a few minutes to evaporate the wine. Add the cream, a generous spoonful of the pesto Genovese and the salt. Cover with a lid and steam for 3–4 minutes until the clams have all opened.

pesto genovese

It's cheaper to buy a basil plant than a plastic bag of basil. After a few days of sunshine on the windowsill, your basil will be the perfect ingredient for home-made pesto.

SERVES 4

1 garlic clove
salt
50g pine kernels
4–5 tbsp extra virgin olive oil
250g basil leaves
75g Pecorino Romano, finely grated

Using a pestle and mortar, cream the garlic with a pinch of salt. Add the pine kernels and loosen the mixture with a little olive oil. Gradually add the basil, blending it into the garlic mixture. Add more oil as required until you have a smooth paste that is the consistency of soured cream. This will take about 10 minutes. Finally add the Pecorino Romano and more salt, to taste.

celery, gooseberry & smoked mackerel salad

Waldorf Salad? Even Cole Porter wrote, 'You're the top, you're a Waldorf Salad'. Four generations of my family, like so many others, have laughed to the point of crying at Basil Fawlty describing this infamous celery salad. Fawlty Towers makes many of us hoteliers and restaurateurs see ourselves through the eyes of our customers. There is no reality TV show or celebrity chef series that can match it. Basil, there are moments (only a couple) when I've been you! The most common Waldorf Salad recipe contains celery, apple, grapes, walnuts, lettuce and mayonnaise. My version is very loosely related – hopefully as loosely as my likeness to Basil!

SERVES 4

200g 'Little Gem' lettuce, divided into leaves, or similar soft salad leaves
4 celery sticks, cut into small pieces
200g ripe gooseberries, halved
4 smoked mackerel fillets
4 small handfuls of ruby chard leaves or micro herbs

croûtons (see recipe below)
4 wedges of unwaxed lemon, to serve

for the dressing
16 tbsp natural yogurt
8 tbsp extra virgin olive oil
salt

Make the dressing by blending the yogurt and olive oil with a few pinches of salt. Mix until smooth and set aside. Scatter the lettuce leaves on 4 flat serving plates, then scatter the celery and gooseberry halves on top. Flake the smoked mackerel, checking there are no bones, and scatter on top of the salad with the ruby chard or micro herbs. Generously spoon the dressing over the salad and finally scatter the croûtons on top. Serve with a wedge of lemon.

croûtons

1 tsp celery salt
1 tsp dried basil
1 tsp dried oregano
1 tsp chilli flakes

1 tsp dried thyme
8 tbsp extra virgin olive oil
approx. 15cm piece of baguette, cut into small cubes

Preheat the oven to 230°C/450°F/Gas 8. Mix together all the ingredients except the cubes of bread in a large bowl. Add the bread and mix well to ensure it is well coated.

Transfer to a baking tray and bake in the preheated oven for 10 minutes until crisp and golden. Turn half-way through to ensure the croûtons cook evenly. Remove from the oven and leave to cool. The croûtons can be stored in an airtight container for up to 1 week.

roast grouse
with crushed new-season potatoes and gooseberry & celery chutney

SERVES 4

4 grouse, cleaned and fat, feathers and giblets removed (ask your butcher)
4 sprigs of rosemary
4 sprigs of thyme
8 rashers of streaky bacon

Preheat the oven to 200°C/400°F/Gas 6. Wash and dry the grouse and stuff with the rosemary and thyme. Wrap the grouse in the bacon and place on a roasting tray. Roast in the preheated oven for about 12 minutes, then lower the heat to 180°C/350°F/Gas 4 and cook for 15 minutes more, until firm to the touch. The meat is best served pink. The juices should run clear when you pierce the underside of a leg. Cut the breast and leg from the carcass and serve with a generous spoonful of the gooseberry and celery chutney and some crushed new-season potatoes.

The glorious Twelfth of August. The official first day of the grouse season in Scotland. The birds shot at this time of year are incredibly tender and don't take as long to cook as game that's killed later in the season. The shot used to bag the bird can easily be missed when you're cleaning it, so when you're enjoying this king of game, check before you bite.

crushed new-season potatoes

SERVES 4
500g new potatoes
3–4 tbsp extra virgin olive oil
salt and freshly ground black pepper
100g watercress, leaves only
50g green olives in brine, pitted
  and coarsely chopped
1 unwaxed lemon or 1 preserved lemon,
  very finely sliced

Wash the potatoes, cut them in half and put in a pan with salt and cold water to cover. Bring to the boil, then lower the heat and simmer for about 15 minutes, until tender but not overcooked. Drain, then add a generous amount of olive oil, salt and pepper. Mash roughly. Just as you are about to serve, mix through the watercress, olives and lemon. Season to taste with salt and pepper.

Crushed new potatoes were a real fad for a while. When I first tasted them I wasn't wooed. Then I realized that often the potatoes had been cooked in advance and reheated. Inevitably they lost that sensation of newness. When they are freshly boiled, drained and then crushed, with a little extra flavoursome ingredient added, they are delicious. This recipe uses watercress leaves. The crisp, bitter watercress and the creamy oil melt into the crushed potatoes. Hopefully you'll be wooed by this tasty combination.

gooseberry & celery chutney

This is a very light and fresh chutney so must be eaten within a few days of making. It's best served hot but can be served cold or quickly reheated if required.

MAKES 1 x 450g jar
2 tbsp extra virgin olive oil
50g celery stick, very finely chopped
2.5cm fresh ginger, peeled and very
  finely chopped
¼ tsp fennel seeds
¼ tsp cumin seeds
salt
300g gooseberries, halved
1 green chilli, deseeded and very
  finely chopped
150g granulated sugar
250ml hot water
freshly ground black pepper

Heat the oil in a pan that is large enough to fit all the gooseberries in as shallow a layer as possible. When the oil is hot, add the celery and fry until soft but not coloured. Add the ginger, fennel seeds, cumin seeds and ½ tsp salt. Cook for a few minutes to release the flavours. Add the gooseberries, chilli and sugar. Finally add the hot water and simmer for about 20 minutes until the gooseberries have started to break down and the water has reduced to a syrup. Season to taste with salt and pepper.

scotch eggs

Scotch eggs were one of the first things I can remember being cooked on TV. I remember thinking two things. One, that it was a load of work and two – wow, those look delicious! I can confirm that both are true and for this recipe I haven't found any short cuts. While I can admit that the Scotch egg is in fact English and was born at Fortnum & Mason in 1738 (Guardian Word of Mouth Blog), with a name like Scotch eggs, I feel that the Scots could grant them a passport to match their name. Nothing complements Scotch eggs better than a potato and pea shoot salad and Margaret's pickled beetroot.

MAKES 6

6 eggs, plus 1 egg for the crumb
100g plain flour, plus extra for dusting
200g fresh breadcrumbs, finely ground (such as from old sourdough bread)
extra virgin oil, for frying

for the sausage-meat covering

300g good-quality free-range or organic pork mince
100g good-quality unseasoned sausage meat, at least 80% pork
small handful of mixed thyme, flat-leaf parsley and sage leaves, very finely chopped
50g fresh breadcrumbs, finely ground
1 tsp cayenne pepper
1 small onion, very finely grated
1 egg
salt and freshly ground black pepper

Scotch eggs can be enjoyed hot or cold. After a morning in the garden, they are the perfect summer lunchtime treat, as long as someone else has made them for you!

To parboil the eggs, pierce the shell with an egg pricker and place in a pan of cold water. Bring to the boil and simmer for 5 minutes. Drain, then run under cold water for a couple of minutes until the eggs are cold to the touch. This will give you a lovely soft yolk. When cold, peel carefully. Place on a plate covered with layers of kitchen paper and set aside to dry.

Meanwhile, make the sausage-meat covering. Using your hands, mix together in a large bowl the mince, sausage meat, mixed herbs, breadcrumbs, cayenne pepper, onion, egg, a pinch of salt and plenty of black pepper. Divide the mixture into 6 equal parts and, working on two sheets of greaseproof paper, gently press each part into a flat circle large enough to wrap an egg. Lay the circles on a floured surface.

To make the double crumb, beat the egg for the crumb in a small bowl, then sprinkle the breadcrumbs onto a dinner plate and set up a small production line: 1) dip the parboiled egg in a little flour; 2) wrap the egg in the sausage meat circle to make a ball, ensuring the edges are sealed all round and the sausage meat is as thin and as even as possible; 3) dip the ball in flour; 4) dip the ball in the beaten egg; 5) dip the ball in the breadcrumbs; 6) dip the ball in the egg again; 6) roll in the breadcrumbs for a second time.

Transfer to a baking tray lined with a sheet of greaseproof paper and refrigerate for at least 30 minutes. This helps the breadcrumbs stick together when frying. Fill a heavy-based casserole dish with oil so the eggs will just be covered and the oil won't boil over when hot. Put the pan over a medium heat. When the oil is hot, test the temperature by adding a drop of beaten egg. If it bubbles instantly but doesn't spit, the oil is at the right temperature. Carefully drop the chilled Scotch eggs into the oil and cook for 3–5 minutes until golden brown. Use a slotted spoon to move the eggs gently around in the oil to ensure they don't stick. Remove from the oil and check with a knife that the sausage meat is cooked. If it isn't, return the Scotch eggs to the pan for a few minutes more. When cooked, remove and drain on a sheet of greaseproof paper.

new potato & pea shoot salad with spring onion & mint

Salads keep me alive more than hot vegetables. Even in winter I prefer to make cold or warm salads rather than hot vegetables. The ambient temperature at which salads tend to be eaten seems to make the flavours more intense and more interesting. I've got loads of big bowls and plates for salads but I usually run out as I have been known to serve several all at once. Plenty of different flavours, in big quantities, for everyone to help themselves to the bits they like the most. We always have a leaf salad in a big mixing bowl. All that tasty, tantalising oil and vinegar left at the bottom, just ready to be soaked up by a big wedge of bread. My dear Uncle Landie, whom Orlando was named after, would visit maybe once a year. I can remember looking shocked. He was sitting with his face in the bowl and the biggest smile you could imagine. In between mouthfuls and in between the big smile he would say, 'Darling, you can't waste the best bit!' My darling best uncle knew what he was talking about.

SERVES 4
500g new potatoes
100g pea shoots, washed
1 spring onion, finely sliced
small handful of mint, leaves only
2–3 tbsp extra virgin olive oil
**salt and freshly ground black
  pepper**

Peel the potatoes and place in a pan with salt and cold water to cover. Bring to the boil, then lower the heat and simmer until the potatoes are tender. Drain and when cool enough to handle, slice thickly and scatter on a large plate. Scatter the pea shoots, spring onion and mint over the potatoes. Drizzle with plenty of olive oil, salt and lots of black pepper.

margaret's pickled beetroot

I have always loved pickled beetroot. I remember Margaret, our fairy godmother, second mother, child-spoiler and all-round lovely lady, who worked for Daddy for over 60 years, with her mother before her working for almost as many years for my grandmother. One hundred per cent Scottish from Peterhead. Our October holiday treat was a visit to Margaret's home town. A week of being absolutely spoiled with the best ice creams, home-made ice lollies, fish suppers, stovies, cinnamon lucky pennies, the best mashed potatoes ever, the most amazing sand dunes at Buckie Lighthouse and, if we were really, really lucky, the aurora borealis! I convinced myself I saw it once. It was probably the oil rigs out in the North Sea and a few clouds bouncing off the moonlight on the clearest, cleanest skies you could imagine. Margaret's beetroot was even better than that.

MAKES approx. 2 x 450g jars
**4 cooked beetroots, peeled and
  sliced, or 12 whole baby beets**
480ml cold water
480ml malt vinegar
225g granulated sugar

Place all the ingredients in a heavy-based pan and bring to the boil. Reduce the heat and simmer for 5 minutes. Transfer to sterilized jars and seal immediately. It will keep for 6 months or longer.

squashed roast chicken
with potato & pea salad with a garlic & lime dressing

Spatchcock chicken always confuses us. Sunday is roast chicken day. When I'm in a rush, I spatchcock the chicken rather than leaving it whole. Hey presto! Depending on the size of the chicken, after 50 minutes in the oven, lunch is served. What confuses us is that a chicken cooked this way is eaten, almost bones and all, but if I roast a chicken whole, there's always some left. That makes me think that this recipe must be tastier. It's also moister as the chicken roasts more in its own juices and, because it cooks more quickly, the white meat is more succulent. Finger-licking good. I don't know why I don't spatchcock the chicken every time.

SERVES 4
1.5kg free-range or organic chicken
3 green chillies, deseeded
2 garlic cloves
1 unwaxed lemon or 1 preserved lemon, halved
  and deseeded
large handful of flat-leaf parsley leaves
large handful of coriander leaves
4 tbsp extra virgin olive oil
salt

Wash and dry the chicken. Cut it in half and remove the backbone. Lay the two halves, skin side up, on a roasting tray. Using the palm of your hand, press each half down either side of the wing to flatten them out. Put the chillies, garlic, lemon, herbs, 3 tbsp olive oil and a generous pinch of salt in the blender or food processor and blend until fairly smooth. Pour over the chicken and gently rub it in. Leave to marinate for at least 1 hour.

Meanwhile, preheat the oven to 220°C/425°F/Gas 7. Sprinkle some more salt over the chicken and drizzle with the remaining olive oil. Roast for 20 minutes in the preheated oven so the skin becomes lovely and tasty, then lower the oven temperature to 180°C/350°F/Gas 4 and cook for another 30 minutes or so, until the legs of the chicken come away from the body easily.

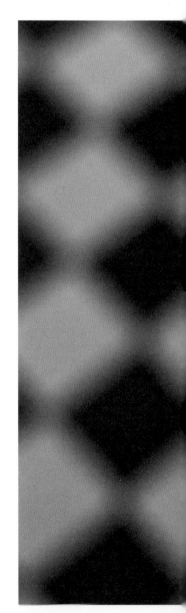

Fresh peas just podded are irresistible. This salad, with the texture of the waxy new potatoes, the crunchy peas and the dressing drizzled over, is a delight.

potato & pea salad with a garlic & lime dressing

SERVES 4

500g new potatoes
150g fresh peas, podded weight
large handful of mint leaves, torn
1 garlic clove
salt and freshly ground black
  pepper
2–3 tbsp extra virgin olive oil
small handful of flat-leaf parsley
  leaves
juice of 1 unwaxed lime

Peel the potatoes and put them in a pan with salt and cold water to cover. If necessary, cut them to ensure they are all the same size. Bring to the boil, then lower the heat and simmer until the potatoes are cooked but still have some bite. Drain and place on a large serving platter or bowl. Scatter the uncooked peas and half the mint leaves on top. Using a pestle and mortar, cream the garlic with a little salt, then loosen with some olive oil. Add the remaining mint and the parsley, together with enough oil and lime juice to make a loose dressing. Season to taste with salt and pepper, then drizzle over the potato and pea salad.

barbecue skewers
with watercress & mixed currant salad and poppy seed rolls

Fresh fruit in salads has been a tradition in our family for generations. When I'm really busy it's one quick step to getting our daily intake of fruit. Apples, pears, melon, grapes, pomegranate seeds, oranges, peaches and figs are often found stealthily and healthily tucked into our salads at different times of the year. Berries give instant bursts of flavour, huge nutritional benefits and fabulous colours. So don't keep the berries for the trifle. Stick them in salads, too. If the weather is being kind and the sun is shining, these barbecue skewers are a perfect partner for this really summery salad.

SERVES 4 (2 skewers per person)
1kg boneless leg of lamb, cut into chunks
8 wedges of unwaxed lime

for the marinade
200ml plain yogurt
100ml cold water
1 fresh green chilli, deseeded
2 tsp ground turmeric
2 cloves garlic
juice of 2 unwaxed limes
100g fresh coriander
1 tsp salt

Blend all of the marinade ingredients in a processor and pour over the lamb. Cover with clingfilm and refrigerate for 6 hours or preferably overnight. After marinating, drain the marinade from the lamb. Soak 8 large wooden skewers in water to prevent them burning and heat the barbecue. Thread the lamb onto the skewers and add a wedge of fresh lime to each skewer. When the barbecue is hot, grill the skewers until the lamb is cooked but still a little pink in the middle. Rest the lamb for 5 minutes before serving.

watercress & mixed currant salad

If you can't find the currants, pomegranate seeds prove a very tasty alternative and also go really well with the lamb.

SERVES 4
100g fine French beans, trimmed and cut in half
salt
50g watercress leaves, washed and dried
50g soft lettuce leaves (such as lollo rosso and lollo bianco), washed and dried
100g mixed white and red currants, or fresh pomegranate seeds

100g tomatoes, cut into quarters
4 tbsp extra virgin olive oil, for drizzling
juice of 1 unwaxed lime, for drizzling

for the dressing
100g Greek yogurt
25g watercress leaves
50ml extra virgin olive oil
juice of 1 unwaxed lime, for drizzling
1 tsp cumin seeds

First make the dressing. Blend all the ingredients in a blender or food processor and chill until required. Meanwhile, blanch the French beans in hot salted water until tender but still al dente. Drain and refresh in cold water. Place the watercress leaves and soft lettuce leaves in a large bowl. Scatter with the white and red currants or pomegranate seeds. Add the tomatoes and season with a little salt. Drizzle with the olive oil and lime juice. Serve the salad witrh the skewers, adding a generous spoonful of the dressing to cool the flavours.

poppy seed rolls

My children love these poppy seed rolls. They are really easy to make and taste even better if you make them a day in advance, cool them, cover them with clingfilm, then remove the clingfilm and reheat them in a hot oven. The poppy seed crust becomes really crispy and the middle is soft and yummy and is especially good with lashings of great butter. For this recipe my favourite flour is Doves Farm Strong White Bread Flour.

MAKES 16

500g Doves Farm Strong White
  Bread Flour, plus extra for dusting
1 heaped tsp fine table salt
2 tsp dried yeast
300ml hand-hot water
1 tsp clear honey
20ml extra virgin olive oil,
  plus extra for greasing
egg wash made from 1 egg, beaten
poppy seeds, for sprinkling

Sieve the flour, salt and yeast into a large mixing bowl. Add the water, honey and olive oil. Mix well in a mixer with an electric dough hook or by hand. Transfer the dough to a floured surface and knead until smooth. Place the dough in an oiled bowl, cover with clingfilm and leave in a cosy spot in the kitchen or larder for about 40 minutes, until the dough has doubled in size. Once it has risen, turn onto a floured surface, knock the dough back and shape it lightly into a ball. Cut the ball into 16 equal-sized pieces. Knead the balls in your hands or roll with the palm of your hand on the work surface until each ball is a smooth, uniform shape. This will ensure that the balls rise evenly. Place the balls on an oiled baking sheet with enough space between to allow them to double in size. Cover with clingfilm and leave in your cosy spot for about 30 minutes, until well risen. Preheat the oven to 230°C/450°F/Gas 8. Remove the clingfilm and lightly brush the balls with the egg wash. Sprinkle with poppy seeds and bake in the preheated oven for 10–12 minutes until golden and risen.

Me, trying to look uninterested in 1987. Victor, still with hair, looking interested.

Victor and I dated for a year before we told the family. I am saying this absolutely tongue in cheek, but it was a bit like the final episode of the Godfather. It was the daughter or the family business. Thankfully, Victor choose the daughter. Victor was best friends with two of my older brothers and his brother was married to my sister. I was Daddy's pet. When your father is 50 years older than you, you can choose to make his life as easy as possible or you can become the rebel without a cause. I chose the goody two shoes option – that was until I dated Victor. What has this to do with barbecues? Well, our clandestine dates had to take place where the rest of the family wouldn't spot us.

The first date, in August, was at the ski chalet at Hill End. No chance of any of my family finding us there. There was Dunbar Harbour for fish and chips in September, but most Saturday nights were spent at Edinburgh's oldest and most authentic kebab shop – Kebab Mahal. Lots of shish and holy men. All those kebabs really ignited my tastebuds. Yogurt, chilli, spices and barbecues. I loved it all and they gradually influenced my cooking. The markets of Milano were replaced by the souks of Istanbul.

roasted veal meatballs
with runner bean salsa

MAKES approx. 12

500g British rose veal, coarsely minced
1 egg yolk
50g fresh breadcrumbs
grated zest of 1 unwaxed lemon
50g golden raisins
25g parsely, coarse stalks removed and chopped
25g thyme, coarse stalks removed and chopped
25g oregano, coarse stalks removed and chopped
salt and freshly ground black pepper

Preheat the oven to 230°C/450°F/Gas 8. Mix together all the ingredients except
the salt and pepper in a large mixing bowl. Season to taste. Divide the mixture
into small balls. You can weigh each ball to about 50g so that they cook evenly.
Squash each ball into the shape of a small clementine, then lay them on an oiled
baking sheet. Roast in the preheated oven for 8–10 minutes until the meatballs
are cooked all the way through. Serve hot with the runner bean salsa.

runner bean salsa

If you are a child of the 60s or 70s you may remember the excitement
over a tin of green beans. We would fight over them but they should have
been labelled 'grey beans'. There was no green in them. We are so spoiled
now, with the readily available variety of fresh beans, but read the labels.
Try and avoid the food miles and buy as locally as you can. French beans,
fine beans and runner beans are also easy to grow. This recipe packs in a
few extra flavours to help make the meatballs just that bit more exciting.

SERVES 4

200g runner beans, tough strings removed
salt
400g firm tomatoes
large handful of coriander leaves
large handful of basil leaves
1 fresh red chilli, deseeded and finely sliced
1 small onion, finely chopped
juice of 1 unwaxed lime
extra virgin olive oil

Cut the runner beans into 2.5cm pieces and blanch them in salted boiling water
until tender but still al dente. Drain and refresh in cold water, then drain again.
Chop the tomatoes into pieces the same size as the runner beans. Mix the tomatoes
and beans with the coriander, basil, chilli, onion, lime juice and a pinch of salt.
Loosen the mixture with enough olive oil to make the salsa glossy. Taste and
check the seasoning.

The only restaurant Mummy and I have ever been thrown out of was Edinburgh's best-known vegetarian restaurant. It involved an incident with a full-length mink coat and a crocodile handbag. I think you can guess the rest. For years, veal aroused the same controversy as animal furs. Now British rose veal is readily available and thanks to great animal husbandry, these wee veal calf beauties have a very happy life and we get a truly world-class ingredient. These lovely little meatballs are roasted in the oven and then served with a delicious runner bean salsa. They are also great with a lovely salad or you can stuff them into baby flatbreads for an on-the-hoof snack, or serve them as you would a beef burger – only a much tastier one.

dried blueberry & cinnamon shortbread
with blackberry soufflé

We make hundreds of thousands of shortbread biscuits every year. We've always served a tiny unexpected treat to our customers with our coffee and tea. The basic mixture can be tweaked to give a whole variety of different characters. Stem ginger, lavender, cranberry and chocolate chip are all classic flavourings but these little dried blueberry and cinnamon sweeties are a seasonal best-seller.

MAKES approx. 70
200g unsalted butter
125g caster sugar, plus extra for sprinkling
300g plain flour, sieved, plus extra for dusting
75g cornflour
100g dried blueberries
½ tsp ground cinnamon

Preheat the oven to 180°C/350°F/Gas 4 and line a baking tray with greaseproof paper. Cream the butter and sugar together in a bowl until light and fluffy. Slowly fold in the flour and cornflour until well incorporated, then fold in the blueberries and cinnamon. Transfer to a floured surface and roll out to a thickness of 3–5mm. Using a scone or biscuit cutter, cut the dough into small rounds. Place on the baking tray and bake in the preheated oven for 8–10 minutes or until golden. Remove from the oven and sprinkle with a little caster sugar, then leave to cool on a wire rack.

blackberry soufflé

They say we eat first with our eyes. Colour can confuse you, deter you or entice you to eat. The vibrant pink colour of this dessert makes it irresistible. Orange, lemon and chocolate are all classic examples of soufflés, but making one from this very juicy, intense berry produces a truly dramatic appearance. Serve with a dusting of icing sugar to really set it off to perfection.

SERVES 4
½ vanilla pod
200g blackberries
2 large eggs, separated
2 tbsp Drambuie
2 tsp plain flour
25g unsalted butter, softened, for greasing
75g golden caster sugar
icing sugar, to serve

Split the vanilla pod lengthways and scrape out the seeds with a sharp knife. Put the seeds in a pan over a low heat with the blackberries and heat gently until the berries have softened – about 5 minutes. Remove from the heat and vigorously beat in the egg yolks, Drambuie and flour. Return to the heat and cook until the mixture starts to thicken. Sieve to remove any seeds and leave to cool.

Preheat the oven to180°C/350°F/Gas 4 and grease 4 individual 150ml ramekins. Beat the egg whites until stiff in a clean, dry bowl, then very slowly add the sugar, a teaspoon at a time, continuing to beat until the mixture is very creamy.

Mix half the egg whites into the cooled fruit mixture, then slowly fold in the remaining half. Spoon the mixture into the ramekins and place in a deep roasting tin. Half-fill the tin with warm water to make a bain-marie and bake in the preheated oven for 12 minutes until the soufflés have risen. Serve immediately with a sprinkle of icing sugar.

cherry pick-me-up
with tipsy cherries

We had a cherry tree in our old garden but never managed to get any cherries from it. We've planted four different cherry trees in the new garden. It will probably take three years before we see any fruit, so we'll have to rely on readily available English cherries or on those amazing Italian stonkers that burst in your mouth. The beauty of this recipe is that the alcohol used to soak the cherries brings even the skinniest ones alive. My cousin Ronnie in London was a champion cherry preserver and still smuggles in incredibly lethal and probably illegal pure proof spirit to soak them. If you can grow your own cherries, the yield will be lower than on the Continent so I think this gives you a really great excuse to soak them and treasure every little gem.

SERVES 4-6

5 eggs
260g caster sugar
235g self-raising flour
200g tipsy cherries (see recipe below)
70% cocoa Valrhona dark chocolate, to decorate

for the cream cheese
5 egg yolks
80g icing sugar
580g mascarpone
580ml double cream
300ml Maraschino or vodka

Genovese sponge is the lightest, best sponge for trifle, baked Alaska or any dessert that needs a sponge base.

Start by making the Genovese sponges. Preheat the oven to 180°C/350°F/Gas 4 and line two 24cm sandwich tins with baking parchment. Beat the eggs in a bowl until light and pale in colour. Very slowly beat in the sugar until the eggs are creamy and fluffy. Sieve in the flour and fold in very gently with a slotted metal spoon. Divide the mixture between the prepared tins.

Bake in the preheated oven for about 15 minutes until the sponge bounces back when you touch it. Remove from the oven and leave to cool on a wire rack. Meanwhile, make the cream cheese. Beat the egg yolks with the sugar in a large bowl until the mixture has thickened and is a light lemon colour. Add the mascarpone and mix thoroughly. Whip the cream in a medium bowl until it forms stiff peaks. Fold into the mascarpone mixture. Slice one of the Genovese sponges into 1cm lengths and dip them in the juice from the tipsy cherries. Use the soaked pieces to line a decorative trifle bowl. Spoon over a layer of the cream cheese mixture, then a layer of tipsy cherries.

Slice the other Genovese sponge into 1cm lengths and dip them in the Maraschino or vodka. Add these to the bowl. Add another layer of cream cheese mixture and another layer of tipsy cherries. Finish with the remaining cream cheese mixture and smooth the top. Refrigerate for 2 hours. Grate some chocolate over before serving.

tipsy cherries

As well as being brilliant in the cherry pick-me-up, these are delicious served on their own as a dessert. When Mummy had her way, she would put them in mini chocolate cup cases and top them with melted chocolate. If only there were more hours in the day!

Makes 1 x 900g jar
½ vanilla pod
500g juicy cherries, pitted
500ml Maraschino or vodka
3–4 tbsp caster sugar, depending on the sweetness of the cherries

Split the vanilla pod lengthways and scrape out the seeds with a sharp knife. Put the seeds in a pan with the remaining ingredients and bring to the boil. Remove from the heat and leave to soak overnight. The cherries can be used the next day or store them immediately in sealed, sterilized jars and they will keep for 6 months.

baked alaska
with hot tayberry sauce

Tayberries have a very short season but more than make up for it with their size and flavour. They are raspberries for kings. When we were little we always had hot raspberry sauce. Lashings, all over the purest pure white Di Ciacca ice cream. It brings back the fondest memories. But the hot sauce was even better when we made it with tayberries. Their flavour is similar but much more intense and when heated the intensity really comes through. Number Seven son, for some reason, would always get a baked Alaska for his birthday.

SERVES 4-6
1 Genovese sponge (make half the recipe on p.206)
250ml vanilla ice cream
300g berries of your choice, washed and dried

for the meringue
3 large egg whites
125g of golden caster sugar

Preheat the oven to 220°C/425°F/Gas 7. Remove the ice cream from the freezer and scoop small balls of it onto a flat tray. Place the tray, with the balls of ice cream, back into the freezer until you are ready to assemble the Alaska. Place the sponge on a large flat baking tray. To make the meringue, beat the egg whites until stiff, then very slowly beat in the sugar, one teaspoon at a time, until the eggs are glossy and form stiff peaks. Remove the ice cream from the freezer and arrange the ice cream balls on top of the sponge. Stud the ice cream with the berries and add berries between the balls of ice cream. Trim away any excess sponge from around the base, leaving less than 2.5cm to help hold the meringue. Using a piping bag or two spoons, very quickly add the meringue, working from the sponge base to the top to cover the ice cream. You don't want any gaps or the heat will get through the meringue and the Alaska will melt to a puddle. Sprinkle a little caster sugar on top of the meringue and bake in the preheated oven for 5 minutes until the meringue is golden and toasted. Alternatively, you can colour the meringue with a cook's blowtorch. It is quicker and less risky for the ice cream if you're brave enough to use one. Serve immediately with the hot tayberry sauce.

Fresh sponge, cold ice cream, fresh fruit and that soft mallow but toasted meringue is a sugar-bomb explosion. You need to work quickly for this dessert so get organized before you start. Home-made berry sorbet or chocolate or strawberry ice cream are favourite partners for baked Alaska, but at this time of year, a filling of good old-fashioned vanilla ice cream and berries, plus the hot tayberry sauce, is pretty perfect.

hot tayberry sauce

SERVES 4-6
300g tayberries
150g caster sugar

Heat the fruit and sugar together in a saucepan until the sugar dissolves. Cook for a few minutes, then sieve through a metal strainer to remove the seeds. Serve hot, but it's also delicious cold.

blueberry & almond tart
with gooseberry & ricotta cream

This tart doesn't need to be blind baked before you fill it so it really is easy to make. The gooseberry and ricotta cream accompaniment makes a change from whipped cream.

SERVES 6-8
250g plain flour
pinch of salt
120g unsalted butter, chilled
70g icing sugar
2 egg yolks

for the filling
125g whole blanched almonds
125g golden caster sugar
125g unsalted butter, at room
 temperature
1 tsp vanilla extract
2 eggs
1 tbsp plain flour, sieved
125–200g blueberries (depending
 on how fruity you want the tart
 to be)

To make the pastry, sieve the flour and salt into a bowl. Grate in the butter and mix with your fingertips to the consistency of fine breadcrumbs. Add the sugar, mix well, then add the egg yolks. Combine to form a dough. If you need a splash of ice-cold water to help, don't resist. Refrigerate for about 1 hour.

Meanwhile, preheat the oven to 180°C/350°F/Gas 4. Remove the pastry from the fridge and allow to come to room temperature. Roll the pastry out to the thickness of a pound coin and use to line a 24cm loose-bottomed tart tin. Refrigerate while you prepare the filling.

Roast the almonds in the preheated oven until golden, then leave to cool. Put in a blender or food processor and blend until fine. Set aside. Beat the sugar and butter together in a bowl until light and fluffy. Fold in the vanilla extract, then beat in the eggs, flour and almonds. Remove the tart tin from the fridge and scatter the blueberries over the bottom of the pastry case. Spoon the almond mixture on top. Bake in the preheated oven for 50–60 minutes until the tart is golden and a knife comes clean from the centre.

gooseberry & ricotta cream

SERVES 6
250g gooseberries, halved
1 piece of stem ginger, finely
 chopped
3 tbsp icing sugar, plus extra,
 to taste
1 tbsp ginger syrup (from the stem
 ginger)
125g ricotta
1 tbsp double cream

Heat the gooseberries in a pan over a low heat with the ginger, icing sugar and ginger syrup until they are soft. This will take about 5 minutes. Leave to cool. Meanwhile, use a fork to mix the ricotta with the cream to lighten it. Fold the cooled gooseberries into the ricotta cream. Check the mixture is sweet enough, adding more sugar if necessary.

GROWING NOTES

garlic
Allium sativum

Cultivars grown at Casa San Lorenzo
- 'Christo' – strong flavour
- 'Early Purple Wight' – really early harvest in mid-June

Cultivation
- Traditionally planted on the shortest day of the year and harvested on the longest.
- We give our garlic a head start by planting in October directly in the soil if weather conditions allow. Alternatively, plant in pots if the ground is cold and wet.
- Garlic thrives on free-draining soil and responds to a good application of potash (found in wood ash) prior to planting.

Interesting fact
- Garlic requires a period of chilling below 10°C for several weeks to initiate the bulbing process. Get them in the ground before the depths of winter to ensure big fat bulbs!

celery, self-blanching type
Apium graveolens var. *dulce*

Cultivars grown at Casa San Lorenzo
- 'Granada F1' – vigorous, self-blanching cultivar

Cultivation
- Seeds should be sown with a little heat in a propagator in early spring.
- Transplant once all risk of frost has past.
- Self-blanching celery requires a sunny site on moisture-retentive but well-drained soil.
- Plants should be arranged in a grid pattern to help exclude light. They can be blanched further – though the stems are naturally pale – by wrapping card around.
- To avoid stringy stems, keep the plants moist.

potatoes
Solanum tuberosum

Cultivars grown at Casa San Lorenzo
- 'Charlotte' – a waxy, early cultivar; great as a salad potato
- 'Pink Fir Apple' – another good salad potato

Cultivation
- Plant into trenches 15cm deep, then cover with a further 10–15cm of compost or soil. This protects the tubers from early frosts.
- As the growth pushes through the soil, 'earth up' with more compost, soil or straw to cover the leaf growth.
- Water in dry spells.
- Second early 'Charlotte' takes four months to harvest; main-crop 'Pink Fir Apple' takes five months to harvest.

Interesting fact
- Fast-growing (early type) seed potatoes can be cold-stored until July and planted into compost bags for a second crop in late autumn and early winter.

september

There is cooling in the air. September can be a beautiful month if you remember to wear your cardigan. There are still a few hints of summer but the available ingredients are changing and you know the seasons are changing, too.

This is the season of celeriac, squash, turnips, pears, apples, carrots, plums, damsons, shallots, peas, duck eggs and scallops.

Black pudding and bannocks say Stornaway more than any other ingredients. Part of our Slow Food beliefs is to do with supporting jobs where people live. Stornaway is about 300 kilometres from Edinburgh and it will take you roughly 8 hours to get there by car. Thankfully, the black pudding is readily available closer to home and the bannocks take minutes, not hours, to prepare. Together they make a great brunch dish.

butternut squash & black pudding
with home-made bannocks

SERVES 2
½ small butternut squash,
  cut into cubes
salt
2 dessert apples
pinch of cinnamon

2 thick slices of Stornaway
  black pudding
2–3 tbsp extra virgin olive oil
2 duck eggs
15g unsalted butter, for frying

Put the squash in a small pan of cold salted water. Bring to the boil, then reduce the heat and simmer until tender. Peel the apples and cut into cubes. Add the apple to the squash and simmer for 2–3 minutes to just soften the apple. Drain, then purée using a hand-held blender. Season with salt and cinnamon. Set aside. Preheat the oven to 150°C/300°F/Gas 2. Fry the black pudding in the olive oil until crispy on both sides. Keep warm in the preheated oven for up to 20 minutes. Slowly fry the eggs in another pan in the butter, just long enough so the whites are cooked but the yolks are lovely and runny. Serve the black pudding and eggs on top of a large spoonful of the squash purée and the warm bannocks.

home-made bannocks

Bannocks can be baked but are traditionally cooked on a griddle. If you get your timing right, cooking on the griddle will give the best and quickest results. Traditional recipes don't use the bicarbonate of soda. I find that this helps make the bannocks less plasticky and less dense. I know 'plastic' is a strange word to use with a recipe that's almost a thousand years old, but trust me.

MAKES approx. 20
100g medium oatmeal
50g barley beremeal flour or plain
  flour
generous pinch of salt

2 pinches of bicarbonate of soda
4 tbsp unsalted butter, melted
15g sage leaves, finely chopped
15g oregano leaves, finely
  chopped

Mix together the oatmeal, flour, salt and bicarbonate of soda in a bowl. Make a well in the centre and add the butter, sage and oregano. Add enough hand-hot water to make a stiff dough. Lightly mix the ingredients together but don't over-knead. Heat the griddle pan over a medium heat. Form the dough into a round flat circle that is the thickness of a fancy chocolate cream. Use a small scone cutter to cut the dough into about 20 circles. Bake on the hot griddle pan or in a hot non-stick pan until golden. When the edges curl slightly, they are ready to be turned. Cook on the other side. Transfer to a clean, dry tea towel until you serve them with plenty of lovely butter.

To lighten this dish and make it more of a meal, serve with mixed herbs and salad leaves drizzled with some cold-pressed rapeseed oil and a splash of cider vinegar.

celeriac, apple & goat's cheese salad

Celeriac is one of the ugly ducklings of the vegetable world but once you've tasted her when she's firm and fresh, she'll be the darling of the salad bowl ball. The apple and celeriac discolour quickly so it's best to make this salad when you're ready to eat it. It doesn't do to leave it hanging around.

SERVES 4
1 firm celeriac
juice of 1 unwaxed lemon
2 dessert apples or sweet
  cooking apples
250g Inverloch goat's cheese,
  cut into cubes
good pinch of sumac

for the dressing
6 tbsp extra virgin olive oil
juice of 2 unwaxed limes
handful of coriander leaves,
  coarsely chopped
handful of flat-leaf parsley leaves,
  coarsely chopped
salt and freshly ground black pepper

Prepare the dressing by mixing the olive oil, lime juice, coriander and flat-leaf parsley in a jug. Add a pinch of salt and pepper to taste. Set aside.

Peel the celeriac, grate it coarsely and arrange it on a large platter. Squeeze some lemon juice over to stop the celeriac discolouring. Core the apples and slice them finely. Arrange on top of the celeriac.

Sprinkle the goat's cheese on top, then pour over the dressing. Finally sprinkle generously with sumac. Serve immediately.

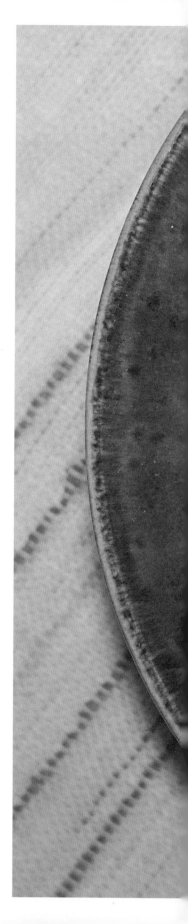

scallops and smoked pork cheek
with a mint & coriander dressing

Scotland has a huge family of food heroes. Guy Grieve of the Ethical Shellfish Company is most definitely one of ours. Having our kitchen garden has allowed us to really appreciate and marvel at nature and at how it rejuvenates itself. With harvest festivals all over the country, September, more than any other month, allows us to celebrate this. The sea's harvest is far harder for us to appreciate so we fail to notice the huge damage that is done by unethical overfishing. The dredged scallop market, which literally drags the ocean floor apart, has done real harm to the ocean bed. Fresh, hand-dived scallops aren't cheap but nature isn't cheap either. Less of better is better than plenty of worse. The lovely thing about this dish is it allows you to beef up the scallops with the lovely little potatoes.

SERVES 2

200g waxy new potatoes
salt
2 small shallots, very finely
   chopped
3 tbsp extra virgin olive oil
50g smoked pork cheek or
   pancetta, cut into small cubes
8 hand-dived scallops, digestive
   tract removed and corals intact or
   removed, according to preference
200g fresh peas, podded weight
mint and coriander dressing
   (see below)
sea-salt flakes

Peel the potatoes and put in a pan with salt and cold water to cover. If necessary, cut them to ensure they are all the same size. Bring to the boil, then lower the heat and simmer until the potatoes are tender. Drain and leave to cool. When cool enough to handle, cut in half. Fry the shallots in a little olive oil. When soft, add the pork cheek and potatoes. Cook until they start to colour.

Meanwhile, wash and dry the scallops. Heat a little olive oil in a clean non-stick frying pan and when the oil is hot, add the scallops and fry until they have caramelized and started to colour. Turn over and cook for just 1 minute more. They shouldn't be overcooked. Add the peas to the pork and potatoes and warm them through. Serve the scallops on top of the potatoes. Drizzle with a little of the mint and coriander dressing and season with a sprinkle of sea-salt flakes.

mint & coriander dressing

SERVES 2

2 sprigs of mint, leaves only,
   coarsely chopped
250g coriander leaves
6 tbsp extra virgin olive oil
zest of 1 unwaxed lemon
15g garlic chives
1 tbsp cold water
pinch of salt

Put all the ingredients in a food processor or use a hand-held blender and blend until smooth.

kitchen garden cottage pie

My nephew Laurence taught me the difference between shepherd's pie (lamb mince) and cottage pie (beef mince) when he was about eight. I remember thinking how clever he was. He lived up to all our expectations. We love you, Laurence, for being such a know-all but for always delivering your knowledge in the nicest possible way. Cottage pie has always been a favourite of his and of most of the rest of the family, especially the wee ones. Adding all these root vegetables to the mince makes this pie lighter and sneaks in all the really good vitamins without anyone under eight even noticing.

SERVES 4 hungry big kids
2 tbsp extra virgin olive oil
2 large onions, finely chopped
1kg beef mince
salt and freshly ground
   white pepper
2 large carrots, cut into
   small cubes
1 small squash, cut into
   small cubes
1 small turnip, cut into small cubes
1 litre hot beef stock or 2 tsp Bovril
   dissolved in 1 litre boiling water
salt and freshly ground black
   pepper

for the potato topping
500g Maris Piper potatoes
salt
50g unsalted butter
100ml full-fat milk

Put the olive oil in a heavy-based casserole dish and when it is hot, add the onion and fry until golden but not browned. Add the mince and fry over a hot heat until browned. Season with salt and pepper, then add the carrots, squash and turnip. Add the stock or Bovril, reduce the heat and simmer for about 1½ hours until the beef is tender. Alternatively, put the lid on the casserole dish and bake in a preheated oven for about 1 hour at 180°C/350°F/Gas 4.

Meanwhile, make the potato topping. Peel and cut the potatoes into quarters and put in a pan with salt and cold water to cover. Bring to the boil, then lower the heat and simmer until the potatoes are tender. Drain and mash with the butter and milk. Leave the mash slightly wetter than normal as it will dry when baked. When the mince is cooked, transfer it to a 1.5kg deep pie dish and pipe the mashed potatoes on top. Alternatively you can use a palette knife to spread the potatoes evenly on top, then drag a fork over from side to side, creating little ridges. These will crisp when baked to give a lovely crunchy topping.

Bake at 200°C/400°F/Gas 6 for 25 minutes if you're cooking the pie straight away or at 180°C/350°F/Gas 4 for 1 hour if you're baking it from cold.

This is a great dish if you've got a few busy days ahead of you as it can easily be made in advance and stored in the fridge for up to four days. With all the root vegetables in it, there is no need to serve other vegetables. That means fewer pots and pans, which somehow makes it even tastier.

roast partridge with nutmeg creamed carrots
and pan-fried plums & parsnips

The world loves Scotland for its great game. Wealthy fanatics head to the hills from all over the world with well-kempt local stalkers who pander to their passion for the incredible wild creatures. These are shot and prized as trophies, not only for the marksman's great ability, but for the flavour and character of all the different birds and beasts. The partridge season kicks off from 1 September. There is no doubt that these tender, young birds are worth playing the game for at this time of the year.

SERVES 4

4 young partridges
8 sprigs of thyme
125g unsalted butter, at room temperature
salt and freshly ground black pepper
12 rashers of streaky bacon
splash of white wine

Preheat the oven to 200°C/400°F/Gas 6. Check that the partridges are clean and the carcasses are empty. Wash and pat them dry. Stuff the thyme into the carcasses, rub with a generous amount of butter and season with salt and a good grinding of black pepper. Lay the bacon over the partridge breasts, tucking it in below the wings. Place in a roasting tin. Roast in the preheated oven for 15 minutes, then reduce the temperature to180°C/350°F/Gas 4. Add the wine to the tin and roast for 15 minutes more. Remove from the oven and leave to rest for 10 minutes before serving. Like all game birds, this is best served pink.

The moistness of these creamy carrots makes them a lighter accompaniment than mashed potatoes.

nutmeg creamed carrots

SERVES 4

250g carrots, cut into chunks
generous pinch of salt

25g unsalted butter
50ml double cream
½ nutmeg, freshly grated

Boil the carrots in cold salted water and when tender, drain and leave to cool slightly. When cool, add the butter, cream, nutmeg and salt. Using a hand-held blender, blend everything until you have a smooth, creamy mixture. Just before serving, transfer to a pan and reheat gently.

pan-fried plums & parsnips

Serve the roast partridge on a bed of nutmeg creamed carrots with pan-fried plums and parsnips. Frying the parsnips and plums just gives a little extra texture to marry with the succulent game and creamy carrots. Remember to warn your guests that there may be shot in the partridges before they get stuck in.

SERVES 4

3 firm parsnips
salt
25g unsalted butter
2 tbsp extra virgin olive oil

8 firm plums, halved and stones removed
2 sprigs of lemon thyme
large handful of watercress leaves

Peel, trim and cut the parsnips into cubes the same size as the plum halves. Blanch the parsnips by plunging them in boiling salted water for a few minutes until tender but not overcooked. Drain well and set aside. Melt the butter and oil in a large frying pan. When they start to bubble, add the plums. Cook for about 5 minutes until they start to soften. Add the blanched parsnips and the lemon thyme. Just before serving, add the watercress and heat through.

apple and rosemary pork parcels
with apple, carrot & sultana salad

This is a perfect Saturday supper for family and friends. The parcels can easily be prepared in the morning and left ready to be popped straight into the oven, with no pots to clean after dinner. Be warned though – use quality baking parchment not greaseproof paper as greaseproof paper may tear if the parcels are left standing. Then the juices will run out and spoil.

Preheat the oven to 180°C/350°F/Gas 4. Cut a square of baking parchment and a square of tinfoil large enough to wrap each pork chop individually. Lay the parchment on top of the foil. Thickly slice the apple and remove the pips. Place the chops on the parchment and scatter with the rosemary and apple. Season well with salt and pepper and drizzle with the oil and honey. Add the Calvados for the adults.

Carefully fold the foil and parchment to form a sealed parcel, leaving the edges at the top of the parcel so it's easy to open and the juices stay inside. Place the parcels on a baking tray and bake in the preheated oven for about 40 minutes, until the meat is tender and comes cleanly away from the bone. Serve with a wedge of lemon.

SERVES 2
1 Cox's apple
2 x 250g pork chops
2 sprigs of rosemary
sea salt and freshly ground black pepper
2 tbsp good-quality extra virgin olive oil
2 tsp Scottish blossom honey
few splashes of Calvados
2 wedges of unwaxed lemon, to serve

Serve the pork in its parcel and let everyone open their own. Be careful, as the steam will be hot. Serve with boiled potatoes, the apple, carrot and sultana salad, and a big wedge of lemon.

apple, carrot & sultana salad

Prepare this just before the pork comes out of the oven so the apples don't have time to discolour.

SERVES 4
50g hazelnuts
2 crisp sweet eating apples
1 tsp mustard seeds
3 carrots, coarsely grated
100g sultanas
50g flat-leaf parsley leaves, coarsely chopped
3–4 tbsp extra virgin olive oil
1 tsp Dijon mustard
juice of ½ unwaxed lemon
salt

Preheat the oven to 180°C/350°F/Gas 4. Put the hazelnuts on a baking tray and toast in the preheated oven until golden but not brown. Remove from the oven and leave until cool enough to handle. Using a clean tea towel, rub off the skins and roughly crush the hazelnuts with a rolling pin. Peel, core and finely slice the apples. Add these to the remaining ingredients, mix together and add salt to taste. Serve with the warm hazelnuts sprinkled on top.

plums with crowdie

Choosing cheese as a course in a meal is a real indulgence. Those swanky restaurants that present their array of cheese on a gilt-edged trolley are just showing off, but I love it. The guilt hits you immediately – can I have pudding and cheese? The alternative is to have pudding and cheese all in one.

SERVES 2
2 plums, halved and stones
 removed
1 tbsp clover honey
2–3 tbsp fruity extra virgin olive oil
freshly ground black pepper
125g Crowdie
10g pansies or pink purslane,
 to decorate
aged aceto balsamico, for drizzling

Preheat the oven 180°C/350°F/Gas 4. Place the plums on a baking tray, skin side down. Drizzle over the honey and 2 tbsp olive oil. Add a very small twist of pepper. Bake in the preheated oven for 10–15 minutes until tender and slightly shrivelled but not burned. Leave to cool. Crumble the Crowdie onto a large serving plate and scatter the baked plums on top. Sprinkle with the pansies or pink purslane, then drizzle with a few drops of aceto balsamico and the rest of the olive oil.

Aceto balsamico, or vin cotto, is a very intense, syrupy vinegar that bears no resemblance to its very poor relation, balsamic vinegar. Yes, aceto balsamico is hugely expensive but being seven, ten or even 25 years old, it will never go off and is as good value as the best Scotch Malt.

apple, sultana and no-clove pie

Mummy's apple pie is a classic. She spent the first 30 years perfecting it and the next 30 years tweaking it. The words 'If it isn't broken, don't fix it' come to mind. When the apple pie arrived with cloves, it was the equivalent of the broken tooth treatment before the trip to the dentist. Living above a sweetie shop I unfortunately remember having a lot of toothache, and the oil of cloves was often rolled out if the toothache arrived on a Saturday when the dentist was closed for the weekend. This may have only happened once, just as the apple pie with cloves only arrived once, but both left a unique and memorable taste that's not to be repeated. So, no cloves but a tiny pinch of cinnamon instead.

SERVES 4-6

7 small or 4 large Bramley apples
1 tbsp water
1 tbsp caster sugar, plus extra
  for sprinkling
small handful of sultanas
¼ pinch of cinnamon
25g unsalted butter, melted,
  for greasing
egg wash made from 1 egg, beaten
pouring cream, chilled, to serve

for the pastry
250g self-raising flour, plus extra
  for dusting
pinch of salt
125g unsalted butter, chilled
100g caster sugar
1 egg yolk
2 tbsp ice-cold water

This pastry is made with self-raising flour and has a lovely light, crisp texture that goes really well with the soft apples.

First make the pastry. Sieve the flour and salt into a large mixing bowl and coarsely grate the butter on top. Dip the butter into the flour to stop it sticking, then rub the butter into the flour using your fingertips until it resembles coarse breadcrumbs. Add the sugar and mix through, then add the egg yolk and bind with the water until the mixture forms a ball. Place on a floured surface and knead gently. Transfer to a bowl and refrigerate for about 30 minutes.

Meanwhile, prepare the apple filling. Peel and core the apples and slice them to roughly the same size. Place in a pan over a low heat with the water and sugar and cook for about 10 minutes, until the apples have collapsed into a soft but slightly chunky purée. Keep the apples moving in the pan with a wooden spoon to stop them discolouring. Remove from the heat, add the sultanas and cinnamon and adjust the flavouring, adding a little more sugar if required. Set aside.

Preheat the oven to 180°C/350°F/Gas 4 and brush a 20cm ovenproof glass pie dish with melted butter. Remove the pastry from the fridge and allow to come to room temperature. Cut the pastry in half. On a floured surface, roll out half to the same size as the pie dish. Line the bottom of the dish with the pastry. Spoon the apple mixture on top and gently spread it over. Roll out the remaining pastry and use to carefully cover the apple mixture. Cut away the excess pastry from the edges and brush with the egg wash. Make one slit in the top to let the air escape.

Bake in the preheated oven for 20–25 minutes until golden, then remove and sprinkle with sugar. Serve hot or cold with a generous spoonful of chilled pouring cream.

Our damsons straight off the tree

When we were little we were spoiled with food. Three courses every night without fail, and that was when we weren't working. When we were working, we ate whatever was left over and as Mummy's food was always great, the workers, the team and the entire entourage were always fed. Often the only thing that was left was the mashed potato. We did spend a lot of our childhood at the outside caterings in the miners' club, the Freemasons' hall or at the bowling club. Whether we were at home or working, there was always food. Mostly soup, followed by a stew or pie, or something that was easy for feeding at least ten people, and then a pudding. Semolina always took the form of Marshall's Farola rather than the slightly coarser durum wheat semolina. Marshall's Farola is very difficult to get a hold of now but it's really light and easy to digest, so if you can find it, buy it.

creamy semolina
with damson compote

I've not got a microwave but would love one for this recipe. The challenge is to not let the semolina stick to the pot. Instead, you have to be stuck to the cooker for 20 minutes. Burnt semolina is a school-dinner horror story but 'two-creams semolina' is a gold-star pudding. Traditionally, semolina is made using milk but this recipe has cream for added cosiness. As a little girl, I always imagined that semolina was what the three bears would have left behind when Goldilocks came visiting. You'll be very hard-pressed to find damsons in your local supermarket or greengrocer. But if you're lucky, there will be a tree nearby. Damsons are one of nature's wonderful free foods if you know where to find them, when to pick them and how to cook them. If the damsons are early in the season and are incredibly tart, then I'd add a vanilla pod cut in half to bring out the sweetness. But if you're very lucky and they've been allowed to ripen in a really sunny spot, then a cube of fresh ginger and a couple of star anise will add a really unusual spicy flavour.

SERVES 4

200ml single cream
600ml full-fat milk
50g semolina
1 heaped tbsp caster sugar
double cream, to serve

Put the cream and milk in a large pan and slowly bring to a simmer. Using a balloon whisk, beat in the semolina and sugar. Beat well to ensure there are no lumps, then stir with a wooden spoon for about 20 minutes until the semolina has thickened and is smooth. Serve hot with a spoonful of damson compote and a drizzle of double cream to make the semolina not too hot, not too cold, but just right.

damson compote

SERVES 4

250g damsons, halved and
  stones removed
125g golden caster sugar
150ml water
1–2 tbsp plum eau de vie or grappa
  (optional)

Put the damsons, sugar and water in a cast-iron pan and bring to the boil. Reduce the heat and simmer for 15–20 minutes until the damsons are soft. Check for sweetness. If you like, you can add 1–2 tbsp plum eau de vie or grappa at this stage. If you do, increase the heat and cook rapidly to burn off the alcohol. Serve the compote hot or leave it to cool and refrigerate it for 3–4 days.

GROWING NOTES

apples
(Malus spp.)

Cultivars grown at Casa San Lorenzo
- Lord Derby – cooker; White Melrose – Scottish cultivar, cooker; Katy – dessert; Peasgood Nonsuch – cooker; Lane's Prince Albert – cooker; Charles Ross – dual-purpose cooker/dessert; James Grieve – Scottish cultivar, dessert, local heritage variety developed by an Edinburgh nurseryman; Ashmeads Kernel – dessert; Chiver's Delight – dessert; Ellison's Orange – dessert

Cultivation
- Young trees are planted whilst dormant from November to March.
- We train the trees as cordons and espaliers so we have both productive and decorative plants. These tree shapes also allow more fruit to be fitted into a small area.
- Young trees can take several years to fruit so are a long-term investment.

Interesting fact
- We have selected our cultivars to give us a range of cooking and eating apples for use over several months and for different end uses (pies, purées, eating).

plums
Prunus domestica

Cultivars grown at Casa San Lorenzo
- 'Victoria' – dual-purpose for eating, but best cooked or as jam

Cultivation
- Plant plums in a sheltered sunny spot, avoiding frost pockets that can damage the early blossom.
- They like a heavier soil with a high moisture content, but never waterlogged.
- Grown as standards or as fans trained against a wall, plums do well in Scotland.
- Only prune in spring and early summer to avoid fungal diseases damaging the tree.

Interesting fact
- In a good fruiting year, the plums may need to be thinned to improve quality but also to avoid the branches tearing off under the weight. Heavy branches can be propped up take the extra load.

celeriac
Apium graveolens var. *rapaceum*

Cultivars grown at Casa San Lorenzo
- 'Prinz' – produces large roots
- 'Monarch' – smoother-skinned

Cultivation
- Seeds need to be sown early under cover in February/March as they are slow to germinate and the plants require a long growing period to develop big roots.
- Plant out when the weather is milder, as sudden drops in temperature can make the plants bolt at the expense of root development.
- Like their relatives, celery, they need rich, moist, soil. Feeding with nettle tea weekly during the summer will help to produce bigger roots.

october

The children love October. It's the start of those long dark nights and the excitement leading up to the 31st is more intense than Christmas. This is the month of Halloween, ghosts and guising – great fun!

In season we have Jerusalem artichokes, apples, horseradish, beetroot, salsify, pumpkin, squash, mushrooms, blueberries, cranberries, elderberries, pears, walnuts, monkfish and woodcock.

pumpkin & pear soup
with onion scones

Pear in soup? It makes a really light, fresh addition to this hearty, earthy autumn dish and the melted cheese on top hits every tastebud on your tongue.

SERVES 4

50g unsalted butter
2 tbsp extra virgin olive oil
400g onions, coarsely chopped
1kg pumpkin, cut into pieces
salt
1.2 litres vegetable stock, hot
50g pumpkin seeds
2 firm pears
freshly ground black pepper
100g mature cheddar (such as Isle
  of Mull, Loch Arthur or Anster),
  grated, to serve

Heat the butter and olive oil in a large pan over a medium heat, then add the onions and fry gently until translucent. This will take about 10 minutes. Add the pumpkin, stir well, then season with salt and add the hot stock. Reduce the heat and simmer for 30 minutes until the pumpkin is tender. Meanwhile, put the pumpkin seeds on a baking tray in an oven at 180°C/350°F/Gas 4. Turn the seeds occasionally, until toasted. Set aside. Peel the pears and chop coarsely, then add to the soup and heat through. If the pears are ripe, they won't need to be cooked but if they are hard, simmer for 5 minutes to soften them. Transfer the soup to a blender or use a hand-held stick blender to blend until smooth, then add salt and pepper to taste. Serve sprinkled with plenty of cheese and the toasted pumpkin seeds to add a little crunch. Onion scones straight from the oven are the final touch.

onion scones

Savoury scones with a hearty bowl of soup make a heavenly lunch at any time of the year but it really hits the spot in these autumn months.

MAKES 10-12

150g unsalted butter, chilled, plus extra,
  softened, for greasing
1 tbsp extra virgin olive oil
1 onion, very finely sliced
300g self-raising flour, plus extra
  for dusting
1 tsp baking powder

100g Isle of Mull or similar mature
  cheddar, finely grated
1 egg
15g chives, finely chopped
200ml natural yogurt
1 tsp cayenne pepper
egg wash made from 1 egg, beaten

Heat 20g butter and the olive oil in a large pan. When they are hot, add the onion and fry gently until translucent. This will take about 10 minutes. Set aside. Preheat the oven to 220°C/425°F/Gas 7 and grease a baking tray. Sieve the flour and baking powder into a large mixing bowl and coarsely grate the remaining chilled butter on top. Dip the butter into the flour to stop it sticking, then add the grated cheddar and rub the mixture with your fingertips until it resembles fine breadcrumbs. Add the egg, chives, yogurt and cayenne pepper. Mix until the ingredients come away from the sides of the bowl. Transfer to a floured surface and knead lightly. The mixture should be soft enough to handle. The yogurt can make the mixture sticky so don't be shy to add more flour if it is too sticky to handle. Roll out to about 2.5cm thick, then use a small scone or biscuit cutter to cut out the scones. Place on the greased baking tray, brush with the egg wash and sprinkle with the fried onions. Bake for 10–12 minutes until risen and golden.

jerusalem artichoke fritters
with foraged leaves, soured cream
& horseradish salad

SERVES 4

350g Jerusalem artichokes
2 shallots
2 tbsp pinhead oatmeal
50g plain flour
½ tsp salt

1 red chilli, deseeded and
  coarsely chopped
2 eggs
50g coriander leaves, finely chopped
2 tbsp light olive oil, for frying

Coarsely grate the Jerusalem artichokes and shallots into a large mixing bowl. Add the oatmeal, flour, salt, chilli, eggs and coriander leaves. Mix to make a batter.

Half-fill a shallow frying pan with the olive oil and put it over a medium heat. When the oil is hot, add a drop of the batter. It should bubble immediately; if it spits, the oil is too hot. When the oil is the right temperature, add a few tablespoonsful of batter at a time and fry slowly, turning occasionally until golden all over. Cut a fritter in half to check it is fully cooked, otherwise the centre can be runny and will taste awful. Remove onto kitchen paper or greaseproof paper to drain. Repeat until all the batter is used up. The fritters will sit in an oven at 150°C/300°F/Gas 2 for up to 15 minutes.

foraged leaves, soured cream
& horseradish salad

There is a huge variety of foraged leaves at this time of year. Cucumber, soured cream and horseradish make a lovely fresh contrast to the flavours of the wild leaves. This salad is incredibly tasty and different.

SERVES 4

1 small cucumber, peeled, halved
  lengthways and deseeded
handful of small capers in salt,
  rinsed and drained
200g soured cream
15g fresh horseradish, peeled
  and finely grated

small handful of sweet cicely mixed
  with other foraged leaves (such as
  Jack by the Hedge, dandelion, etc.)
juice of ½ unwaxed lemon
pinch of salt

Cut the cucumber very thinly into crescent shapes. Add the capers, soured cream, horseradish, sweet cicely and foraged leaves, and a squeeze of lemon juice. Taste and season with the salt and an extra squeeze of lemon if needed. Serve with the fritters. The walnut chutney (page 245) also works really well with this.

Pinhead oatmeal adds an extra crunch to these very tasty fritters.
You could also make them with freshly grated celeriac instead of the
Jerusalem artichokes. Don't bother to form the fritters into perfect
shapes: the rough edges end up lovely and crispy.

pumpkin dumplings
with sage & almond butter

SERVES 4

500g pumpkin, prepared weight, peeled and deseeded

2–3 tbsp extra virgin olive oil, for drizzling

salt and freshly ground black pepper

500g floury potatoes

500g plain flour, plus extra for dusting

1 egg yolk

Oh, a little bit of Italy is sneaking in again! Gnocchi, or dumplings, are so easy to make. They were a Saturday treat for us. If there was a big catering on a Friday night and there were loads of cold mashed potatoes left over, we would make gnocchi on the Saturday. They were like lead bricks. But they were Italian and the *sugo* (sauce) was great and the Pecorino from Picinisco that Nonna had sent over would melt on top and become stringy - and the gnocchi were tasty. Now, thankfully, I don't need to use leftover potatoes from the old folks' treat, so I can make them fresh, fresh, fresh. And that's they way they like to be.

The flavour of the butter, almonds and sage with the pumpkin is amazing. You'll be pleasantly surprised to realize that you won't even need any Pecorino on your dumplings.

Preheat the oven to 180°C/350°F/Gas 4. Cut the pumpkin into small pieces and place on a roasting tray. Drizzle with some of the olive oil and add a generous pinch of salt and some pepper. Bake in the preheated oven for about 30 minutes until the pumpkin is soft. Meanwhile, line a baking tray with greaseproof paper. Peel and cut the potatoes into quarters and put them in a pan with salt and cold water to cover. Bring to the boil, then lower the heat and simmer until tender. Drain and mash, then leave in the pan, covered, with a clean tea towel under the lid to help absorb any steam. Pass the cooked pumpkin through a mouli or mash it until smooth. Transfer the mashed potatoes and pumpkin to a floured surface. Mix together well with your hands. Having the mixture warm will help to keep the dumplings light but be careful not to burn your hands.

Create a well in the centre of the mixture and add the egg yolk and flour. Working quickly to keep the mixture as light as possible, gently knead together to form a dough. Add a little more flour if necessary. Roll the mixture out to a thickness of about 1cm. Cut into 2.5cm strips and gently roll these into long, smooth sausage shapes. Cut into small cubes using a sharp knife. To add texture, press the back of a fork on top of each cube and quickly move the fork back to make the dumpling curl. This takes a little skill and time but the end result is worth it. Place the dumplings on the prepared baking tray. This way you won't need to add more flour and the dumplings won't go mushy or chalky when cooked.

To cook, bring a large pot of salted water to the boil. Lift the greaseproof paper and dumplings off the tray and immerse the whole lot in the boiling water. The dumplings will be released from the paper. Remove the paper and bring the dumplings to the boil. Once they rise to the surface of the water, reduce the heat and simmer for 2 minutes. Drain and toss in the sage and almond butter (see below).

sage & almond butter

SERVES 4

100g whole blanched almonds

sprinkle of granulated sugar

125g unsalted butter

4 sage leaves

salt

Put the almonds in a dry non-stick pan and toast over a medium heat until golden. When they start to colour, add the granulated sugar and cook until the sugar has crystallized. You don't want to make toffee almonds – you're just looking for a tiny sweet crunch. Remove from the heat and leave to cool. When cold, crush with a pestle and mortar or in a food processor. Melt the butter in a small pan and add the sage leaves. When they start to bubble, season with salt. Add the crushed almonds and warm through.

fennel & coriander roasted pork belly
with herby roasted pumpkin & mr apple sauce

There are two complaints that we've had at various occasions over the years. The first is, 'Why does my cappuccino have to have milk?' (Thankfully we don't get this one as much as we used to.) But the second and the worst is, 'My pork belly is too fatty!' Aaargghh! We buy most of our pork from Chris and Denise at Peelham Farm on the River Tweed on this side of the Scottish border. Peelham is 100 per cent organic and its Tamworth pigs live a happy, free-range, well-fed life. Thankfully, they are also a little fat. Fat comes with the territory and most visibly with pork belly territory. No, there shouldn't be too much fat but you need enough to give the melt-in-the-mouth flavour your expect from this cut of pork.

SERVES 4

1 tbsp fennel seeds
1 tbsp coriander seeds
½ fennel bulb, cut into small pieces
2 garlic cloves
1 tsp salt
200ml Greek yogurt
2 tbsp honey
2 tbsp extra virgin olive oil
1.5kg pork belly, skin
  removed, reserved and scored
  (ask your butcher)
sea salt

The day before, heat the oven to 180°C/350°F/Gas 4. Put the fennel seeds and coriander seeds on a baking tray and roast for 3–4 minutes until all the flavours are released. Remove from the oven, leave to cool and set aside. Put the fennel bulb, garlic, the teaspoon of salt, the yogurt, honey and olive oil in a food processor or blender and blend until smooth. Add the toasted seeds. Put the pork belly in a dish and pour over the yogurt mixture. Cover with clingfilm, put in the fridge and leave to marinade overnight. The next day, remove from the fridge and allow to come to room temperature. This will take about 30 minutes. Preheat the oven to 150°C/300°F/Gas 2. Place the pork on a roasting tray fitted with a rack and cover first with clingfilm, then with tinfoil. The clingfilm stops the foil sticking to the pork and melting into it. Roast in the preheated oven for 3 hours. A knife should slip easily through the belly when cooked.

Meanwhile, prepare the pork skin for the oven. Line a large baking tray with greaseproof paper and place the skin on top. Sprinkle with a generous amount of sea salt. Place another sheet of greaseproof paper on top and then put another baking tray of the same size on top to weigh it down.

Place in the oven when the pork belly has been cooking for 1½ hours. Roast for 1½ hours, then remove the pork belly and the skin from the oven. Carefully remove the top baking tray from the skin: the skin – it's now crackling – should be dry and crunchy. Set aside.

Remove the foil and clingfilm from the pork belly and, for the final cooking, increase the oven temperature to its highest setting. Return the pork belly to the oven and roast for 15 minutes more to crisp up the meat. Serve the pork belly with the herby roasted pumpkin and a generous spoonful of hot or cold Mr Apple sauce. Break the crackling into pieces and serve a generous piece to each person.

herby roasted pumpkin

The onion caramelizes in the olive oil to create a really tasty and easy-to-make side dish.

SERVES 4

500g pumpkin
500g Jerusalem artichokes
1 large onion, cut into wedges
2 tbsp extra virgin olive oil

salt
1 tsp dried thyme
1 tsp dried oregano
1 tsp chilli flakes

Preheat the oven to 200°C/400°F/Gas 6. Cut the pumpkin and Jerusalem artichokes into half-moon shapes and place in an ovenproof dish with the onion. Drizzle with the olive oil, salt to taste, thyme, oregano and chilli flakes. Roast in the preheated oven for 30–40 minutes until golden and tender.

mr apple sauce

Hot or cold apple sauce with roast pork is a darling combination. This is so easy to make and so homely. We also serve this apple sauce with scones for afternoon tea and Victor's dad would sometimes have some on toast as an alternative to jam or marmalade. It's really different and definitely worth a try.

SERVES 4

300g cooking apples
4 tbsp fresh apple juice
1 star anise
pinch of salt
caster sugar, to taste
20g unsalted butter

Peel, core and coarsely chop the apples. Place in a pan and add the apple juice, star anise and salt. Add a little sugar at a time to get the sweetness you like. Cook over a low heat until the apples have collapsed into a smooth pulp. When the apples are cooked, remove from the heat and beat in the butter. Taste and add a little more sugar if you think it needs it. Serve hot or cold, or refrigerate for up to 3 days. It reheats well.

wild mushrooms
with walnut chutney on toast

Simple but brilliant. Artisan sourdough bread, pan-fried wild mushrooms and this really fresh chutney make a super-fast but tasty tea. Chanterelles, porcini, chestnut, blewits, hedgehog, morels are all in season. Any combination works, depending on your preference. I prefer the more fragrant varieties but use whatever you can get your hands on. In Italy the local pharmacy or police station will have a trained expert who will identify whether the variety of mushroom you've chosen is edible and, more importantly, if it's poisonous. Botanic gardens here have experts you can consult and there are many fungi forays around the country that you can join to get one-to-one knowledge and advice. The golden rule is, though, if you don't know and you're not sure, don't eat or touch.

SERVES 4

500g mixed wild mushrooms, cleaned, wiped and trimmed
2 sprigs of thyme, leaves only
1 garlic clove, finely sliced
salt
5–6 tbsp extra virgin olive oil
50g flat-leaf parsley leaves, finely chopped

to serve

4 slices of sourdough bread, toasted
extra virgin olive oil, for drizzling
1 small garlic clove

Preheat the oven to 200°C/400°F/Gas 6. Coarsely chop the mushrooms, making sure they are all the same size so they cook evenly. Scatter them onto a baking tray and add the thyme, garlic and salt to taste. Drizzle with the olive oil.

Bake in the preheated oven for 10–15 minutes until the mushrooms are soft and golden. Remove from the oven and mix the chopped parsley through the mushrooms.

Serve on toasted sourdough bread drizzled with olive oil and rubbed with a tiny little garlic clove. Drizzle the walnut chutney over the mushrooms and serve hot.

walnut chutney

SERVES 4

50g walnuts
2 tbsp walnut oil
2 sprigs of mint, leaves only, washed and dried
1 small garlic clove
salt
1 tbsp runny honey (such as clover honey)
100ml Greek yogurt

Preheat the oven to 180°C/350°F/Gas 4. Put the walnuts on a baking tray and toast in the preheated oven until golden but not brown. Remove from the oven and leave to cool. Blend the walnuts and walnut oil in the blender, then add the mint, garlic, salt to taste and honey. Blend until smooth. Fold in the yogurt and add more salt if needed.

halloween mince
with thyme dough balls

The first meal I cooked when we moved into the house was mince and dough balls. It was a bit of bribery to get the main joiner to finish his to-do list. When we were little, Margaret would often make dough balls for us and we always had some Atora or Trex suet in the fridge at the ready. All through the 90s and noughties, the word 'lard' was as dangerous as Dracula out during daylight. Now, thankfully, there is an awareness that not only is a little animal fat ok, but it's actually quite good for you. And, like many calorific things in life – in moderation, it can't do too much harm. In my world, dough balls can only do good, especially on cold dreak late October nights. And what could be better after a night of guising than to come in for a hot, tasty one-pot meal with minimal washing-up and some very interesting 'eye balls' as an extra little trick or treat.

SERVES 4 hungry guisers
1–2 tbsp extra virgin olive oil
1 large onion, finely chopped
800g best beef mince
salt and freshly ground
  white pepper
2 heaped tbsp HP sauce
1 litre boiling water
2 carrots, cut into small cubes
2 parsnips, cut into small cubes
1 small turnip (preferably white),
  cut into small cubes

for the dough balls
100g self-raising flour
1 sprig of thyme, dried in a
  moderate oven for 5 minutes
generous pinch of salt
25g unsalted butter, chilled
25g suet (preferably Atora)

Preheat the oven to 180°C/350°F/Gas 4. Heat the olive oil in a large heavy-based casserole dish. When it is hot, add the onion and fry until soft and golden. Increase the heat and add the mince. Cook until browned, stirring regularly to stop it sticking. Season with salt, pepper and HP sauce.

Add the boiling water and stir to release all the lovely caramelized bits that are stuck to the casserole dish. Add the carrots, parsnips and turnip, then cover with a lid and transfer to the preheated oven. Cook for 1½–2 hours until the mince is tender and the vegetables are soft. Alternatively, you can simmer over a low heat for about 2 hours.

Meanwhile, make the dough balls. Sieve the flour into a large mixing bowl. Crumble in the dried thyme leaves and add the salt. Coarsely grate the butter on top and add the suet. Rub all the ingredients together with your fingertips until they resemble coarse breadcrumbs. Add enough cold water to bind until the mixture forms a dough. It should be the texture of a soft scone mixture. Divide the mixture in half, then in half again and in half again to make 8 little dough balls. Roll in the palm of your hand to form even balls.

Carefully remove the lid from the casserole dish. Stir the mince and adjust the seasoning. Gently place the dough balls evenly on top of the mince, leaving enough space between each to allow them to swell up. Replace the lid and cook over a low heat for 15–20 minutes until the dough balls are lovely, light and fluffy.

'Machek and Swaveck, our two pastry boys at Ristorante Contini, make these delicious muffins. Thank you, boys.'

blueberry muffins

Machek and Swaveck, our two pastry boys at Ristorante Contini, are my sweethearts. The whole team knows that I have a soft spot for these boys. They are reliable, trustworthy, dedicated and very hard-working. We have a wonderful team, all of whom fit this description, but my two sweethearts have opened up Ristorante Contini almost every day for six years and haven't let us down once. They run the breakfast service, make our bread and pasta – and they make these delicious muffins. Thank you, boys.

MAKES 12
365g plain flour
1 tsp baking powder
125g golden caster sugar
2 large eggs
125g full-fat natural yogurt
125g full-fat milk
125g unsalted butter, melted
125g blueberries
icing sugar, to decorate

Preheat the oven to 180°C/350°F/Gas 4. Sift the flour and baking powder into a large bowl and mix in the sugar. In another bowl or jug, mix together the eggs, yogurt, milk, melted butter and blueberries. Very quickly add this to the flour and mix together very loosely. You don't want the mixture to be smooth like a batter; it should be lumpy and uneven. Spoon into 12 muffin papers sitting in a muffin tray and bake in the preheated oven for 12 minutes until risen and golden. Remove from the oven and cool on a wire tray. Serve with a generous sprinkle of icing sugar.

vanilla pudding
with apple & ginger compote

A classic rice pudding is baked and the sticky skin is highly prized, but I've always preferred a soft, runny rice pudding. It takes a little more effort as you need to keep an eye on the pot to ensure it doesn't bubble over and burn but, like the best things in life, it's worth waiting for. Treat this like a risotto. Don't be tempted to walk away!

SERVES 4
200g pudding rice
1 litre full-fat milk
150g caster sugar
½ vanilla pod

Put the rice in a pan, cover with cold water and bring to the boil. Drain and put in a large heavy-based pan. Add the milk and sugar. Split the vanilla pod lengthways, scrape out the seeds with a sharp knife and add the seeds and pod to the pan.

Bring to the boil, then quickly lower the heat to a very slow simmer. Stir regularly to stop the rice from sticking. Cook for about 40 minutes until the rice is soft and the milk has been absorbed. Be patient and keep stirring as the pudding will stick when it starts to thicken. Discard the vanilla pod and serve hot with a dollop of apple and ginger compote.

apple & ginger compote

SERVES 4, with a little left over
250g cooking apples (such as Bramley)
250g caster sugar
1 chunk of stem ginger in syrup, drained and finely chopped

Peel, core and cut the apples into chunks. Put in a pan with the sugar and 1 tbsp cold water. Bring to the boil and add the stem ginger. Lower the heat and simmer for about 10 minutes, until the apples have started to collapse but there is still some sign of the chunks. Remove from the heat and serve straight away with the vanilla pudding. This compote is also tasty served cold.

blueberry & banana ice cream

The children love this recipe as the ice cream is as purple as a bruise. My very smart brother (they can fight over which one I'm talking about) always makes such a fuss when Orlando chooses blue ice cream on holiday. Many of the costal resorts in the south of Italy make blue ice cream. 'Azzuro' is what they call it – blue like the colour of the sea. Strangely, blue ice cream is one of the few dairy ice creams made without eggs, so with Orlando's food allergies, the 'Azzuro' seemed the safest. He was always as high as a kite for a few hours afterwards but it was worth it, even though his tee shirts never recovered. The egg-free blue ice creams are made with bananas, blueberry juice and a secret 'Engredient'. Here's our easy-peazy variation that has a similar colour but with a little less of the high blue sky.

SERVES 4

400g blueberries
200g golden caster sugar
2 tbsp blueberry juice or cranberry
  juice or a liqueur of your choice
200g ripe banana
400g double cream

Heat the blueberries, sugar and juice or liqueur in a pan over a medium heat until the sugar has dissolved. Reduce the heat and simmer until the blueberries are soft. Remove from the heat and leave to cool. When cool, strain through a sieve. Put in a blender, add the banana and cream, and blend until smooth. Transfer the mixture to an ice-cream maker. If you don't have one, put it in a plastic container and freeze it, stirring after about 1 hour to stop crystals of fat forming. This quantity will take about 2 hours to freeze.

GROWING NOTES

pumpkin and squash
Cucurbita pepo, C. maxima and *C. moschata*

Cultivars grown at Casa San Lorenzo
- 'Baby Bear' – small pumpkin
- 'Celebration' – sweet-flavoured squash

Cultivation
- We start the seeds off indoors in April to ensure germination.
- They are then potted on and kept in large containers in the polytunnel. We plant outside only once all risk of frost has passed.
- They love moisture-retentive soil so we add loads of organic matter and water them liberally to keep them happy.
- We only allow two or three flowers to set per plant to encourage larger fruits.

Interesting facts
- Pumpkins and squashes can be used to suppress weeds as their leaves sprawl over the ground and exclude light from other seedlings.
- Planting through or in anything black (permeable fabric, old tyres) helps to hold in the warmth, which they love.

jerusalem artichokes
Helianthus tuberosus

Cultivars grown at Casa San Lorenzo
- 'Fuseau' – less bumpy than other cultivars, so easier to prepare

Cultivation
- Tubers are planted mid-March, depending on the weather.
- Plants grow very tall so they are good used as a shelter barrier for other crops.
- They require very little maintenance; just cut down the stems to a few centimetres in late autumn and lift the crop as required. Cover with the cut stems or with straw to protect from frost.

Interesting fact
- A word of warning – grow Jerusalem artichokes somewhere as a permanent bed as once planted, they are tricky to remove. Their flowers look like sunflowers.

blueberries
Vaccinium corymbosum

Cultivars grown at Casa San Lorenzo
- 'Bluecrop' – heavy-cropping cultivar
- 'Earliblue' – produces pale blue fruits

Cultivation
- Blueberries require acidic soil that is moist but free-draining. We grow them in raised beds so we can adjust the soil pH.
- Plants will fruit better when cross-pollination takes place, so we grow two different cultivars together.
- Prune out one or two old stems at the base each year, and cut away any strong, new growth back to a healthy bud to encourage branching.

november

The leaves have now all fallen from the trees and the colours in the garden have almost gone. It's cold, it's wet and it's windy. We need hearty, cosy, warming food.

In season we have onions, potatoes, red cabbage, carrots, parsnips, chicory, chanterelles, crab apples, quinces, apples, pears, cod and halibut.

creamed carrot & parsnip soup
with salted apple compote

Soup can be a shining star or a watery mess. If you're not addicted to making soup – I have many soup expert/addict friends – it's easy to put too much liquid in or not enough seasoning. Lunch then proves to be a real anti-climax. Soup is simple but you need to grasp the basic rules to get a really satisfying tummy warmer.

SERVES 4

100g unsalted butter
2 tbsp extra virgin olive oil
400g onions, coarsely chopped
600g carrots, coarsely chopped
400g parsnips, coarsely chopped

salt
1 litre hot home-made stock or
 1 litre boiling water
freshly ground black pepper, to
 serve

Cook this soup either on the hob or in the oven. If cooking it in the oven, preheat the oven to 200°C/400°F/Gas 6. Melt the butter and olive oil in a large casserole dish over a low heat. Add the onions and sweat slowly until they are soft and look as if they can't absorb any more butter. Don't let them caramelize or brown. Add the carrots and parsnips, season with a good teaspoonful of salt, then add the hot stock or water. Either simmer for 45 minutes with the casserole dish half-covered with a lid or cover completely, transfer to the preheated oven and bake for 40 minutes. When the vegetables are tender, transfer the soup to a blender or food processor and blend until smooth. Add salt to taste, if necessary, and sprinkle with freshly ground black pepper. Serve with the salted apple compote.

salted apple compote

Because so much butter is used to make the soup, you don't need to finish the dish with any cream – but of course you can if you're looking for a little more luxury. Or, for a different taste experience altogether, this chunky salted apple compote spooned through the soup really delivers.

SERVES 4

2 apples
1 tsp coriander seeds
pinch of salt

Peel, core and cut the apples into small chunks. Place the apples, coriander seeds, salt and 1 tbsp water in a pan and simmer gently for 5 minutes until the apple has cooked through. If you choose dessert apples they won't collapse so you'll have pieces of apple in the soup. A puréed compote is also delicious but I rather like the smooth soup with the bits of apple. It reminds me of a starry sky!

parsnip kedgeree

This kedgeree has more vegetables than most so it's lighter but just as tasty. The parsnips can either be grated or cut into small cubes. If you grate them, they'll dissolve into the rice and give a light background flavour whereas little cubes will give more of a contrast. I've left the eggs out of my kedgeree but have added extra smoked haddock. This is simply to keep my family happy, which can be tricky at the best of times. Many recipes use easy-cook rice but I prefer basmati. The flavour and texture are in another league.

SERVES 4

4 parsnips
2 tbsp extra virgin olive oil,
  plus extra for drizzling
generous pinch of salt
2 tsp ground cumin
600g undyed smoked haddock fillet,
  skin left on
600ml full-fat milk
6 cardamom pods
100g unsalted butter, plus extra
  to finish
1 onion, very finely chopped
400g basmati rice
1 tbsp home-made curry powder
  (see below)
600ml vegetable stock or light
  fish stock
handful of flat-leaf parsley,
  coarsely chopped
handful of coriander, coarsely
  chopped

to serve
cayenne pepper (optional)
4 wedges of unwaxed lemon or
  lime

Preheat the oven to 200°C/400°F/Gas 6. Peel the parsnips and cut them into pieces or grate them. Place on a roasting tray with a drizzle of olive oil, the salt and the cumin. Bake in the preheated oven for 10 minutes until tender and slightly golden. Meanwhile, prepare the haddock. Place in a pan, cover with milk and add the cardamom pods. Bring to the boil, remove from the heat and leave to cool for 5 minutes.

Remove the haddock from the milk and flake the fish from the skin. Be sure to remove any bones. Set aside. Strain the milk and set aside. Heat the butter and remaining olive oil in a large casserole. When they are hot, add the onion and fry until soft and translucent. Add the rice and curry powder and cook for a few minutes to release the flavours. Add half the haddock-poaching milk and the stock. Simmer for about 12 minutes until the rice is cooked but still has some bite. It should be flaky and fluffy. Remove from the heat. Fold in the roasted parsnips, flaked haddock, parsley, coriander and a generous knob of butter. Serve with a sprinkling of cayenne pepper, if you like it hot, and a wedge of lemon or lime.

home-made curry powder

This can be stored in a sealed jar for up to two months.

MAKES enough for 2 batches of kedgeree
1 tsp cumin seeds
2 tsp coriander seeds
1 tsp dried red chilli
1 tsp ground turmeric
1 tsp ground cardamom
½ tsp ground cinnamon
1 clove
1 tsp whole peppercorns

Roast the cumin seeds and coriander seeds in a dry non-stick frying pan until they start to pop. Add the chilli, turmeric, cardamom and cinnamon. Heat through for a few seconds. You don't want the spices to burn or they will become bitter and unusable. Put everything, including the clove and peppercorns, in a pestle and mortar and grind to a fine powder. When cool, store in an airtight container.

baked cod, potatoes & olives in a bag
with beetroot, orange & mustard-seed salad

Intimate gatherings are occasions all on their own. Enough people not to be private but not so many people that it's a crowd. Cooking for these sorts of occasions requires organization and as few dishes as possible. Et voilà! The French say 'en papillote'. The Italians say 'in cartoccio'. We'll just say 'in a bag'. If you are making this dish in advance to save time on the day, it's really important to choose baking parchment that won't disintegrate when it's sitting in the fridge. Otherwise the fish will be having an intimate experience with the oven.

SERVES 4

4 waxy potatoes
salt
800g cod fillet, skin left on
4 small garlic cloves
32 Taggiasche olives
8–12 sprigs of flat-leaf parsley,
  chopped
freshly ground black pepper
extra virgin olive oil, for drizzling

Peel and slice the potatoes into rounds, then put in a pan with salt and cold water to cover. Bring to the boil, then lower the heat and simmer until the potatoes are parboiled. Set aside. Preheat the oven to 200°C/400°F/Gas 6. Cut four 30 x 30cm squares of baking parchment and of tinfoil the same size. Lay each square of parchment on top of each square of foil. Arrange a flat layer of parboiled potato in the centre of each square of baking parchment and place 200g cod on top. Peel and slice the garlic and scatter on top. Scatter with the olives and parsley, then season with salt and pepper. Drizzle with a generous amount of olive oil.

Carefully fold the foil and parchment to form a sealed parcel, leaving the edges at the top of the parcel so it's easy to open and the juices stay inside. Place the parcels on a baking tray and bake in the preheated oven for 20 minutes until the paper has puffed up.

Cod works really well but halibut, hake or megrim will do a great job.

beetroot, orange & mustard-seed salad

SERVES 4

4 purple beetroots, peeled, cooked and
  sliced
2 large navel oranges, chilled (they are
  easier to cut when cold)
25g flat-leaf parsley leaves or basil
  leaves

2 large carrots
juice of ½ orange
zest of 1 orange
4–5 tbsp extra virgin olive oil
1 tsp Dijon mustard
1 tsp yellow mustard seeds
sea-salt flakes

Those lovely big navel
oranges are just coming
into season. They add
colour and real zing to
this beautiful salad.

Put the beetroot on a large platter. With a sharp serrated knife, cut the skin and
pith from the oranges. Slice into rounds and remove any pips. Layer on top of the
beetroot. Sprinkle with the parsley or basil. Use a potato peeler to cut the carrot
into thin ribbons. Scatter on top. Mix together the orange juice and zest, olive oil,
mustard and mustard seeds. Add salt to taste and drizzle the dressing on top.

pan-fried halibut with chanterelles

My two favourite ingredients. I've probably said this loads of times about other larder gems, but for once I'll be like Mummy. She says she doesn't have any favourites but likes best whichever of her eight children is with her at that moment. So, at the moment, halibut and chanterelles can be my favourites. Chanterelles. I have the warmest feeling just thinking about them. Their sparkling golden colour lets you spot them lying low tucked under mossy, grassy glades in the depths of the forest. Then there's the seductive perfume that surrounds them when they have been freshly picked, and the singularly unique, almost designer-boutique flavour when you eat them. They are gems indeed. Talking of gems, I can't resist mentioning Victor's all-time hero, Sir Sean Connery. We've had the privilege of cooking for him at Ristorante Contini and at Bute House on many occasions and each time he has been an absolute gentleman. Yes, Daniel Craig is making very good progress but with our Scottish colours flying, Sir Sean is our 007 favourite. I cooked this dish at Bute House years ago when he was President of the Edinburgh International Film Festival and it was the halibut that stole the show. Line-caught wild halibut is the Number One. Most halibut sold in this country is from Canada and is frozen. There are some very good organic halibut farms but when the halibut is line-caught, the size will be the best and the flesh the most succulent. So make sure you check your halibut's credentials – we don't want any imposters.

SERVES 2

2 x 200g halibut steaks, bone in
plain flour, for dusting
salt
light olive oil, for frying
200g chanterelles
2–3 tbsp extra virgin olive oil
1 garlic clove, sliced
1 dried red chilli
small handful of flat-leaf parsley
  leaves, coarsely chopped

to serve
salad leaves
2 wedges of unwaxed lemon

There are hundreds of ways to cook both chanterelles and the halibut but pan-frying is the simplest.

Preheat the oven to 180°C/350°F/Gas 4. Wash and dry the halibut with kitchen paper and set aside. Sieve some flour onto a large plate and season with a little salt. Put at least 5mm of light olive oil in a deep frying pan over a medium heat. Dip the halibut in the flour to coat it lightly on all sides. Shake off any loose flour and gently place the fish in the hot oil. When the oil is hot, the halibut should sizzle but the oil should not spark.

Very gently move the halibut in the pan to prevent it from sticking. Fry for about 3 minutes, depending on the thickness. The underside should be golden but not brown. Very carefully turn the fish over and continue cooking. It will be cooked when you can easily remove the flesh from the central bone.

Remove the halibut from the pan, place it on baking tray and keep it warm in the preheated oven while you fry the chanterelles. Ensure all the chanterelles are clean. Use a sharp knife to scrape off any moss or earth, then gently wipe them with a damp kitchen cloth. Don't wash them as this will make them too wet and they will go mushy when cooked.

Put the olive oil in a large frying pan over a medium heat. Add the garlic and crush in the chilli. Fry for a few minutes to release the flavours but don't let the garlic brown. Add the chanterelles and increase the heat. Fry very quickly, keeping the pan moving so they cook evenly. Season with salt and add the parsley. Cook for another few seconds until the chanterelles are al dente. Serve hot with the pan-fried halibut, a few salad leaves and a big wedge of lemon.

beef shin in stout

This hotpot is a perfect supper for the boys and will make them feel like men. The flavours are rich and strong and the texture is tender and lean. We use a local stout but Guinness or a dark ale will work equally well.

SERVES 4

2 tbsp extra virgin olive oil
2kg shin of beef, bone in
500ml stout
approximately 200ml home-made
  vegetable stock
200g shallots, coarsely chopped
2 celery sticks, coarsely chopped
2 parsnips, coarsely chopped
2 carrots, coarsely chopped
1 bayleaf
1 sprig of rosemary
1 sprig of thyme
1 sprig of marjoram
salt and freshly ground
  black pepper

Choose a casserole dish that will fit the joint. It's worth taking your casserole dish to the butcher and asking him to give you a cut that fits!

Preheat the oven to 160°C/325°F/Gas 3. Heat the oil in a large flameproof casserole dish. When it is hot, add the beef. Brown on all sides, then add the stout and enough stock to reach three-quarters of the way up the sides of the casserole dish. Bring to the boil, then add the shallots, celery, parsnips and carrots, together with the bayleaf, rosemary, thyme and marjoram. Season with salt and pepper.

Cover with a tight-fitting lid and bake in the preheated oven for 3–4 hours. When it is ready, the meat will be tender and falling from the bone. Test it after 2½ hours. Remove the herbs before serving.

pear & praline tart

I've probably made this tart more than any other. The volume of almonds and the moisture in the pears help it keep for a good few days. It never hangs around that long in my house but it's good to think that it could. Take the time to roast and grind the hazelnuts and almonds yourself. The difference is like that between supermarket-brand whisky and an 18-year-old single malt from Glengoyne. Both are good individually but there's no comparison when matched. Serve this tart with some chilled crème fraîche – with a few drops of whisky in it if you're in the mood.

SERVES 4

1 quantity pastry (see pastry
  recipe, p.209)
50g whole blanched hazelnuts
200g whole blanched almonds
250g unsalted butter, at room
  temperature
250g golden caster sugar
1 tsp vanilla extract
2 eggs
4 firm pears

Prepare the pastry and refrigerate for 1 hour. Remove from the fridge and allow to come to room temperature. Roll the pastry out to the thickness of a pound coin and use to line a 24cm loose-bottomed tart tin. Return to the fridge for 30 minutes.

Meanwhile, preheat the oven to 180°C/350°F/Gas 4. Remove the tin from the fridge and line the base of the pastry with greaseproof paper. Fill with baking beans and bake in the preheated oven for 10–15 minutes until the pastry is lightly cooked and golden. Remove from the oven and discard the baking beans and greaseproof paper. Set aside. Lower the temperature of the oven to 160°C/325°F/Gas 3.

Put the hazelnuts and almonds on a non-stick baking tray and toast in the oven for 8–10 minutes until golden but not brown. Remove from the oven and leave to cool. Put the cooled hazelnuts and almonds in a food processor or blender and blend until fine. Transfer to a bowl and add the butter, sugar and vanilla extract. Slowly fold in the eggs. If you beat them, the mixture will contain too much air and will overcook.

Peel the pears, cut them in half and layer them on top of the pastry in the tin. Spoon the hazelnut and almond mixture on top of the pears and bake in the preheated oven for 35 minutes until golden. Leave to cool slightly, then carefully remove from the tin. This is best served slightly warm.

nonna olivia's pancakes
with crab apple jelly

Before we moved out to the garden in the country, Sunday mornings for my children meant church. The reward for an hour's sitting very patiently was pancakes at Nonna's. She hasn't made them for several years now but we'll never forget the tea towel covering the plate with the most delicious pancakes sitting on the hotplate. Lashings of home-made crab apple jelly or strawberry jam, a good spreading of butter, and the angels are singing.

SERVES 4 Contini children
200g self-raising flour
1 tsp baking powder
85g granulated sugar
200ml full-fat milk
2 eggs
pinch of salt

These are so easy to make and absolutely delicious. Once you start you can't stop. Nonna's two top tips are: 1) use a good non-stick griddle pan and 2) have a clean tea towel to hand to cover the pancakes once they're cooked. In Mum's words, this keeps them 'lovely and soft'.

Put the flour, baking powder and sugar in a glass bowl. Slowly blend in the milk and eggs with a balloon whisk, then add the salt. The mixture should be wet but not too runny. You don't need to leave the batter to rest but you can keep it for 3–4 hours in the fridge if required. Place the griddle pan over a medium heat. When it is hot to the touch (be careful not to burn yourself), add 1 tbsp of the batter at a time. The mixture will spread a little but it shouldn't run. After a few moments, you'll see tiny bubbles appearing on the surface of the pancake. As soon as 8 or 10 bubbles appear, quickly flip the pancake over. It should be a lovely light golden colour on the underside. Cook for another 10–15 seconds, then remove to a plate covered by a clean tea towel.

Continue until all the batter is used up. Try not to eat the pancakes, otherwise you'll get distracted. And then, before you know it, they'll be all gone and there will be none left for the children.

crab apple jelly

MAKES 2 x 500g jars
2kg crab apples

1kg caster sugar
juice of ½ unwaxed lemon

Remove any stalks and remnants of blossom from the crab apples and cut away any bruised or damaged parts. Wash them, then put in a large preserving pan and add just enough cold water to cover. Bring to the boil, then reduce the heat and simmer for about 30 minutes until the crab apples are soft. Don't stir or squash them at any stage as this will make the jelly cloudy and it will lose the lovely sparkle for which it is known.

Some flavours never leave you. I clearly remember, at the age of five, making crab apple jelly at school and I've loved it ever since. I proudly came home with my little plastic cup of jelly that had been filled with our two-minute fluoride mouthwash the week before. Patience is required to make this as it's not like most jams that you can make and eat the same day. This will take an overnight if you want to do it properly and get a lovely clear jelly.

Set up a muslin strainer over a large jug or pan and pour the soft crab apples into it. Allow the liquid to drain through the muslin. This will take at least 12–14 hours. Measure the strained liquid and add 70g of sugar to every 100ml of liquid. You may want to add more sugar, depending on the sweetness of the crab apples. Place the strained liquid with its sugar and the lemon juice in a clean preserving pan. Bring the liquid to the boil, then reduce the heat and simmer until the jelly starts to thicken. Skim off any foam while it simmers as this will also make the jelly cloudy. Test the jelly has set by placing a spoonful on a chilled saucer. It will wrinkle when you run your finger through it. When it has set, transfer the jelly to sterilized jars and seal while still warm. It will keep for 6 months.

coffee buns

I started making choux buns when I was a tot. Mummy would have them on the menu for special parties. If she was catering for a golden wedding or golf club annual dinner, she rolled out the choux buns. The buns can be made a couple of days in advance and reheated to help crisp them up, but they have to be eaten as soon as they've been filled with cream and iced. The flavour and texture are second to none. You can serve them either with decadent hot melted chocolate or, as here, with my Scottish favourite – chilled coffee icing.

MAKES 10-12
80g strong white flour
pinch of salt
50g unsalted butter, plus extra
  for greasing
120ml cold water
2 large eggs
300ml double cream

for the coffee icing
250g icing sugar
1 shot of espresso coffee or
  1 heaped tsp instant coffee
  dissolved in 2 tbsp hot water
1 tbsp double cream

To make the coffee icing, beat all the ingredients together until thick and glossy. Set aside.

Cut a large sheet of greaseproof paper to about A3 size and sieve the flour and salt on top. Set aside.

Heat the butter in a pan with the water over a low heat until the butter starts to melt. Don't let it boil. Add the sieved flour and salt and stir with a wooden spoon to make a roux. Cook until the mixture forms a stiff ball. Beat in the eggs. The mixture should be firm enough to spoon or pipe. If it isn't thick enough, return it to the pan over a low heat and cook slowly until it forms a ball. You need to keep beating it with a wooden spoon so it doesn't stick to the pan.

Preheat the oven to 230°C/450°F/Gas 8 and grease a baking tray. Spoon golf-ball size balls of dough onto the tray, then splash the tray with a little cold water. Bake in the preheated oven for 10 minutes. Remove and turn the buns over, then reduce the temperature of the oven to 180°C/350°F/Gas 4 and cook for 15 minutes more. When the buns are risen and golden, remove them from the oven. Prick each bun with a skewer or toothpick to help the hot steam escape so when the buns cool, they don't go soggy. Leave to cool completely on a wire rack.

Meanwhile, whip the cream until it forms soft peaks. Split the buns and fill with the cream. Spoon over the coffee icing and serve within an hour or two. Do not refrigerate.

- Root removal u
- Tidy & Weed to
- Bark chip & path
- Boards walls
- *Collect manur
- Prune Parthen
- Plant out gar

GROWING NOTES

carrots
Daucus carota subsp. *sativus*

Cultivars grown at Casa San Lorenzo
- 'Amsterdam Forcing 2' – ideal for an early crop
- 'Cosmic Purple' – purple-skinned with orange core
- 'F1 Rainbow' – colourful mix of white, yellow and orange carrots
- 'Autumn King 2' – sown mid-summer for a late autumn crop

Cultivation
- Carrots like a light soil, so if your soil is heavy, grow in a raised bed.
- Always sow direct once the soil is warm enough.
- Sow as thinly as possible to avoid wasting time by thinning out later.
- We sow our autumn carrots in the polytunnel to produce large carrots late in the season, but we produce baby carrots during the summer months outside.

parsnips
Pastinaca sativa

Cultivars grown at Casa San Lorenzo
- 'Tender and True' – heritage cultivar from the late nineteenth century; produces long roots
- 'White Gem' – shorter roots and with good resistance to canker

Cultivation
- For the longest parsnips, ideally grow on deep, poor, sandy soils.
- Seeds can take a while to germinate if the soil is cold. We pre-germinate (chit) the seeds on damp kitchen paper in a warm, dark place like an airing cupboard to get a head start.
- Chitting also helps to avoid sowing too thickly and having to thin the young seedlings, so you save time in the long run.

Interesting fact
- Parsnip seed does not keep so buy and sow fresh seed each year to ensure successful germination.

onions
Allium cepa

Cultivars grown at Casa San Lorenzo
- 'Stuttgarter Giant' – white and semi-flat
- 'Long Red Florence' – Italian cultivar, red/pink and slender

Cultivation
- You can grow onions from seed in January/February or from sets (small bulbs) in March/April. We use seed to give us a greater choice of cultivars. Grown from seed, the onions are less prone to bolt, plus it's cheaper.
- Start the seed off in modules indoors, and transplant in April as the temperature and light levels increase.
- Keep plants weed-free, but avoid damaging the roots if using a hoe.
- They are ready to harvest when the tops start to yellow and fall over.
- Lift gently with a fork, then dry in a well-ventilated space prior to storage.

december

December in our house is all about Christmas and Christmas is all about the family. We take turns in our family for the big feast. There can be anything up to 30 of us. If it's your turn, the month revolves around planning for the big day, but if you're off the hook – every other year – there's time for a little easy entertaining, present-wrapping parties and general fun.

In season we have Jerusalem artichokes, Brussels sprouts, leeks, kale and winter salad leaves.

The Vegetable Stall by William York MacGregor

This large, bold, still-life painting is considered by many to be William York MacGregor's (1855–1923) masterpiece. The robust character of the vegetables is conveyed by the rich colours and thick square brush strokes. Originally, the figure of the stallholder, a young market girl counting her takings, was included on the right. MacGregor's decision to concentrate on the still life, however, resulted in this highly original picture. He produced the painting while living in Crail, the historic old harbour town in Fife on the East Coast, during the summer of 1884. The vegetables in this painting are typical of Scotland's produce and of the vegetables we grow at Casa San Lorenzo.

John Di Ciacca

48 High Street,
Cockenzie,
East Lothian.

Tel: Port Seton 811550

MENU 1

Choice of two Home-made Soups

* * *

Steak & Kidney Pie, 2 Vegetables & Potato
or
Braised Steak, 2 Vegetables & Potato
or
Home-cooked Ham, Salad & Potato

* * *

Fresh Cream Trifle
or
Di Ciacca's Ice Cream, Meringue & Fresh Cream
or
Fruit Salad & Di Ciacca's Ice Cream
or
Chef's Choice

* * *

Tea or Coffee
Home-made Shortbread

Alternative Sweets may be provided if desired.

ham hough & a pot of lentil soup for a rainy day

The trick about becoming a practical cook is learning how you can get more than one meal from the same amount of effort. This can have two very practical advantages. The first: it saves time and we can all enjoy a little more time. And the second: it can also save money. Making a pot of soup with a ham hough (end) is the perfect example of how to be a thrifty cook who also has time to paint her nails or, in my case, bake a cake. This is a really old-fashioned, simple and very hearty recipe. There are no spices or gimmicks or extras; it's just good, old-fashioned, healthy comfort. Mummy used to make lentil soup for the caterings. She always used the ham stock that was left over from the boiled ham used for the vegetarian ham salads. Yes, Mummy thought that if you chose a salad over steak pie or braised steak, regardless of the fact that it contained part of a pig, you were a vegetarian. Oh! The 1970s in Cockenzie were revolutionary in culinary terms. Each pot of her lentil soup would hold over 50 litres – enough to serve about 100 guests. It would be heated in the Wemyss Café, then Daddy would drive the VW van very cautiously the five or six kilometres all the way to Wallyford, Tranent, Musselburgh or Portobello, if it was a posh party. On arrival it was transferred to Bunsen burners that were sitting ready. Within 20 minutes it would be served piping hot to the very happy guests who would expect nothing more than deliciously hearty home-made soup.

SERVES 4

1 smoked ham end
2 litres cold water
salt
2 carrots, chopped
2 onions, chopped
200g red lentils
freshly ground black pepper

Rinse the ham end and place it in a large pan with the cold water. Add just a pinch of salt to help clarify the water while the ham is cooking. Don't oversalt the water as the ham is salt-cured and can make the stock very salty. Bring the water to the boil, then reduce the heat to a simmer and carefully skim off any scum until the broth is clear.

Check the seasoning and add a little extra salt if required. Add the carrots, onions and lentils. Simmer for 1½ hours until the ham is falling off the bone. Remove from the heat. Remove the ham end from the pan and set it aside.

Transfer the soup to a blender or food processor and blend it until smooth. Season to taste with salt and pepper. Cut the tender ham off the bone. Carefully reheat the soup in a clean pan, taking care not to let it stick to the pan. Serve the soup with the cooked ham for an all-in-one pauper's (or prince's) feast. Or keep the ham for lunch the next day and eat it with a little mustard and some delicious mashed potatoes.

marie rose cocktail

Fresh fish is a vital part of our diet and our menus. There are many regulatory bodies that tell us what fish to eat at what time of year. We have a very simple rule in the restaurants. We only serve fresh fish that is landed in Scottish ports by Scottish boats. We could buy fish from the Americas, Dubai or the Far East that is certified sustainable, but it is frozen and has been transported by air. I've always felt this was a contradiction in terms. Supporting our fisherman in local ports is vital and we must champion the men who put their lives at risk week in and week out. Of course, at home I'll have a tin of tuna fish and salted cod or ling, but unless I'm abroad I never buy swordfish, tuna, catfish or prawns as they won't be fresh. From 22 December, the vast majority, if not all, of the boats that fish in the waters around the Scottish coast take their annual holidays, so unless you know someone with a rod and line, it will be impossible to get fresh fish at this time of year. I used to indulge in a secret fetish for frozen prawns but now I prefer to use smoked trout as a really local and delicious alternative. That 1970s sweet cocktail sauce dates me almost to the month. The addition of the melon really works with the smoky flavour of the trout. All are as 70s as Abba and just as good. Christmas and cocktail go so well together. Or as Abba would sing, 'Happy New Year'.

SERVES 4

250ml double cream
300ml home-made mayonnaise
  (see p.51)
60ml Heinz tomato ketchup
½ tbsp Tabasco sauce
½ tbsp Lea and Perrins
  Worcester sauce
juice of 1 unwaxed lemon
splash of brandy
1 tsp cayenne pepper, plus extra,
  to serve
salt and freshly ground
  black pepper
500g smoked trout (or frozen
  prawns if you can't resist)
1 Ogen or Cantaloupe melon,
  cut into cubes
125g seasonal salad leaves

Whip the cream in a bowl until it forms soft peaks. Set aside. Put the mayonnaise and ketchup in a large glass bowl and use a balloon whisk to mix them together. Add the Tabasco sauce, Worcester sauce, lemon juice, brandy and cayenne pepper, then fold in the whipped cream. Add salt and pepper to taste.

Flake in the smoked trout or wash, rinse and dry the prawns, if using, and fold them into the mixture. The washing removes the excess fishy water but also removes the salt, so add a tiny pinch of salt to balance the flavour. Fold in the melon.

Refrigerate until required. Serve in pretty glasses with teaspoons for a party or in glass bowls. Arrange the salad leaves at the bottom and a good sprinkle of cayenne pepper on the top for an extra kick.

scotch barley & bean broth
with almond pesto

Scotch broth has its passport stamped SNP (Scots National Potage). The traditional barley and vegetable soup has been made for thousands of years. Hearty, slightly creamy in texture, very healthy and very reliably Scottish. I love adding a few other nationalities to give it a sense of being a world-wide traveller.

SERVES 4

100g cannellini beans
100g red kidney beans
100g split green peas
100g pearl barley
2 litres mutton stock or
  vegetable stock
1 carrot, finely chopped
2 baby turnips, finely chopped
2 leeks, finely chopped
2 onions, finely chopped
200g curly kale, finely chopped
salt and freshly ground black
  pepper

If you can get some mutton bones, make your own stock. Vegetable stock will work very well, too, but gives a different character to the soup and less depth of flavour.

The day before, put the cannellini beans, red kidney beans and split peas in a large bowl and cover with cold water. Leave to soak overnight. The next day, rinse in fresh water and put in a pan. Add the barley and cold water to cover. Bring to the boil. Meanwhile, put the stock in a large pan over a medium heat. Drain the beans, peas and barley and add to the hot stock. Add the carrot, turnips, leeks and onions and simmer for 1 hour until the beans are tender. Add the kale and cook for 15 minutes more until it has disintegrated and the soup is thick. The kale adds the most wonderful colour and really brings the soup to life. Season to taste with salt and pepper.

almond pesto

To transform the character of this broth, add a tablespoon of this almond pesto and serve it with some garlic toast. It's a December holiday served up in a bowl.

SERVES 4

100g whole blanched almonds
4–6 tbsp extra virgin olive oil
2 tbsp cold-pressed rapeseed oil
2 small garlic cloves
25g basil leaves
25g flat-leaf parsley leaves
zest of ½ unwaxed lemon
salt and freshly ground black pepper

Preheat the oven to 180°C/350°F/Gas 4. Put the almonds on a baking tray and toast in the preheated oven until golden but not brown. Remove from the oven and leave to cool. Put the almonds, olive oil and rapeseed oil in a blender or food processor and blend until smooth. Add the garlic, basil, parsley and lemon zest, and blend again. Season to taste with salt and pepper. The pesto can be stored in the fridge for up to 1 week. Cover with a little extra oil to stop it oxidizing.

The first time I tried goose was when I was 16 on holiday with Number One brother in Cork in Ireland. I can still remember the taste and I loved it. All three of my babies were due on 25 December, which meant that when I was nine months pregnant, I wasn't really up for Christmas with the family. We never cooked goose at Christmas because there were just too many of us in the family. So being pregnant presented the ideal opportunity to celebrate Christmas in style and cook the goose. Number One child, Orlando, was born in early January, Number Two, Carla, was born in early December but Number Three, Arianna, was born bang on the button. She was our Christmas panettone!

So for Numbers One and Two we had goose and it really was a treat. For Number Three, it was turkey. It was stuffed and ready to go in the oven just as I headed into triage. Mummy was left to look after the children. When I got back from hospital on 26 December, I was starving and expecting a fantastic lunch on a table that had already been set. But then Mummy dropped the bombshell. She 'wasn't feeling well' and hadn't done anything. Needless to say, it was me who put the turkey in the oven. Four hours later we ate it, and five hours later I burst into tears and almost throttled my mother. Ever since then I've definitely preferred to eat goose.

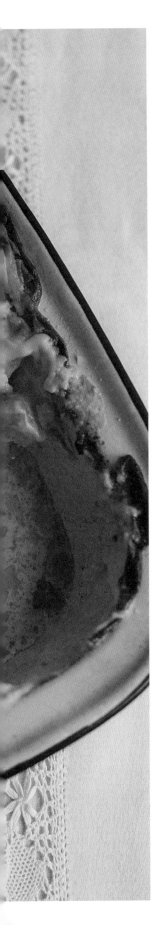

roast goose
with potato & leek dauphinoise

SERVES 4

4kg goose
3 oranges
2 tbsp clover honey
1 tsp Chinese five-spice powder

4 tbsp extra virgin olive oil
salt and freshly ground black
  pepper
4 sprigs of thyme, leaves only
2 onions

Preheat the oven to 200°C/400°F/Gas 6. Wash and trim the goose. Make sure the body cavity is empty and pat it dry with kitchen paper. Place on a metal rack in a deep roasting tin. Grate the zest of the oranges into a mixing bowl and add the honey, five-spice powder and olive oil. Season with a generous amount of salt and pepper. Prick the skin of the goose with a needle to help release the fat, then rub the spicy mixture into the skin. Place the oranges inside the carcass with the thyme and whole onions. Roast in the preheated oven for 30 minutes. Remove from the oven, baste with the juices and remove any excess fat. Cover the back and legs with tinfoil to stop them burning, then return the goose to the oven. Lower the temperature of the oven to 180°C/350°F/Gas 4 and cook for another 1½ hours until the goose is cooked through. The juices should run clear when you pierce the underside of a leg. Remove from the oven, cover with tinfoil and a clean tea towel and leave to rest for 30 minutes before serving with the potato and leek dauphinoise, if you fancy.

potato & leek dauphinoise

The creamy sauce from this classic dish works so well with the potatoes. In our house there is always a fight for any leftovers.

SERVES 4

500g roasting potatoes
salt
1 leek, thickly sliced
freshly ground white pepper

1 garlic clove, peeled and
  crushed
1 litre double cream
50g unsalted butter

Peel and thinly slice the potatoes and put in a pan with salt and cold water to cover. Bring to the boil, then lower the heat and simmer until tender. Drain, then cover the pan with a clean tea towel and place the lid on top. Set aside. Blanch the leek by plunging it in boiling salted water for a few minutes until tender but not overcooked. Drain well and set aside.

Preheat the oven to 180°C/350°F/Gas 4. Put the potatoes and leek in a 1kg deep baking dish. Season with salt and pepper. Mix the garlic and cream and pour on top. Dot with the butter and finish with white pepper. Bake in the preheated oven for 30 minutes. Remove from the oven and press the potatoes down with the back of a large spoon. This will help them to stay firm. Cover with tinfoil and bake for 45 minutes more, removing the foil after 10–15 minutes to allow the top of the dauphinoise to get golden brown, bubbling and piping hot.

red deer with pan-fried cabbage

The red deer is the Monarch of the Glen. It's also the food of kings so it's not cheap but rather a treat for that special occasion. This dish can be really hearty or remarkably light, depending on the accompaniment. Red deer is a deliciously lean meat and is best served rare. It is therefore really important to seal it in a very hot pan, then transfer to the oven to finish cooking.

SERVES 4

800g loin or fillet of red deer
150g Savoy cabbage
salt
250g waxy potatoes
freshly ground black pepper
2–3 tbsp extra virgin olive oil
4 sprigs of thyme, leaves only
50g whole blanched almonds
1 garlic clove, thinly sliced
1 dried red chilli, crumbled
50g sultanas
redcurrant jelly (see recipe, p.286),
 to serve

Leave the loin or fillet of deer at room temperature for about 30 minutes. This is important as the meat is so tender that it doesn't require a huge amount of cooking but you must ensure it gets hot in the middle. Meanwhile, shred the cabbage and blanch it by plunging in boiling salted water for a few minutes until tender but not overcooked. Drain and refresh in cold water, then drain again thoroughly and set aside. Peel the potatoes and cut them into equal-sized chunks. Put them in a pan with salt and cold water to cover. Bring to the boil, then lower the heat and simmer until the potatoes are tender. Drain well and leave to cool.

Preheat the oven to 180°C/350°F/Gas 4. Ensure the deer is well trimmed. The loin may require more trimming than the fillet. Season with salt and pepper and place in a cast-iron pan or roasting tray that is big enough for the whole piece of meat. Add enough olive oil to coat the bottom of the pan. Place over a medium heat and when the oil is hot, add the meat and sear it on all sides until golden and crisp. Season with a little more salt and add the thyme. Cook in the preheated oven for 10 minutes.

Remove from the oven, cover with tinfoil and a few tea towels to keep the meat warm. Leave to rest. Meanwhile, heat 1 tbsp olive oil in a large frying pan. When the oil is hot, add the almonds and fry until golden. Remove from the pan and leave to cool.

Heat enough olive oil in the same pan to partially coat the bottom. When it is hot, add the garlic and chilli. Cook for 1 minute over a medium heat to release the flavours. Add the sultanas and warm through for 1 minute. Add the blanched cabbage and increase the heat, then add the potatoes. Season to taste with salt and pepper. Keep moving the pan to warm everything through, adding a little more oil if required. Add the fried almonds.

Carve the deer meat into 8 slices and serve 2 per person with a helping of the cabbage and potato mixture and a generous spoonful of redcurrant jelly, warmed in a small pan.

redcurrant jelly

Get to know your local fruit farmer. When redcurrants are in season they are plentiful and really easy to pick, especially for little fingers. This makes three 450g jars of jelly and really couldn't be simpler.

MAKES 3 x 450g jars
1.5kg redcurrants
squeeze of lemon juice
2 star anise
1.5kg granulated sugar

Perfect with the red deer on page 284, this jelly is also delicious with the chicken liver parfaits on page 96 or with a large sharing cheese board.

Sterilize the kilner or jam jars according to your usual method. Place the redcurrants in a preserving pan with the lemon juice and star anise and slowly bring to the boil. Stir continuously to break down the redcurrants and release their juice. When they have all burst, add the sugar and increase the heat. Bring to the boil, stirring continuously so the sugar doesn't burn. Boil for 10 minutes until the colour changes.

Place a double layer of fine cotton or muslin over the top of a large double-handled pan and tie it loosely around the handles. Gently pour the hot jelly onto the cloth and let the juices drain through. Squeeze a little of the fruit through the cloth, but not too much or it will make the jelly cloudy. Remove the star anise. Transfer the strained jelly to the sterilized jars, cover each with a circle of greaseproof paper and seal while still hot. Leave to cool. The jelly will keep for up to 6 months.

cherry madeira cake

I usually can't resist cakes with icing but there are times when a classic non-iced cake comes into its own. This one is particularly tasty served warm with a cup of freshly brewed tea from a fine bone china teapot with matching cup and saucer, of course. It's also a great standby as it keeps very well in a cake tin for up to a week and will easily impress those lovely old aunties who pop in unexpectedly with the Christmas envelopes for the children.

SERVES 4-6

225g unsalted butter, at room temperature
225g golden caster sugar
finely grated zest of
   1 unwaxed lemon
1 tsp vanilla extract
4 eggs
125g self-raising flour, sieved
125g plain flour, sieved
3 tbsp double cream
200g glacé cherries, dipped in flour, excess flour
   shaken off
50g flaked almonds

Preheat the oven to 180°C/350°F/Gas 4 and line a 25cm cake tin with greaseproof paper. Put the butter and sugar in a bowl and beat until light and fluffy. Add the lemon zest and vanilla extract.

Slowly add 1 egg and 1 tbsp flour, beating after each addition until all the eggs and both flours have been added. Using a metal spoon, fold in the cream and glacé cherries. Pour the mixture into the prepared cake tin and sprinkle with the almonds.

Bake in the preheated oven for 1 hour, then place a sheet of greaseproof paper over the cake to stop it colouring too much and bake for 20 minutes more until it is cooked through. Leave to cool for a few minutes in the tin, then transfer to a wire cooling rack.

poached pears
with butterscotch sauce

The quality of the pears and wine you use for this recipe are equally important. Choose firm pears and a fresh, fruity, light wine, not one with heavy oaked or mineral flavours. I much prefer pears poached in white wine to red. With white wine, the white flesh of the pears becomes almost translucent.

SERVES 4-6
500ml white wine
500ml water
500g caster sugar
4 cardamom pods
1 thick slice of orange peel
4–6 under-ripe (but not too hard)
  pears

If you're serving the pears with just a little cream and a sprinkle of ground cinnamon, then continue simmering the syrup until it thickens slightly. But if you're serving them with the butterscotch sauce, there is no need to thicken the syrup.

Put the wine, water, sugar, cardamom pods and orange peel in a deep pan. The pears must sit in the pan, up to their stalks in the liquid. Bring the liquid to the boil, then reduce to a simmer. Meanwhile, prepare the pears. Peel them, leaving the stalks intact, then trim their bottoms slightly so they can stand upright. Don't be tempted to prepare the pears too early or they will start to discolour and while the taste won't be impaired, they will look less attractive.

Carefully lower the pears into the syrup and simmer very gently for about 30 minutes or until they are tender. Leave to cool in the syrup and serve hot, warm or cold – whatever you're in the mood for or whatever suits your dinner plans.

butterscotch sauce

Butterscotch sauce is heaven. Yes, it's a sweet-toothed person's nirvana and a sticky hell for lovers of savoury, but for me it's ecstasy in liquid form. This recipe is the classic starting point. If you're looking for a bit more adventure, you can add a crumbled pinch of Hebridean salt or the seeds from a vanilla pod. Either can be added to the sauce while it's hot.

SERVES 4-6
125g unsalted butter, cut into small cubes
100g dark brown sugar
125ml double cream

Put all the ingredients in a heavy-based cast-iron pan over a medium heat. Using a balloon whisk, beat until the sauce is smooth and glossy. This will take 3 or 4 minutes. Remove from the heat and either leave to cool or serve hot.

pear, banana & cranberry jelly trifle

Scotland has one special claim to fame at this time of year and that's Hogmanay. The restaurants are open on 31 December and Victor will always be at Ristorante Contini to see in the bells, but by quarter past midnight, he'll be home with us, welcoming in the New Year with his nearest and dearest. This trifle is a festive celebration centrepiece. It's perfect as a Hogmanay party show-stopper – or for Christmas if you're not a Scot and up at midnight to bring in the bells.

SERVES 8-10

1 Genovese sponge (see recipe, p.206)
2–3 bananas
500ml–1 litre double cream (depending on the size of your bowl)
70% cocoa Valrhona dark chocolate, coarsely grated, to decorate

for the cranberry jelly
2 leaves of gelatine
500ml premium 100% cranberry juice
2 tbsp golden caster sugar

for the custard
400ml single cream
50g caster sugar
5 large egg yolks

for the pears
6 small firm pears
400ml Crabbie's Green Ginger Wine
400ml water
200g golden caster sugar
cinnamon stick

Following the instructions on page 206, make a Genovese sponge and set it aside. To make the cranberry jelly, put the gelatine in cold water to soften for a few minutes, then remove from the water and squeeze out any excess. Set aside. Put the cranberry juice and sugar in a pan over a low heat until the sugar has dissolved. Don't let the mixture boil. Remove from the heat, add the gelatine and leave to cool. Transfer the mixture to a glass bowl and refrigerate until the jelly is soft-set. It must be soft enough to pour with a little help from a spatula. If it's too set, you won't get the lovely, even layers in the trifle that are always so appealing.

To make the custard, put the cream and half the sugar in a pan over a low heat until the cream starts to steam but doesn't boil. Whisk the egg yolks and remaining sugar by hand in a bowl and slowly add to the warm cream, using a balloon whisk to prevent lumps forming. Continue to beat the mixture over a very low heat until it starts to thicken. Remove from the heat and strain through a metal sieve. Transfer to a glass bowl and leave to cool. To prevent a skin forming, place a sheet of greased greaseproof paper on top of the custard.

Meanwhile, prepare the pears. Peel them, cut them in half and remove the cores. Put the ginger wine, water and sugar in a deep pan over a low heat until the sugar has dissolved. Reduce the heat to a simmer. Put the pears and cinnamon stick in this syrup and cook for 15–20 minutes until the pears are tender. Leave to cool in the syrup.

To assemble the trifle, choose your swankiest glass bowl. The showier the better but make sure it fits in the fridge. Start by placing a circle of Genovese sponge in the bottom of the bowl. Add a little of the pear syrup to moisten but not soak the sponge. Cut the bananas into rounds and arrange on the sponge, leaning against the sides of the bowl. Arrange the pear halves in the centre of the sponge. Pour the cranberry jelly over the fruits, cover with clingfilm and refrigerate until set.

Only when the jelly has set, pour the cooled custard on top, cover again with clingfilm and return to the fridge. When the custard has set, softly whip the cream and spoon it on top. Decorate with the grated chocolate and serve straight away.

GROWING NOTES

brussels sprouts
Brassica oleracea Gemmifera Group

Cultivars grown at Casa San Lorenzo
- 'Trafalgar' – sweet-tasting

Cultivation
- Sown in pots in April and planted out in June into fertile soil.
- Plants should be firmed in when transplanted and planted slightly deeper than in their pot to help support the stem.
- Add a cabbage collar to prevent cabbage root fly from laying eggs near the roots.

Interesting facts
- Harvest the sprouts from the base of the stem and work your way up as they develop.
- Be sure to use the top leaf growth as you would cabbage greens.

kale
Brassica oleracea Acephala Group

Cultivars grown at Casa San Lorenzo
- 'Red Russian – rough leaf edges with a purple midrib
- 'Black Tuscany' or 'Cavalo Nero' – Italian cultivars with dark green, deeply textured leaves

Cultivation
- We make three sowings – the first direct into a polytunnel bed in February for cut-and-come-again leaves and the second and third pot-sown in May and July for harvesting from September right through to winter.
- Kale is susceptible to the usual brassica pests and care needs to be taken to cover plants to protect them from pigeons and moths/butterflies.

Interesting fact
- Kale is versatile as cut-and-come-again leaves for salads in spring and as a wonderful green in its own right as it matures. It is also one of the most beautiful-looking vegetables when covered in frost on a winter's day.

winter salad

Cultivars grown at Casa San Lorenzo
- Lamb's Lettuce (*Valerianella locusta*) 'Vit' – small rosettes of smooth leaves
- Mustard Frills (*Brassica juncea*) 'Ruby' and 'Golden' – decorative leaf with a mild mustard flavour
- Mizuna (*Brassica rapa* var. *nipposinica*) – serrated leaf with a mild cabbage flavour
- Lettuce (*Lactuca sativa*) 'Winter Density' and 'Valdor' – hardy lettuces

Cultivation
- All these leaves are sown in late August/early September and are overwintered in the polytunnel or under cloches of horticultural fleece outside.

Interesting fact
- All leaves are hardy and, if harvested with care, can provide an interesting mix of leaves even in the depths of winter.

suppliers

We're really lucky to have access to so many excellent,-quality producers. And we're happy to share our luck with you!

Vegetables / Herbs
Phantassie
East Linton
East Lothian
EH40 3DF
Tel: +44 (0) 1620 861 531
www.phantassie.co.uk
This lovely organic fruit and vegetable grower is based just a few kilometres from Casa San Lorenzo and has been supplying us for years. They are regulars at the farmers' markets and deliver great veg boxes all year round.

Potatoes
Carroll's Heritage Potatoes
Tiptoe Farm
Cornhill-on-Tweed
Northumberland
TD12 4XD
Tel: +44 (0) 1890 883833
www.heritage-potatoes.co.uk
Suppliers of wonderful varieties of heritage potatoes, many of which you will never have seen in your life. They provide us with a staggering array of different seasonal varieties, all with different characters, tastes and uses.

Garlic
Simply Garlic
Cumbers Farm
Rogate
Petersfield
Hants
GU31 5DB
www.simplygarlic.co.uk
When we first found this supplier we were amazed that garlic could be grown in Scotland. It's hearty, seasonal and excellent quality.

Haggis
Findlay's of Portobello
116 Portobello High Street
Edinburgh
EH15 1AL

Tel: +44 (0) 131 669 4559
www.findlayofportobello.co.uk
Supplies award-winning haggis and pies. They are real family butchers and can advise on different cuts of meat. They also always offer a little cooking tip for fun!

Pork / Lamb / Veal
Peelham Farm Organic
Foulden
Berwickshire
TD15 1UG
Tel: +44 (0) 1890 781 328
www.peelham.co.uk
Our special friends at Peelham are true experts. They are passionate Slow Food supporters and passionate farmers producing world-class home-reared produce.

Black Pudding / Bacon / Ham on the Bone
Ramsay of Carluke
22 Mount Stewart Street
Carluke
ML8 5ED
Tel: +44 (0) 1555 772277
www.ramsayofcarluke.co.uk
A wonderful supplier for the Christmas or New Year ham on the bone. Beautiful, traditional produce. The black pudding has to be our favourite.

Shetland Lamb PDO (Protected Designation of Origin)
Richard Briggs
Briggs' Shetland Lamb
Cuckron
Stromfirth
Weisdale
Shetland ZE2 9LH
Tel: +44 (0) 1595 840227
www.briggs-shetlandlamb.co.uk
Native whole Shetland lamb from another Slow Food family member. A farmer who knows and loves each of his animals. Lamb

is available mainly available from September to December. Mutton and Hogget also available.

Pheasant / Wild Duck
Burnside Farm Foods
Burnside Farm
Kelso
Roxburghshire
TD5 8NR
Tel: +44 (0) 1573 229890
www.burnsidefarmfoods.co.uk
Burnside provides a wonderful range of Scottish birds, such as pheasant and wild duck. They work in tune with the seasons and are regarded as one of the country's leading gamekeepers.

Chicken / Duck Eggs
Linda Dick Poultry
Peebles
Scottish Borders
Tel: +44 (0) 1721 752297
www.lindadick.co.uk
Many top chefs feel that Linda's free-range, organic chickens are the best in the UK. We agree and have been saying so for years. Be prepared to get a fright, though, when you see the chickens – they are more like tiny turkeys! She also supplies free-range duck eggs.

Turkey / Guinea Fowl / Duck
Gartmorn Farm Poultry
Alloa
Clackmannanshire
FK10 3AU
Tel: +44 (0) 1259 750549
www.gartmornfarm.co.uk
Great value and great-quality turkeys – ideal for Christmas celebrations. They also supply chickens, guinea fowl, ducks and geese.

Beef / Lamb / Pork / Chicken
Hugh Grierson Organic
Newmiln Farm

Tibbermore
Perth
PH1 1QN
Tel: +44 (0) 1738 730201
www.the-organic-farm.co.uk
Another jewel of the Scottish farming community. Dedicated to and determined to spread the word about good, clean, fair growing practices.

Organic Smoked Salmon
Inverawe Scottish Oak
    Smokehouse
Taynuilt
Argyll
PA35 1HU
Tel: 0844 8475 490
www.smokedsalmon.co.uk
Internationally recognized award-winning producer of smoked salmon that is hand-smoked over slow-burning oak log fires. Their smoked salmon is delicate, light, very sophisticated and elegant.

Oak Smoked Salmon
James Dickson & Son
West Harbour Road
Cockenzie
East Lothian
EH32 0HX
Tel: +44 (0) 1875 811301
www.jamesdicksonandson.co.uk
Family friends for over three generations. Their rustic, rich and intensely flavoured oak-smoked salmon is full of happy memories.

Sausages
Crombies of Edinburgh
97–101 Broughton Street
Edinburgh
EH1 3RZ
Tel: +44 (0) 131 557 0111
www.sausages.co.uk
If you ask nicely, the Crombies will make your own sausages for you. We did and they now make our Contadino sausages for us three times a week to our own recipe, with our own spices and with their best 100 per cent Borders pork.

Rare Breed Pork
Clash Farm Pedigree Saddlebacks

Clash Farm
Port Logan
Stranraer
Wigtownshire
DG9 9NL
Tel: +44 (0) 1776 860246
www.clashsaddlebacks.co.uk
Clash Farm produces the best pork belly. We think it's not too fat and not too thin – but just right.

Loch Arthur Farmhouse, Kriffel and Kebbuck
Loch Arthur Camphill Community
Loch Arthur
Beeswing
Dumfries
DG2 8JQ
Tel: +44 (0) 1387 259669
www.locharthur.org.uk/creamery-and-farmshop
Part of the Camphill Trust Community. They make and sell fabulous cheeses and now have a farm shop serving quality organic produce to the Borders locals.

Isle of Mull Cheddar
J & C Reade & Sons
Isle of Mull Cheese
Sgriob-ruadh Farm
Tobermory
Isle of Mull
PA75 6QD
Tel: +44 (0) 1688 302627
www.isleofmullcheese.co.uk
Champions of the cheese world. One hundred per cent sustainable production and their Isle of Mull cheddar has superstar taste! Macaroni cheese will never be the same again!

Connage Crowdie / Smoked Dunlop / Clava
Connage Highland Dairy
Milton of Connage
Ardersier
Inverness
IV2 7QU
Tel: +44 (0) 1667 462000
www.connage.co.uk
Crowdie is a new love in my life. Low-fat and fantastic, versatile, tasty and Scottish! Definitely a

cook's ingredient. The Connage Highland Dairy also sells delicious Smoked Dunlop and Clava.

Lanark Blue
Errington Cheese Ltd
Walston Braehead Farm
Ogscastle
Carnwath
Lanark South
Lanarkshire
ML11 8NF
Tel: +44 (0) 1899 810257
www.erringtoncheese.co.uk
How do you describe a family led by hero who challenged meritocracy all the way to the High Court? If it weren't for dear Humphrey, Scotland wouldn't have any raw milk cheese production. He is our food hero. They don't have an online shop but their website lists the many places that stock their cheeses.

Honey
Heather Hill Farms
Bridge of Cally
Blairgowrie
Perthshire
PH10 7JG
Tel: +44 (0) 1250 886252
www.heather-hills.com/about-us.php
Scotland has hundreds of honey producers – including Victor. Many make such small quantities that they don't have online shops. Heather Hills does. Thanks, honey!

Mustards / Edible Dried Flowers / Natural Extracts
Uncle Roy's Comestible Concoctions
6–7 Buccleuch Street
Moffat
Dumfriesshire
DG10 9HA
Tel: +44 (0) 1683 221076
www.uncleroys.co.uk
The most unusual food website you can find. They have an incredible array of foodstuffs that you never even knew existed. It's the Harry Potter food emporium!

Cold-Pressed Rapeseed Oil / Fruit Vinegars
Summer Harvest
Ferneyfold Farm
Madderty
Crieff
Perthshire
PH7 3PE
Tel: +44 (0) 1764 683288
www.summerharvestoils.co.uk
Olive oil is definitely in my DNA but rapeseed oil is in my cooking. When matched with local and regional ingredients, the flavours of rapeseed oil balance so very well. Ferneyfold Farm's fruit vinegars are particularly special, too.

Cider
Thistly Cross Cider
The Cidershed
South Belton Farm
Nr Dunbar
East Lothian
EH42 1RG
Tel: +44 (0) 7960 962510
www.thistlycrosscider.co.uk
Seriously good local cider. A new Scottish favourite.

Beer
Williams Bros Brewing Co.
New Alloa Brewery
Kelliebank
Alloa
FK10 1NU
Tel: +44 (0) 1259 725511
www.williamsbrosbrew.com
Great people make great things. I don't like beer but this is a best-seller with our customers. And you know what they say – the customer is always right.

Stewart Brewing
26a Dryden Road
Bilston Glen Industrial Estate
Loanhead
JEH20 9L
Tel: +44 (0) 131 440 2442
www.stewartbrewing.co.uk
Another local microbrewery that delivers wonderful award-winning beers.

Whisky
Royal Mile Whiskies
379 High Street
The Royal Mile
Edinburgh
EH1 1PW
Tel: +44 (0) 131 524 9380
www.royalmilewhiskies.com
One of Victor's best friends. If you're stuck, Arthur will source the rarest varieties of Scotch whisky for you.

Fruit Wines
Orkney Wine Company
Lamb Holm
Orkney
KW17 2SF
Tel: +44 (0) 1856 781736
www.orkneywine.co.uk
A local, sustainable range of wines from Scotland. Almost unbelievable!

Seeds
Moles Seeds (U.K.) Ltd 2013
Turkey Cock Lane
Stanway
Colchester
Essex
CO3 8PD
Tel: +44 (0) 1206 213213
www.molesseeds.co.uk

Calendula, Viola and Nasturtium Seeds
The Organic Gardening Catalogue
Riverdene Business Park
Molesey Road
Hersham
Surrey
KT12 4RG
Tel: +44 (0) 1932 253666
www.organiccatalogue.com/index.html

Soft Fruit and Fruit Trees
Agroforestry Research Trust
46 Hunters Moon
Dartington
Totnes
TQ9 6JT
www.agroforestry.co.uk

Keepers Nursery
Gallants Court
East Farleigh
Maidstone
Kent
ME15 0LE
Tel: +44 (0) 1622 726465
www.keepers-nursery.co.uk

Compost and Growing Media
Caledonian Horticulture
East Fenton
Dirleton
East Lothian
Tel: +44 (0) 1620 850 853
www.caledonianhorticulture.co.uk/contact.html

Clydeside Trading Society Ltd
89 Vere Road
Kirkmuirhill
ML11 9RP
Tel: +44 (0) 1555 894151
www.clydesidets.com

Gardening Tools and Materials
LBS Horticulture Supplies
Standroyd Mill
Cottontree
Colne
Lancashire
BB8 7BW
Tel: +44 (0) 1282 87333
www.lbsbuyersguide.co.uk

Wood and Building Supplies
Mayshade Garden Centre
Mayshade Park
Bonnyrigg Road
Eskbank
Dalkeith
EH22 3LA
Tel: +44 (0) 131 663 1093
www.mayshade.co.uk

... and finally, our own shop!
Our little online shop. Some lovely gifts, our favourite olive oils and a few other foodie treats.
www.contini.com

index

author's acknowledgments

There are some things that you dream about doing – losing weight, travelling to the markets of Marrakech, making that perfect soufflé, running that race and just reaching the finish line . . .

For years I've been dreaming about writing this book and I've loved the dream. But I've cherished writing it even more. Every stage has been fun but it has been a team effort.

My cast of characters played the biggest part in getting my dream into book form, but there have been so many more influences and experiences that have helped along the way.

Each of the restaurants I've eaten in over the years has left its impression. Every one of our customers who passes a comment has helped us evolve from good to great. Suzanne has worked extra hard while I've been dreaming and writing. I've been inspired by all those steamy cookbooks that have been at my bedside as an alternative to saucy novels. None of this would have been possible without our suppliers, who give us the best raw ingredients. In the background have been all those celebrations around the table, the laughs, the jokes, the comments ('Oh, that was better last Christmas'). These have inspired us to tweak, tamper and deliver better next time.

My lovely family, Victor, Orlando, Carla and Arianna, have 'suffered' while I've celebrated. They've put up with countless recipes being tested, tasted and discussed. When you're seven, nine and eleven, eating seasonally at every meal can have its challenges but they did well! Victor and I have both put on kilos eating all the food that I've made to check it's just right.

Living my dream has also helped me look at what I need to do to be a better Mummy. That may be another story but it's true, and acknowledging it is not only wonderful for me but hopefully, in the years to come, it will be great for my beautiful babies and my darling husband and best friend, Victor.

While my children have suffered with me, I've suffered with my mother. I say this with a cheeky smile. Like many daughters, I see myself as a younger version of my mother. Mummy never resists making a comment, a suggestion, a remark. At times it can feel a little rough but her intentions are as good as a glass of champagne on Christmas Day. Now that I'm a mother, I can appreciate it; her comments are most welcome and are often badly needed.

If Mummy is a steady, traditional, reliable cook, Nonna Olivia, Victor's mother, is the creative risk-taker. She taught me to experiment. She's not only my mother-in-law and auntie, but also my friend and mentor.

Andrew, Jo and the wonderful Hilary joined my dream during its last year. This amazing publishing, designing and editing team at Frances Lincoln have brought my dream to life and made it reality.

Finally, there's Margaret. Second mother to my seven siblings and me. She's modest, marvellous and majestic. She's also the salt of the earth and no matter how bad or sad life may be, Margaret has taught us all to appreciate it.

Thank you! Grazie molto and, most importantly, Buon Appetito!

publisher's acknowledgments

The publisher would like to thank the Scottish National Gallery for permission to reproduce the paintings on pages 30, 150, 175 and 276. They would also like to thank Zoe Barrie for all the photographs, apart from the following: Jo Grey, pages 162, 181, 256, 274; Manel Quiros, pages 30, 97, 107, 214, 239, 263; Erica Randall, page 91; Shutterstock, pages 195, 230, 275.